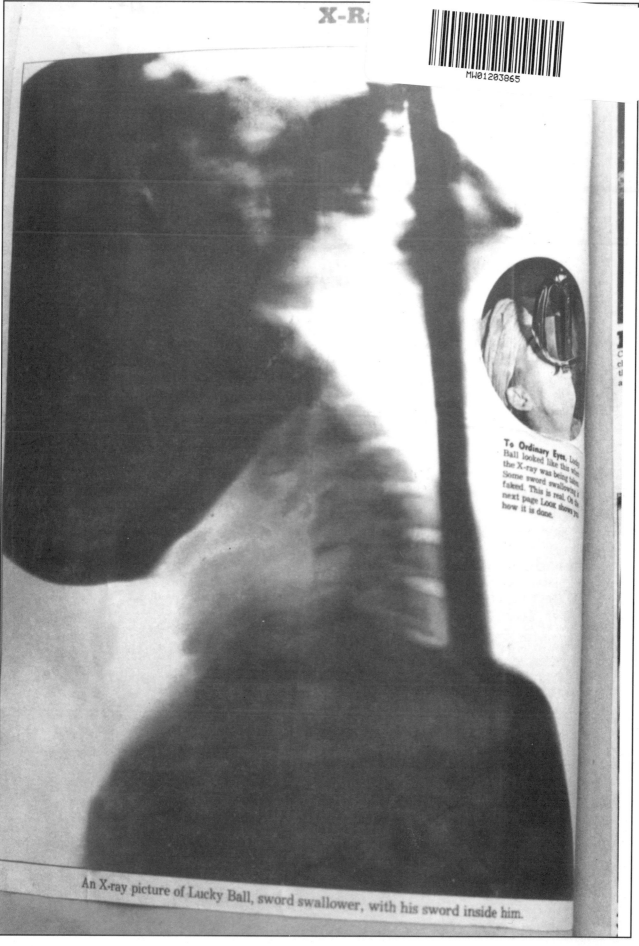

X-R...

To Ordinary Eyes, Lucky
Ball looked like this when
the X-ray was being taken.
Some sword swallowing is
faked. This is real. On the
next page LOOK shows you
how it is done.

An X-ray picture of Lucky Ball, sword swallower, with his sword inside him.

X-Ray of sword swallower.

PUBLISHER/EDITOR: V. Vale
PRODUCTION MANAGER: Marian Wallace
TYPESETTING: Andrea Reider
PHOTOSHOP/SCANS: Thaddeus Croyle
GRAPHIC DESIGN: Matthew Petty
TEXT: Yimi Tong, Catherine Wallace, Andrea Fortus
PRODUCTION CONSULTANT: Valentine Marquesa Wallace
LAWYER: David S. Kahn, Esq.

Memoirs of a Sword Swallower
First photo-illustrated edition
©1950, 1951 by Daniel P. Mannix
Additional material and design ©1996 V. Vale
ISBN: 0-9650469-5-8

Library of Congress Number 96-90463

BOOKSTORE DISTRIBUTION: SUBCO, PO Box 160 or 265 South 5th, Monroe OR 97456.
TEL: 800-274-7826 FAX: 541-847-6018
NON-BOOKSTORE DISTRIBUTION: LAST GASP, 777 Florida St, San Francisco CA 94110.
TEL: 415-864-6636. FAX: 415-824-1836.
U.K. DISTRIBUTION: AIRLIFT, #8 The Arena, Mollison Ave, Enfield, Middlesex U.K. EN3 7NJ.
TEL: 181-804-0400. FAX: 181-804-0044.

For a catalog send SASE or 2 IRCs to:
V/SEARCH PUBLICATIONS
20 Romolo #B
San Francisco CA 94133
TEL: (415) 362-1465
FAX: (415) 362-0742

Printed in Hong Kong by Colorcraft, Ltd.

10 9 8 7 6 5 4 3 2 1

Cover: Design and Photoshop by Matt Petty. Sword swallower/Fire eater: Daniel P. Mannix.

Table of Contents

Fountain of Fire act (1887).

CHAPTER 1

I probably never would have become America's leading fire-eater if Flamo the Great hadn't happened to explode that night in front of Krinko's Great Combined Carnival Side Shows. The tragedy—if such it may be called—took place at eleven o'clock when there's only time for one more show before the carnival closes for the night, so all the concessions compete for the late crowd at the same time. The side show had a bad location, being next to the Oriental Dancing Girls ("Fugitives from a Life of Shame in the Sultan's Harem") and it's pretty hard to compete with ten naked girls for the public's interest.

But a good side show can compete with anything. When Flamo stood up on the platform outside the side show tent, naked to the waist with the two great torches in his hands throwing up plumes of golden fire topped by black smoke that reached above the ferris wheels—well, it was something that nothing in the *Arabian Nights, Grimm's Fairy Tales* or an opium smoker's dreams could top. People left all the other concessions to rush to the side show, and I led the rush.

Some of the other acts had come out on the platform to join Flamo: a cowboy playing his guitar, a Hindu fakir sticking hat pins into himself, a gypsy palmist, and an almost nude girl hopefully holding up a fifteen-foot rock python. As I say, in a side show there's something to appeal to every taste. But none of them could touch Flamo as a public attraction.

Slowly the fire-eater put back his head and thrust one of the burning torches between his lips. Flames rushed out of his mouth like the backlash of a blast furnace, making his cheeks and throat glow like a jack-o'-lantern and throwing a witch glow over the other acts. Women screamed in the rapidly forming crowd and a man beside me suddenly turned sick and tried to force his way out through the mob. Flamo gradually closed his lips over the flame until the fire went out, leaving only the dancing light of the torch in his other hand to illuminate the platform. Taking care to hold the lighted torch well away from his body, he filled a drinking glass half full of gasoline from a scarlet tin marked DANGEROUS. Instantly the Hindu fakir grabbed up a potbellied flute and began to play a wild chant into the microphone while the side show talker beat on a metal triangle and shouted, "This is it, folks! Something you'll never see again."

I'd seen fire-eaters work before, so I guessed that Flamo was going to do the Fountain of Fire. Not many fire-eaters care to try this stunt because even if they don't blow themselves up they're liable to set the audience on fire. To perform the Fountain, the fire-eater takes a mouthful of gas, blows it out in a fine stream, and then lights it. Some fire-eaters will even puff out circles of flame that go undulating up into the air like burning smoke rings. I'd never seen a fire-eater do the stunt except in a dead calm and this evening little gusts of wind were flapping the side show banners—the big canvas pictures of the performers that hang outside a side show.

Flamo hesitated. He probably wouldn't have attempted the Fountain if the Oriental Dancing Girls hadn't suddenly turned loose a series of bumps and grinds that began to draw away some of the side show crowd. Then the fire-eater made his decision. He took a mouthful of gasoline and stood waiting for the wind to die down. I was in the front row of the crowd and by the leaping light of the torch in his hand I could see the fire-eater's face, thin and sunken in spite of his puffed-out cheeks, as he watched the breeze bellying the banner line. He was a swarthy man, apparently of South European blood, his thick black hair carefully combed, and his bare hairless chest as scrawny as an emaciated child's. Suddenly a little trickle of gas leaked from the corner of his mouth and ran down his chin. Instantly a tiny flash of fire from the torch leaped toward it, running through the air as though along an invisible fuse as it ignited the gasoline vapor. The little trickle blazed up and his whole mouthful of gas exploded.

I was blinded for a second by the flash. The fire-eater's whole face was burning and he threw himself off the platform and rolled on the ground, trying to put out the fire. I tore off my coat and tried to smother the flames. The frenzied man beat me off, but the cowboy jumped off the platform and together we put out the fire.

"Hadn't you better call a doctor?" I asked the cowboy.

"What for?" he said in honest surprise. "He'll be all right in a couple of weeks."

The crowd was pressing in around us so closely that I had to fight to keep from being trampled. People kept asking, "Is he dead?" with the same interest that they'd shown while watching Flamo do his act. I helped the cowboy carry Flamo toward the tent. The talker grabbed the mike and shouted, "All right, folks. The show is closed for the evening. There's a fine show on either side of us." The old lady in gypsy costume dropped the tent flap behind us as we carried Flamo inside. A moment later the sidewalls of the tent, which were gleaming a translucent rose from the bright lights on the banner line, suddenly went black as someone disconnected the outside circuit.

The cowboy and I laid Flamo on the thick rosin-scented sawdust. I stood there helplessly, but the carnival people seemed to know exactly what to do. There was no question of the show having to go on. Unlike a circus, a carnival concession is a small, intimate group and the performers were only interested in helping Flamo. The Hindu fakir, a squat old man with a face that seemed to have been whittled out of a hickory knot by a dull knife, stumped in with a saucepan full of warm water he had apparently grabbed from one of the carnival's refreshment booths. A moment later, the girl with the python ran in with a box of baking soda in her hand and the snake still slung around her neck.

Unwrapping the reptile as though he were a feather boa, she handed him to me saying casually, "Here, hold him. He won't bite but don't let him get a turn around you with his tail."

The snake and I looked at each other uncertainly. Instead of being slimy, he felt smooth and slightly cool like a pair of snake-skin shoes left out overnight. As soon as I took him in my arms I could feel the power pulsing through his coils as though I were handling a fire hose under strong pressure. The python reared the upper yard of himself and looked at me, his triangular head only a few inches from my face. Suddenly he shot

his head forward and began to pour himself over my shoulder. I gently and respectfully restrained him and, after getting a purchase on my left ankle with the tip of his tail, he seemed to quiet down.

His mistress had begun pouring baking soda into the saucepan while the old fakir patted the solution onto Flamo's face. There was nothing I could do to help except hold the snake. I looked around the tent. The top was held up by two lines of poles about ten feet apart running down the middle. A long chain was run through holes in the poles and from the chain red canvas had been hung to the ground. Down the center of this chained-off space ran a line of little platforms only a few inches high. Each platform contained the paraphernalia of a different performer. An international madman could not have brought together a more exotic collection. I identified the bullwhips and lariats of the cowboy, the jade-headed hatpins belonging to the fakir, the glass-fronted snake boxes of the snake charmer, and a tattooing outfit with stencils showing South

Krinko.

Pacific hula girls and old frigates under full sail. At one end of the tent was a platform littered with playing cards, silk handkerchiefs, and the apparatus for sawing a woman in half. On a crossbar above the platform sat two little ringdoves as comfortable as though in a tree, snuggled together and watching the proceedings with bright black eyes. The other end of the tent was curtained off, but the curtain had been pulled back at one corner and a little ticket box erected, bearing such signs as IS SEX WORTH IT? and YOU OWE IT TO YOUR FUTURE WIFE TO SEE THIS EXHIBIT!

The rest of the side show performers had entered the tent and were collecting around Flamo. The old fakir who had taken over the doctoring of Flamo seemed to be the head of the show. His stumpy fingers moved with surprising gentleness over the fire-eater's face where masses of blisters were beginning to swell. Occasionally he gave orders in an almost unintelligible gibberish that the others instantly obeyed.

Flamo spoke for the first time. "How do I look— pretty bad?" He put his hand up to touch the blisters and the snake charmer gently stopped him.

"Why, you'll be giving another bally in a week," said the show's tattooed man. He was a powerfully built fellow in his late fifties with a fringe of white hair around his bald head. He was bringing a horse out of the curtained-off recess of the tent. He led the animal past me toward a stall behind the platform at the other end. I was so fascinated watching the network of blue-green tattoo marks which covered not only his body but also his bald head that the horse had gone by me before I noticed that she had five legs.

"Lucky thing it was only your face," continued the tattooed man, putting the horse in the stall and shaking some oats into a nose bag. "I worked with a Human Salamander once who used to introduce his act with a flourish by drinking several glasses of gasoline. One evening the fumes from the gas got into his left lung and when he tried to swallow a lighted torch the lung exploded. He didn't die, but he developed a dislike of fire-eating and had to make a living burning designs on himself with a blow torch."

"I'll be laid up a month with this thing," said Flamo sadly. "The carny moves tomorrow. You leave me here in a hospital and take the show on. I'll go back to my wife when I feel better and stay with her. I may even give up fire-eating and get a regular job. Krinko, you better call the hospital."

The fakir grunted. "You married girl who wants to live in a house and not travel with side show. Why any man in his right mind marry woman like that—But I go phone."

He rose and waddled out of the tent. Flamo sank back with a sigh. The elderly lady in the gypsy outfit sat down beside him and began tearing up strips of cloth for bandages with the dispassionate expertise of a professional seamstress. She was a plump, pleasant-faced woman with iron-gray hair done in a pompadour style like an 1890 Gibson girl. The snake charmer sat on the fire-eater's other side and took the cloth strips as they were finished. She soaked them in the warm solution and put them on Flamo's face. The snake charmer still had the body of a young girl but the harsh overhead lights showed that the texture of her skin was coarsening and she was approaching middle age.

The cowboy had sat down on the platform beside the magical apparatus and, pulling a little bag of tobacco from his vest, he began to roll a cigarette without even looking at his fingers. He was a thin, long-legged young man, his face tanned the color of the brown canvas tent. He looked as though he'd be more at home in Levi's than the embroidered outfit he was wearing. I wondered what had made him leave the West for life in a carnival. Beside him was sitting a cute, brown-haired girl wearing only a spangled bra and tight red shorts which she filled nicely. She and the cowboy seemed very intimate, for he rolled her a smoke and she accepted the cigarette without comment, as though it were a usual procedure.

The wailing moan of an ambulance's siren sounded outside the tent, growing louder as the car rushed up the midway. The siren stopped with a groan outside the entrance, and Krinko came in with a young intern and two orderlies carrying a stretcher. The intern examined Flamo casually.

"Just regular second-degree burns," he said to the orderlies regretfully. "I hoped it might be something special."

The elderly lady went into the ambulance with Flamo to make sure everything would be all right. The tattooed man put on a heavy leather glove, and went about turning out lights by unscrewing the big, thousand-watt bulbs that hung in a chain around the tent. He left one bulb burning in the middle. Instantly, the shadows that had been hanging heavily in the corners leaped forward like a flood of black water to the limits of the light. The red lacquer finish of the magician's props glowed in the subdued light like dull neon and the clutter of esoteric props made the tent look more like an alchemist's workshop than ever.

Krinko, the old fakir, pulled off the brilliant green turban he was wearing, disclosing a close-cropped turf of gray hair. He plunged his stubby hands into the scrub and pulled nervously.

"Now I lose an act. What I do? Got to have fire act for bally. This bad."

I spoke up. "How about teaching me fire-eating? I'd like to join the show."

Everybody stared at me. But to my surprise no one asked why I wanted to work in a carnival as a fire-eater. No one even asked my name.

The tattooed man said gently, "I don't know if you'd like carny life, son. There're plenty of nice people living on carny lots. But plenty of misfits end up here, too."

"That's O.K. I've always been a sort of misfit myself," I told him. ✒

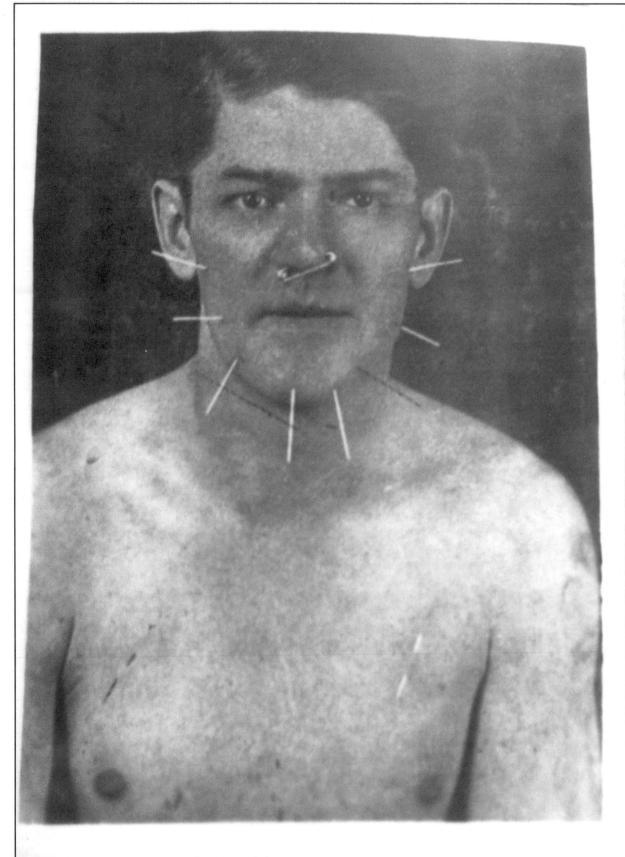

...mhoff his nerve did not register pain at all and he
...e numerous pins through his cheeks without feeling.
...ove It Or Not" shows at the Chicago World's Fair 1839.

Human pincushion (unknown performer).

CHAPTER 2

Ever since I was a kid, I've been interested in the strange and unusual. My father was a captain in the Navy and as he and my mother were often away from home, I was raised by my grandparents in their home on the Philadelphia Main Line. In those days, the Main Line was composed of big estates and farms where a small boy could run wild. I didn't have many playmates. I was always so much taller than other kids my own age that I felt almost freakish. Today I'm six feet, four inches tall and most of my growth came between the ages of eight and fourteen. My contemporaries regarded me as a sort of Frankenstein's monster who was too clumsy to throw a baseball and too uncertain on his feet to make a good football guard. But I didn't mind being by myself. I liked to dream about traveling to strange places and seeing strange people. There aren't many strange people on the Philadelphia Main Line, but I was sure that one day I'd run into some.

When I was eight years old, I was crazy about magic. We had an Irish cook and when things got too tough at school, I'd sit by the old-fashioned coal stove in our kitchen and she would tell me stories of the elves, leprechauns and fairies who, she assured me, were as common as rabbits in Ireland. I learned to read early and soon became an authority on Hans Christian Andersen, the Grimm Brothers, and Andrew Lang. Everybody in fairy stories accepted magic as a matter of course and I was sure I could learn to be a magician if I only knew how to go about it.

One memorable day, I decided to try out some of the spells described in the books. My attempts to turn my sister into a rabbit didn't work but then I didn't have all the ingredients necessary—I was missing some bone from a unicorn's horn. However, there was another incantation that was guaranteed to enable you to fly through the air on a broomstick. All the materials needed could be gotten right around my home, although I had to spend several evenings in a neighbor's barn before I got the heart of a bat. I coated myself with the muck, borrowed the cook's broom without saying what I wanted it for, climbed up on the roof and hopefully stepped off. Fortunately, I only broke my ankle, but the broomstick was never the same again.

That experience discouraged me, especially as the cook admitted she'd colored up her stories about Irish wild life considerably. But I still wanted to be a magician. A few years later I began buying magic tricks from a mail order house and by practicing arduously I was able to give a show at the school's commencement. There was a dime museum in Philadelphia near the Old Chinatown section that featured a magician who kept the kiddies amused while their fathers went in to see the Beautiful Undraped Models. I hung around the magician and he took enough interest in me to explain some of the basic sleight-of-hand moves. When I was in high school I met another young fellow named Arthur Strafford who was also interested in conjuring. We formed a team and went around giving shows to anyone who would watch us.

Arthur and I had diametrically opposite views on magic. He was a magnificent manipulator and could make cards form into waterfalls and fans as though the pasteboards had become living liquid. Clusters of coins materialized at the tips of his fingers. Arthur despised patter and always worked silently, letting his hands talk for him. He regarded magic as an ocular puzzle— his dexterity and misdirection against the audience's powers of observation.

I didn't like this point of view at all. I was resorting to sleight-of-hand only because I couldn't do the real thing. I resented having the audience know I was nothing but a trickster. If I could have pretended to be a genuine magician I would have gladly done so. I still had a sneaking hope that some day I'd learn how to do real magic. There are plenty of people in America today who claim to produce genuine supernatural phenomena— the voodoo doctors in the South, the powwow healers in the Pennsylvania Dutch country, various occult societies, and the spirit mediums. There weren't any voodoo doctors or powwow men around Philadelphia, but eventually Arthur Strafford and I did run into a spirit medium.

Arthur and I often picked up pocket money by giving shows at clubs, banquets, and debutante parties where regular performers were considered a little too *outré* for Philadelphia society. At one dinner party, Arthur climaxed the evening by escaping from a locked mailbag. After polite applause, several people came up to speak to us, including an impressive dowager wearing heavy heirloom jewelry and an expensive but shapeless evening gown.

"I enjoyed that mailbag trick especially," she told us. "My husband can do several things like that."

"Is your husband a magician?" I asked politely.

"Oh no, he's dead," was the astonishing answer. "But he comes back in spirit form. It's simply unbelievable what he can do now. Did you have to dematerialize yourself to escape from the bag?" she asked Arthur.

Arthur nervously replied that there were several different systems and the lady moved on. A moment later an elderly gentleman with a shrewd, kindly face strolled over and introduced himself as the lady's family lawyer.

"A spirit medium who claims to be some sort of a yogi has gotten hold of that woman and I don't consider him a very healthy influence," the lawyer told us. "Why don't you boys see if you can find out how this fellow does his tricks? It might bring her to her senses."

Arthur and I were flattered and delighted. We knew a great deal about spirit mediums—all from reading books, of course—and we were delighted to see a real one. The lawyer said he could arrange to have us attend one of the medium's séances and for the next week we feverishly read up on electric table-rapping, cheesecloth ghosts and bogus slate writing. Equipped with our mass of book learning, we went to the séance.

The séance was held in the elegant drawing room of the medium's home. About twenty people were present, mostly women, although there were a few men. We sat around a long oak table in the center of the room while a concealed phonograph played sacred music. The room was darkened except for a chandelier, hung with cut-glass prisms, and containing a weak red bulb. After an impressive wait, the medium entered garbed in black. He wore a small goatee and looked like a prosperous physician.

As the medium seated himself at the head of the table, some hidden mechanism switched off the red bulb in the chandelier and turned on a dim white light set into the table directly in front of the medium. This light was focused full on the medium's face like a miniature spotlight. It threw hard, definite shadows. The medium began to move his head slightly. At one moment his nose would cast a shadow over his upper lip and then a few seconds later his chin would throw his throat into deep shadow. When his upper lip darkened so as to form a crude mustache, a woman called out, "That's Grandfather David. I recognize him by his mustache. Grandfather's spirit has possessed the medium." A few seconds later, the medium's throat went black and gave the illusion of a beard. A man explained to us, "Now he's become Brigham Young. Has anyone here any Mormon relatives or are any of us interested particularly in Mormonism?"

Suddenly a lady sitting next to me said in a hushed voice, "Mrs. Marshall, a violet light is forming over your head."

I stared at Mrs. Marshall. She was sitting very stiff and proud, but I could see no sign of a violet light. I glanced at Arthur Strafford and could tell by the expression on his face that he wasn't seeing a violet light either. Yet as soon as the lady spoke, other sitters began seeing lights. A man across the table from Mrs. Marshall said in an awestruck voice, "Yes, I can see the light, too. It is assuming the outlines of a cross. I can also see an orange-colored aura forming around Mrs. Benedict."

"That means that Rajah Lalloo, my spirit guide, is coming," Mrs. Benedict told us eagerly.

During the next half hour, everyone saw lights except Arthur and me. The lights took the forms of esoteric symbols. They floated around the room and even rapped on the table. I couldn't hear the raps, but several other people did. It must have been a wonderful demonstration for someone who knew what the hell was going on. When the medium finally awoke from his trance and the séance was over, Arthur strode over to the man indignantly.

"This whole thing is nothing but a form of hypnotic suggestion," he announced angrily. The sitters listened in shocked silence while Arthur went on. "Not a thing happened—no lights, no knocks, nothing. You're a complete fake."

The yogi lost his temper. "Look here, you young punk," he said ("punk" no doubt being an Oriental term for a skeptic). "Wait till you can take a bunch like this, sit 'em down in a room and make 'em see lights. Then you can start talking about occult subjects."

Outside, Arthur burst forth angrily, "Why, there was nothing to expose. No fake tables, no trick slates, no cabinets with secret compartments. That man isn't even a good fraudulent medium. He's a complete failure."

"What does he want with trick cabinets or phony slates?" I asked. "He gets better effects just using suggestions than a magician could with a million dollars' worth of apparatus."

After that experience I began to understand that there was more to occultism than the magicians who write exposés claim. Arthur and I made it our business to call on a large number of spirit mediums. According to the exposés, mediums produce their effects by trapdoors and revolving mirrors. Our experience with one well-known medium, who lives in Harlem, will give a fair idea of how most spirit mediums operate. We had read of this lady in a book written by an exposer who described her devilish ingenuity. After reading the exposé, we decided that the lady must maintain a corps of trained physicists to produce her marvelous effects. No other explanation was possible. So Arthur and I traveled to New York to see this incredible woman.

The medium was a circular colored lady who talked like Uncle Remus and lived in a second floor walkup. We made a "love-offering" of five dollars each and then sat in her front parlor on hard wooden chairs with some ten other clients. The lights were turned low and the medium went into a trance. After a few minutes a man's voice came out of her throat speaking in close-clipped British accents.

"I am Sir Arthur Conan Doyle," said the voice. "Let me assure you that we of the spirit world feel deeply gratified that you Yankees are striving to pierce the veil between life and death."

The effect was quite startling, especially as the "control voice" later became a little child, a Harvard college professor, and a French woman. But after listening for a while it became obvious that the medium was simply "throat talking" like a ventriloquist without moving her lips. The different voices were remarkably good but the timbre of the woman's voice running through them all was unmistakable. Also, there were occasional slips. Sir Arthur had a tendency to say "dat" for "that" and the French lady's accent was more Haitian than Parisian.

Before the séance, Arthur had asked to speak to his Uncle Frank, a mechanical engineer who had died the year before. Arthur had prepared some "test questions" that only his uncle could answer. About halfway through the séance, the deep voice of a man cut through the French woman's rapid clatter.

"I believe that my nephew, Arthur, is in the congregation tonight," said the voice. "I want you to know, my lad, that we are all happy in Summerland and that . . ."

"Uncle Frank," said Arthur, firmly interrupting, "I have a problem."

"I'm sure I can straighten that up for you, my lad," said Uncle Frank happily. "Some little affair of the heart, perhaps, or . . ."

"My problem is this. In preparing a two-way rotary induction coil, should the ammeter receive vibrations from the tensile strength of the hookup or from the Cooke thermal tube?"

There was a long pause from Uncle Frank.

"I see what you mean when you say you have a problem," he remarked. "Now as the power is getting weaker, I must return to Summerland. However at some future date . . ."

"If the power is getting weaker, the medium won't be able to answer these other people's problems and must refund their money," Arthur pointed out. He was really a very unpleasant fellow.

Uncle Frank was so clearly in a horrible position that I took mercy on him.

"Don't you think by increasing the pressure on the coil . . ." I began.

That was all Uncle Frank needed. He knew what "pressure" meant and he took full advantage of it.

"Dat's it!" he shouted, much relieved. "You ain't got enough pressure, son. Put on de pressure! Put on de pressure!"

Uncle Frank returned to Summerland before anyone could stop him, but he came back at intervals during the rest of the séance breaking through the other spirits and shouting gleefully, "Dat problem of yours, son! I got it solved! Put on de pressure, put on de pressure!"

After the séance, Arthur marched over to the medium and denounced her as a fake and a complete incompetent.

"What do you mean, incompetent?" asked the fat lady with imperturbable good humor. "I got youh five dolla', didn't I?"

The Philadelphia dowager's yogi and this old lady marked about the zenith and nadir of occult work, but both of them were real magicians. Unlike stage performers, neither of them had to use mechanical tricks. They had both developed some unusual skill—the old woman her ability as a mimic and the yogi his powers of hypnotic suggestion—but most important they knew how to influence the minds of their clients. I

began to realize that there is almost no similarity between a sleight-of-hand worker and an occultist. An occultist may base his work on some unusual physical device, such as ventriloquism or hypnosis, but mainly he depends on his ability to handle people and create a certain atmosphere.

The modern conjurer with his sleight-of-hand and flashy props has ceased to be a magician—he has become a juggler. No one thinks that a prestidigitator pulls a rabbit out of a hat through supernatural ability. But many people believe that an Oriental fire-walker can walk over hot coals due to some occult power. "If not, then how does he do it?" they argue. The conjurer can't give any logical answer because it's not worth his time to go through the trouble and danger involved in learning fire-walking. So the fire-walker continues to be a real magician because people believe he is genuine.

When I graduated from high school, I wanted to be a real magician. Unfortunately, my parents didn't see things that way. For the last four generations, my family has been in the Navy, so it was more or less taken for granted that I'd go to the United States Naval Academy at Annapolis, Maryland. I didn't want to be a naval officer; I wanted to be a witch doctor. But everyone assured me that once I got into the academy, I'd be carried away by the spirit of the place, so I left for Annapolis.

The next year was the most unpleasant period I've ever spent. I didn't like the discipline, I didn't like the hazing, and I didn't like being kept behind a ten-foot wall patrolled by guards. I guess I just didn't get into the spirit of the academy. The commandant of midshipmen expressed what was wrong with me very well. One afternoon, some VIP paid a visit to the academy and the corps of midshipmen was paraded for his benefit. You've often seen similar reviews in the newsreels. It was a very impressive ceremony—or would have been except for me. After the review was over, the commandant asked to see me. He had me march up and down in front of him with my rifle for nearly half an hour before he expressed himself.

"I don't know what it is," said the commandant, mystified. "His brace is correct, his rifle is correct, and his uniform is correct. But somehow when the rest of the corps is passing in review, he always looks as though he's going duck hunting."

After leaving the Naval Academy, I went to the University of Pennsylvania. I'd always had a hazy idea that someday I might be able to write, so I sent one of my English I themes to the *Saturday Evening Post*. The subject of the theme was keeping pet animals. I'd always liked animals and knew quite a lot about them. To my astonishment, the *Post* accepted the article and sent me a check for five hundred dollars.

I decided that being a writer was easy. I saw no reason why I couldn't sell an article a week to the *Post*, but to be conservative, I thought I'd better not count on selling more than one a month. At my next English class, the professor read one of my themes aloud and then remarked, "Mannix, this is fairly good. I think the college literary magazine might take it. What do you do with your old English themes?"

"I sell them to the *Saturday Evening Post,*" I said.

The professor reeled in his chair while the rest of the class stared at me goggle-eyed. At last the professor gasped, "I've been trying to sell something to the *Post* for the last forty years. Tell me, how did you do it?"

I spent my next four years in college trying to sell to the *Post* again. Everything bounced right back. Finally one of the editors called me in.

"That first article was good because you were writing about something you knew," he explained. "The rest of the things you've been submitting show that you don't have any real knowledge of your subjects. Pick an interesting subject, get some real personalized information on it, and then try the magazine again."

There didn't seem to be any subject on which I had real, personalized information so I decided that I'd have to find some other way to make a living.

But I did derive one great advantage from college. The university had inherited the Lee Library on occultism and witchcraft. Mr. Lee, who is famous for his great work *The History of the Inquisition*, had been preparing another many-volumed account of witchcraft. He died before the series was completed and his collection of reference books, together with the beautiful library in which they were housed, was moved to the university. I spent many happy days in this library reading up on witchcraft, as completely cut off from the college campus as though I were in another world.

But I couldn't treat occultism as though it were a purely academic subject. I wanted to find out if there were anything to the business. Occultists are doing better today than they ever have. Fortunetellers take in over thirty million dollars a year. In addition, there are hundreds of companies manufacturing charms, talismans, crystal-gazing balls, spirit trumpets, magical candles, incenses, and oils. One of these companies in Chicago puts out an annual catalogue containing 780 pages of fine print listing paraphernalia used in sorcery. There are scores of thriving magical groups, several of which have founded communities for the study of the esoteric arts. I wanted to find out if these organizations were completely fraudulent or if they did possess some strange secrets unknown to science.

When the time came for me to graduate from college, I would gladly have become an occultist, but I didn't know how to break into the business. How do you go about becoming a wizard? Then I found there is a place where, for an admission fee of twenty-five cents you can see feats that for centuries have been the property of occultists. This place is the side show of a traveling carnival.

In a side show, you can see dwarfs and giants, gypsies who foretell the future, and men who lie on beds of spikes. You can work with mind readers, astrologers, and fortunetellers. You can see fire-eaters demonstrating their immunity to fire much as the priests of Zoroaster did two thousand years before Christ. How is fire-eating done? I'd read exposés that explained how the performers coated their mouths with chemicals to protect their flesh from the flames. Did Polynesian fire-walkers, Navajo fire-dancers, and carnival fire-eaters all know about these chemicals and have access to them? That seemed hard to believe. But if they didn't, how was the feat performed?

Then there are the men in side shows who do torture acts—thrust pins through their bodies without drawing blood or apparently feeling pain. I knew Indian fakirs had been performing this feat for centuries. My professors had occasionally mentioned the phenomenon. Some of them believed that it was due to self-hypnosis and others claimed that the fakir had first to work himself into a religious frenzy. But none of them seemed really to know.

I had often watched carnival snake charmers handle rattlesnakes as though the reptiles were coils of rope. I had always been interested in reptiles and the curator of the local zoo, an expert herpetologist, had often taken me in the runway behind the cages and opened the plate-glass doors. But he always treated the poisonous snakes with great respect. How were snake charmers able to push rattlesnakes around with impunity? Were the snakes' fangs extracted? If so, how did they eat and why didn't they die of the fatal mouthrot that affects virtually all reptiles with a mouth injury?

Within a side show tent are people dealing with mysteries as old as the human race—and dealing with them in the same cool professional manner that Pharaoh's magicians must have shown when they duplicated Moses' feat of turning his rod into a serpent. But I realized that whatever secrets they knew would always be hidden from me unless I joined a side show.

I was a reasonably good magician and I thought some carnival might give me a job. If you can be a success in side shows, it may be the beginning of a career. Harry Houdini started working in carnivals. He learned the techniques there with which he later astonished the world. Many people still believe that Houdini had supernatural powers because no other magician has ever been able to duplicate his feats. W. C. Fields learned how to juggle in traveling shows, but he also learned something more important—how to gauge audience reaction so perfectly that he was able to eliminate his juggling routine and use straight comedy. Ripley haunted carnivals and got many of his best "Believe It or Not" items from the side show. All these famous men were able to absorb the strange blend of humor, magic, and grotesqueness that is the spirit of carnival life.

So when Flamo blew up that night outside the side show tent, there were a thousand questions I wanted to ask the performers. But looking around the darkened tent, I doubted if these performers would want to teach me the secrets of their business. I stood there waiting hopefully but no one spoke. ✎

Snake charmer.

One of The Impossible Possible's papers.

CHAPTER 3

While we were standing there, the sidewall of the tent near the horse's stall began to sway and billow in. Someone was trying to crawl under the canvas from the outside.

The cowboy shouted out warningly, "Hey you, keep out! There's a vicious horse in there!"

The shaking stopped and a voice like a foghorn said, "M'boy, the only thing that can hurt me is something worse than I am—and I ain't likely to meet that." Then the sidewall was jerked up and a lean, elderly man with a bushy beard came crawling in on his hands and knees.

Krinko gave a joyful bellow and went stamping over toward this apparition with his arms out. "This is wonderful! How you get out of jail?" he roared. "Look, I still got one of your throwaways." He stopped at a massive teakwood chest by his platform and, rummaging through a rat's nest of newspaper clippings, proudly came up with a much-creased piece of paper. "Hey, everybody!" he called. "You know who this man is?"

The paper was passed around and I finally stole a look at it. The "throwaway" was a long slip of glossy paper. On it was a picture of the stranger without his whiskers and wearing a white turban. Above the cut was printed, THE IMPOSSIBLE POSSIBLE! and under it THE INCREDIBLE TRUE!

"We old friends," said Krinko happily. "He do fine fire act." Turning to the stranger, he went on, "Our fire-eater just blow up, so you do fire act for me, eh?"

"I haven't done any fire-eating since I grew this beard," said the Impossible Possible, sitting down familiarly on the platform. "And if I shaved I'd look like my picture in the post office. Anyhow, I got a concession here already fixed up."

Old Krinko shook his massive head as though he refused to believe it. "You stay with me, eh?" he said cozily. "I need fire act bad."

"Honest to God, I'd like to, Krinko. That fire-eating routine of mine was a good effect, all right, but the effect was mainly on me. I began to turn blue from lead poisoning when the gas companies put lead in their gas."

Suddenly I saw a wonderful opportunity to learn fire-eating. Two voices were talking inside of me. One said, "Don't be a damn fool. Suppose you blow up as Flamo did?" The other voice said, "No one really knows anything about side show life and the curious tricks side show people can do. You've always been

crazy about carnivals. Stop reading books about them and join this outfit."

I spoke up. "I'd like to join this show. How about teaching me fire-eating?" It's astonishing how loud your own voice sounds under certain conditions. The Impossible Possible shook his head regretfully.

"Naturally, it's every young man's ambition to be a fire-eater, m'boy. They argue that sometimes you go for weeks without having a really serious accident. But it's a tough thing to teach anybody. All you can do is tell 'em to fill their mouths with gasoline, touch a lighted match to it, and await developments."

"Isn't there some chemical you use that keeps you from getting burned?" I asked.

No one answered and I had an uneasy feeling I'd asked a stupid question. At last the Impossible said gently:

"You forget that chemical stuff, kid. Every now and then someone writes a book on carnivals and decides to expose fire-eating. So he calls up some university chemistry professor and asks how it's done. The professor tells him the fire-eater must coat the inside of his mouth with a chemical formula that resists heat. I used to carry around a number of these formulas supposedly used by all fire-eaters that I'd clipped out of Sunday supplements as a joke. They all contained mercury which is a deadly poison. But every year a bunch of kids who read those stories get poisoned trying out the exposers' systems, which they always describe as 'extremely simple, once the secret is revealed.'"

"Then how is it done?" I wanted to know.

"Fire-eating is an art. I can show you the routine and after that you'll just have to practice until you can do it. But you're going to get pretty badly burned while you're learning."

"What do you want to learn fire-eating for, son?" asked the tattooed man, who quietly materialized by the tent entrance. He had put on a coat and with the amazing tangle of tattoo marks covered, his round red face and fringe of white hair made him look like a benevolent retired sea captain.

"I'd like to learn all the carnival acts," I told him. "I've never seen anything like this before and I don't believe the public realizes that you people aren't fakes. You've really got some wonderful techniques here but no one knows about them. I'd like to be able to do everything—fire-eating, sword-swallowing, handling snakes, maybe even sticking pins in myself like this gentleman who's the Indian fakir."

Old Krinko had been staring at the sawdust. He awakened with a sigh. "He called me fakir. Long time since I heard that word. That's what I am—not just carny bum. I real fakir! That boy smart, got good education."

"He has at that," said the Impossible thoughtfully. "Say, Krinko, I'll tell you what I'll do. I'll teach him fire-eating if you lend him to me for my little concession a couple of times an evening. I was going to get a canvas boy to work as a stick for me, but this kid is better because he don't look carny—which God knows, he's not."

"What's a stick?" I asked.

"I run a Wheel of Fortune and you come up and bet to draw the crowd," the Impossible explained. "To be a good stick you need to be an actor. You've got to throw your soul into it."

"I pay you thirty dollars a week," said Krinko, making up his mind. He came over to me and put his heavy hand on my arm with a smile.

"I show you how to do torture act—stick pins in yourself, dance on broke glass, drive nails into your eyes—you be real fakir like me, eh?"

"It's a chance not many people ever have," I said perfectly sincerely.

The tattooed man walked over and shook hands. "I lay on a bed of spikes," he explained with quiet pride. "If you want any tattoos put on you, I'll do it for free. It's been my experience that every man has wanted to be tattooed at one time or another."

"I'd appreciate that," I told him.

The old lady in the gypsy costume held out her hand without getting up. "I have a mitt camp here . . . that's palmistry, you know. If you're interested I'll show you how to tell what a person is and what's going to happen to him from the lines on his palms."

"I'd give a lot to have that knowledge," I assured her.

Last to come over were the cowboy and the pretty girl in the bra and shorts. "It's sure a pleasure to have you with this outfit, mister," said the cowboy, grabbing my hand in a grip as hard as a T-clamp. "Anything you want to know about guns, ropes, or whips, you come to me. I reckon you don't know that there's over thirty ways to spin a rope, but I can do 'em all. And I'll show you how to flick a fly off the ear of your lead horse usin' one of my bullwhips. This little lady here is my wife, Lu."

Lu grinned all over her little round face as we shook hands. "You're a nice-lookin' kid," she said kindly. "You look kinda like a Swede—your hair's so light and you're tall. But you're awful skinny. I'm goin' to call you Slim."

"Slim it is, Lu," I said.

"Maybe we can get you a nice girl from one of the other shows so you won't be lonely," added Lu benevolently. "But you'd have to have your own livin' top—that's a little tent you sleep in. You got one?"

"I've got some camping equipment—sleeping bag and cooking stuff, but no tent," I said.

"You sleep on inside platform here," said Krinko, kicking one of the wood supports. "You stick pins in yourself all day and you don't want no girl. That's what I do . . . . I old bachelor," he opened his big mouth and laughed like a lion roaring.

"I'll get my stuff and be back here at eight in the morning," I told him.

"Eight in the morning?" said Lu in horror, while the others stared at me. "Nobody gets up on a carny lot before noon."

"I've got to fix my wheel tomorrow so I'll be up," said the Impossible good-naturedly. "You be here around ten and I'll give you a lesson in fire-eating and show you how to cap."

"I'll be there," I said happily and ducking out under the tent flap I walked down the deserted midway toward the glare of distant street lights where I'd parked my car.

I arrived at the carnival lot a little before ten o'clock. There seemed to be no signs of life. The rides and swings were wrapped in their canvas covers, looking like sleeping brown cows. The little booths where you could win a prize by knocking a stuffed cat off a board with a baseball or by throwing darts at rubber balloons still had their front curtains securely tied down. I walked along the empty midway to the side show tent. The great canvas banners had been lowered and the tent flap was lashed closed. I looked around the quiet grounds wondering where I could find the Impossible Possible.

Most people vaguely think of a carnival as a sort of rough-and-ready circus but actually the two institutions are completely different. A circus is a single organization and everything takes place under the big top. A carnival is a collection of small concessions each operating independently but moving around the country together for the sake of convenience. The concessionaires pitch their tents in a great oval, all facing inward. In the center of the oval are the shows that do not require covering, such as the ferris wheel, the merry-go-round, and the open restaurant booths. Between the tents and this central group is an open space, covered with sawdust, called the midway. The midway is the carnival's boulevard along which people stroll in the evenings, stopping at the different concessions to watch the outside platform demonstrations and buying cold drinks from the refreshment stands. At one end of the oval is the entrance, surmounted by a brightly lighted marquee. Admission is charged to enter the carnival and each show also has its own admission charge. To give the customers a return for their entrance fee, the carnival provides a Free Act every evening at eleven o'clock, usually some spectacular acrobatic feat. After you have paid your entrance fee to the lot, you can spend the entire evening wandering around the midway watching the outside demonstrations and buying nothing except a bottle of pop or a hot dog. On the other hand, I'd often spent thirty or forty dollars by going to all the shows and playing the gambling games.

Now I was a member of the organization, but I still felt a little strange as I pushed between the side show tent and the girl show canvas next to it and came out behind the ring of tents.

Behind the tents was a circle made by the parked cars and trucks of the carnival people. The line of cars, parked side by side much as the pioneers used to ring their wagon trains against Indian attacks, formed a wall that protected the carnival from the outside world.

Between this ring and the rear of the show tents was an open space full of soft green grass. This was where the carnival folk lived. A whole crop of little living tents had sprung up here like an Indian village. Some of the trailers had smoke beginning to rise from their chimneys but there was no other sign of life except for a parrot swinging by his beak in a cage hung from the door of a trailer, and a monkey on a long string tied outside one of the tents. When I started to walk among the tents, half a dozen dogs came bursting out, barking at me. A little gypsy kid, naked as a goldfish, crawled out from under a car and stood staring at me with his finger in his mouth. I stared back at him and after a minute he turned and ran.

I walked along, expecting every minute to be challenged, but no one appeared. I saw some girls hanging out their wash on the tent ropes, but they paid no attention to me. I wanted to ask them about the Impossible, but as I didn't even know what his real name was I felt a little shy. Then, rounding the corner of a small tent, I saw the Impossible sitting by a campfire heating a soldering iron. He waved to me and I thankfully hurried over.

"Glad to see you, m'boy," said the Impossible. "I thought you might have turned chicken after thinking things over. I'm getting my props ready for tonight." He was working on a big board with a map of the United States painted on it. Each state had a little electric light set into the center of it and when the Impossible spun a wheel the lights flickered on one after another until the wheel stopped spinning and there was only one light left lit.

"What's that for?" I asked, sitting down on the grass beside him. The Impossible had built his campfire in a little pocket among the tents and although there were scores of people separated from us by only the thickness of thin canvas walls, I had a curious feeling of complete, secret privacy. I felt as though the Impossible and I could have committed a murder there and no one on the lot would have made any comment. The cluster of tents and trailers seemed to form an impenetrable barrier cutting us off from the ordinary life.

"This is my concession," said the Impossible, giving the wheel a whirl and making the little lights dance over the map like drunken fireflies. "People pay a quarter to spin the wheel and then bet where the light will stop. If they guess right, I pay them ten dollars."

"And what's this for?" I asked, pointing to a wire ending in a button that ran off from behind the map.

"That's in case I start winning too much money. I can stop the light anywhere on the board by pressing that button and that allows the people to win more."

"It seems to me you could also use it to keep somebody from winning," I remarked.

The Impossible slowly brought his hand down and slapped the side of his leg. "By golly, that's right!" he exclaimed in amazement. "I never thought of that until this very minute."

I looked up quickly but the lean face was very serious and there was not the slightest twinkle in his deep-set black eyes.

"And what about this bar?" I asked. There was another wire running to a long bar that didn't seem to be of any use.

"Well, I don't like that button much. It stops the wheel too suddenly. Looks unnatural. Also, I have to put my hands under the counter to operate it and there's a certain class of customer you get who notices things like that. So most of the time I use the bar. It runs along the front of the joint under the counter and I work it by my foot. Just a little pressure on it slows the wheel down. And I don't need to go near the map while I'm doing it."

"Is that important?"

"It surely is, m'boy. That gives a mark confidence that he's got complete control of the wheel and the map. It's very important to give people confidence in themselves," the Impossible pointed out virtuously. "Why, a lot of marks make a real scientific study of just how hard they have to spin the wheel to make the light stop on a certain state. Keep notes on it and come back night after night. Sometimes I even let them practice free for a while."

"It's a wonderful machine," I told him. "But it's even more interesting how you've got everything figured out."

"M'boy, in carny life you've got to have a real sympathetic understanding of the public," said the Impossible with what seemed to be genuine sincerity. "When I got this wheel from the manufacturer, it was just an ordinary wheel. Of course, they included printed instructions showing how to install the control button with a warning that dishonest operators occasionally resorted to such devices and offering to sell the necessary parts for a small additional sum. Being a reputable company, they naturally couldn't install the device themselves. Well, I picked up the parts myself from a hardware store during the rush hour when the clerks were busy elsewhere. But the thing didn't bring in the marks. So I sat down and studied the situation out."

"How?" I asked, fascinated.

"M'boy, there's nothing the public likes better than to feel they've swindled somebody," said the Impossible, spitting on his soldering iron to see how it was coming along. "When I was busy trying to collect a tip—that means a crowd—some mark would always start fooling with the wheel when he thought I wasn't looking. I hitched another stop-wire to this bar so I could work the map while I was at the other end of the joint. With a little quiet help from me, the mark would learn how to spin the wheel just hard enough to stop the light on a certain state. Then he'd call me over and we'd start betting. Remember that to be a successful businessman you must have a tender spot in your heart for the foibles of humanity."

A shrill voice called, "Hi, you fellers et yet?" Lu, the cowboy's wife, was standing in the entrance of a little living tent a few yards away grinning at us. With her brown hair hanging over her shoulders she looked about fourteen years old.

"Got some extra food, Lu?" shouted the Impossible, dropping his soldering iron and rising on his long legs like an eager stork.

"I'll cook breakfast if you two'll wash the dishes. This is a hell of a lot . . . no water." Lu's girlish face clouded over and suddenly she looked old and shrewish. "That son-of-a-bitch of an advance man ought to check on them things."

Lu had a little gasoline stove with a double burner. While the Impossible pumped up the gasoline cylinder, I went into the tiny tent to help Lu carry out the food. The cowboy was sitting up on the camp cot that nearly filled the small space rubbing his tousled, curly hair. He was unshaven and still partly asleep. Lu kicked at him with one foot shod in a scuffed green mule.

"I ain't goin' to bring you breakfast in bed, so don't think it!" she shouted in her shrill voice. "Here, Slim, you take the stuff out. This damn top ain't big enough fer a louse, let alone three people."

I received an armful of paper bags, tin plates, knives and forks, and a coffee pot. The Impossible had the stove going and, while I was getting the stuff sorted out, Lu bustled out again.

"Here, you let me cook," she said shouldering me out of the way. With astonishing dexterity, she cooked us a very good breakfast of bacon and eggs with excellent coffee. Without stopping to eat herself, Lu heaped a tin plate with the choicest victuals plus a steaming cup of coffee and headed back for the tent. "That lazy bastard Bronko ain't goin' to get up so I'll have to bring in his breakfast," she shouted over her shoulder.

Bronko was already up and shaving in front of a mirror tied to the centerpole of the tent. Lu came out to get him some hot water, cursing him for not eating his breakfast before it got cold. In a few minutes Bronko came out wearing what was apparently his second-best cowboy outfit and looking very handsome.

"Sure like to sit a spell and chat with you boys," he said gravely, "but I reckon I better look at the stock."

He headed off among the tents, his big wheel spurs catching in the grass.

"I guess he means he's got to look after the five-legged horse?" I said inquiringly.

"You mean Dot?" Lu poured herself a cup of coffee and sat down cross-legged beside us. "Naw, he don't pay no mind to that old wreck. He's goin' to go over our car. We got a miss in the engine somewheres."

"I suppose a five-legged horse is something of a comedown after handling range ponies," I admitted.

"Well, real cowboys nowadays don't fool none with horses. It's all mechanized now."

"What part of the West does Bronko come from?" I asked curiously.

"Oh, he ain't never been out West. He wouldn't go if you paid him. Them cowboys out there ain't real cowboys no more. Bronko's made a study of it."

"You mean he isn't a real cowboy?" I asked in astonishment.

"Sure he's a real cowboy," Lu squeaked indignantly. "It's them cowboys out West that ain't real. Why, last winter we was playin' in a museum in New York— that's a dime museum, you know—and they had a big rodeo at Madison Square Garden. Some of them cowboys came to see Bronko's act and was they surprised! He showed 'em lots about rope-spinnin' and whip-crackin' they never knowed about. Why, they couldn't hardly understand a lot of the real cowboy talk he uses."

"But how did he learn all the stuff he knows about whips and ropes?" I demanded.

"Well, it's like this," explained Lu, wriggling her trim little bottom down into the soft grass. "Bronko used to work for a firm in Brooklyn that made tin cans. The tin cans used to come out of a shute into a basket and he had to select the different kinds and put them into boxes. He worked there five years and he's a big strong guy so it got kind of boring. He lived in a little room over a Kosher restaurant and every night he'd read about cowboys and how they shot it out in the streets and herded cattle and such. He saved up to take riding lessons at Central Park, but the first time he went a horse bit him, so he didn't go back no more. Bronko is awful sensitive, although you wouldn't think it to look at him. Well, he kept on readin' and went to the libraries and read some more, and then he got a book on rope-spinnin' and another on whip-crackin' and studied them up. He got to be awful good and joined a carny."

"What are those notches on his gun for?"

"He won three shootin' contests for being able to draw and shoot the quickest of anybody at the West End Wild West Club. Bronko is the only man in America that ever won that contest three times."

"I see," I said thoughtfully. I sympathized with Bronko. Life had gotten too dull for him to stand it and yet he didn't have the nerve to strike out West and become the man of his dreams. Yet even if he had become a cowboy, would that have been any satisfaction? As Lu said, the West has become mechanized. The West that Bronko loved didn't exist—in fact, probably never had existed. It was the West of the motion pictures where the hero is always clean-shaven, the heroine wears hoop skirts and make-up, and the cattle rustler is always shot down by a six-shooter that fires twenty times without reloading. That was the land that Bronko loved so intensely he had devoted his life to trying to find a way to enter it, just as a child tries hard to find the magic gateway into fairyland. As we grow older, we give up trying, but Bronko had succeeded. He was the mythological cowboy of the past and believed it so sincerely that he had finally succeeded in convincing even his tough, cynical little wife.

Lu.

After we had finished eating, I lay back on the soft grass feeling completely contented. These carnival people suited me exactly. I knew how Bronko, the cowboy, felt with his dull routine job and his desire to be a unique, colorful character. I knew how the Impossible felt with his quiet pleasure in outwitting the crafty suckers who thought they were fleecing him. In the bright blue sky above me, fat white clouds were floating by, slowly forming themselves into castles, dragons, and strange, mystic shapes. I remembered how I used to watch clouds as a child and pretend that they were carrying me into another land, full of strange adventures and weird people, as different as possible from the routine life and prosaic schoolboys I knew. I felt for the first time that the clouds were going to fulfill their promises.

"I got you Flamo's torches as he won't be wanting them any more," said the Impossible. He unfolded his lazy-tong legs and walked back to the campfire. I reluctantly followed him. Lu screamed after us, "Don't you forget to do the dishes!" But when I turned back, she had filled a dishpan with hot water and was washing the dishes herself, whistling a cowboy song and doing a little jig step as she worked.

The Impossible had the torches wrapped up in a rag smelling strongly of gasoline. He unfolded them carefully. "You ought to have a couple extra," he remarked as he laid the smoke-blacked rods out on the grass. "The metal rods that hold up store awnings make good torches. Maybe we can promote some in the next town."

I examined one of the torches. So these were the instruments that the priests of Mazda had used to maintain domination over an empire thousands of years ago. Medieval jugglers had used them—and been hanged for witchcraft. Hawaiian kahunas had demonstrated their imperviousness to fire, and travelers had returned swearing that these men possessed some strange power that more civilized cultures had lost. Now I was going to learn this power—supposing, of course, that I didn't blow myself up first.

The torch looked like a big buttonhook with a handle at one end and the other end twisted into a hook. The Impossible tore off a strip of the rag, wadded it into a ball, and put it into the hook, hammering the soft wire down to hold it in place.

"Now we need some gas," he went on, producing a length of rubber hose and a tin can. "You hunt up a parked car."

He said it as naturally as though telling me to run down to the store. Reasoning that taking gas from any of the cars parked on the lot would be considered stealing by carnival ethics, I hunted up a parked car on a side street outside the carny grounds and nervously filled the tin. No one saw me, but my legs were still shaking when I got back to the lot. This had been my first expedition into crime, but I had a notion that if I stayed with the Impossible, it wouldn't be my last.

The Impossible carefully poured the gas into a glass preserve jar. "I never like to leave gas around in an open tin," he explained. "Did it once while a friend of mine was frying eggs in a pan over a fire. He thought the gas was ham gravy and poured it over the eggs." The Impossible left a little gas in the tin, then clamped down the lid on the jar, and put it well away from the fire. "Made quite a little flare-up. Burned off most of his face and raised hell with the eggs."

The Impossible soaked the cloth end of the torch in the can, and then squeezed the cloth against the side to get rid of the surplus gas. He struck a match on his boot and lit the torch. I was disappointed to find that the fire which had glowed so magnificently by night was almost invisible in daylight. But when I took the torch, I could feel the heat of the six-inch flame.

I tried to hold the torch as Flamo had. The steel was black and I wondered how many times the fire-eater had used this particular torch and how he was feeling now.

"The great secret of fire work is not to allow the fumes of gas you're eating to explode in your lungs," the Impossible explained.

"Once you've learned how to avoid that, your only worry is how to keep from being burned by the fire coming out of your mouth."

"That's the part I'm particularly interested in," I assured him.

"Well, first make sure your mouth and lips are wet." I licked my lips, surprised at how dry my mouth had suddenly become. "Now you have to put the torch in at just the right angle, or the flames will bounce off the roof of your mouth and burn your cheeks and lips. And, listen, m'boy. Don't inhale!"

I wiped off the sweat that was dripping into my eyes and lowered the torch toward my mouth. "Get your head farther back," instructed the Impossible. "Keep the torch at just about that slant. Don't make a mistake and miss your mouth. Make sure you're breathing out a little all the time, or you'll get gas fumes into your lungs, and there'll be an explosion there like in the cylinder of a car. Only your lungs ain't built to take it."

I breathed out very conscientiously, and stuck the torch into my mouth. I felt the fierce heat and pulled it out again quickly. I could taste the gasoline, and after a few seconds the left corner of my mouth began to hurt. I touched the spot with my tongue and found I had a blister.

"You see, you can always tell when you're doing it wrong," remarked the Impossible. He dug up a little mud and put it on the blister. "Try again."

I did, and was so anxious to keep the flame away from the blister that I got my head too low. I could feel the gas fumes rush through my lungs, and I thought for a moment that I was going to explode. But the fumes came out my nose instead. As the vapor hit the air, the torch ignited it so a little puff of flame came out either nostril.

"I can smell the hairs in my nose burning," I said in amazement.

"That's nature's way of telling you that you've made a mistake," said the Impossible, pouring a little more gas onto the tin. "You had your head way too low that time. You even singed off one of your eyebrows."

I practiced until I had a fair amount of blisters. A little breeze had sprung up, making the torch's flame flicker, and the Impossible said we'd stop for the day. "This is tear-down night, and the carnival moves tomorrow, or I'd give you some more lessons after the show. We'll knock off a day and let the blisters heal, and then on the next lot we'll start working seriously. You can shill for me this evening."

"Is that the same as being a stick?" I asked.

"Sure, stick, capper, shiller—same thing." He hunched himself up like a tapeworm and got a dollar out of his pocket.

"You bet this dollar on the wheel. You can keep the dollar afterward, m'boy."

"You mean I'm pretty sure to win?"

"Win some, lose some. But you'll be left with a dollar."

I pocketed the dollar. Old Krinko was walking among the tent ropes toward us. He was wearing overalls and looked like a chunky farmer.

"I see you learn fire-eating," he said, grinning at my blisters. "How you like it, eh?"

"I'll like it better when I can keep from getting burned."

"You do good fire act, I know," he said encouragingly. Then he turned to the Impossible. "I got news. I found a fat lady who wants to join show. She come tonight and open with us on new lot tomorrow."

"She going to work the blow-off?" asked the Impossible.

"Sure. She carry nut by herself," said Krinko, grinning until his big mouth seemed to reach the back of his ears.

I must have looked puzzled for the Impossible turned to me.

"The blow-off is the extra feature attraction in a side show, m'boy. It's presented in a curtained-off space at one end of the top—top means tent—and you have to pay extra to see it. A good blow-off attraction like the fat lady will carry the running expenses of the entire show—that's called the nut."

"That's right. She fine freak and freak most important person in a side show," said Krinko seriously. Gently, as though warning me that there were heights which I could never attain, he added, "You may do great fire act, be sword swallower, be good acrobat, but you never get to be freak, son. You must be born that way. If you not born a freak, you never can get to be one. I been in show business all my life, but even I never important as good freak."

I had always thought of a deformed person as someone worthy of pity. But I now began dimly to realize that these people thought of deformity as a God-given attribute as others might think of a great operatic voice or startling beauty. I wondered how the fat lady felt about it. Making a living by exhibiting your deformity seemed horrible to me.

As five o'clock drew close, the carnival gradually awoke to life. The merry-go-round was the first show to open because it catered mainly to children. When the cheerful, irregular strains of the "Beer Barrel Polka" began to roll out over the midway, the performers with our show started to filter into the side show tent. I helped the tattooed man run up the banners which had been taken down during the day. The banners were hung on two long frameworks that ran along the front of the top, one on each side of the entrance. There was a wonderful feeling of exultation in seeing the great banners with their huge, brightly colored figures go soaring up to flap in the evening breeze. All around us carnival life was beginning to stir. The ride boys were taking the canvas covers off the rides and the small concessionaires were rolling up the fronts of their joints. The smell of sawdust, that seemed to lie dormant during the day, grew more intense. The spicy odor of popcorn and the sweet scent of spun candy mingled with it. From the entrance marquee two loudspeakers blared out "The March of the Gladiators," and little dribbles of people began to leak through the entrance onto the bare midway.

In the side show top, I tried to help the performers get ready for the evening. Most of them preferred to lay out their own props, working with the fast sureness of people who know exactly what they are doing. I helped May, the snake charmer, rub the body of her big python with a polishing cloth so he would shine in the lights, and later gave the tattooed man a hand with the bed of spikes he used in his act.

"What's your name?" I asked, while we were putting stones under the legs of the bed to keep it steady.

The tattooed man didn't answer for a moment. "People on this lot call me Captain Billy," he said at last. "But don't ask people on a carny lot what their names are. They might think you meant their real names and that's their own business."

"I'm sorry."

"That's O.K. You're here to learn."

"Do you really lie down on that bed of spikes?" I asked, hoping to make up for my slip. "That must be a terrific act."

"Well, it's a good act, son, a good act," said Captain Billy modestly. He sat down casually on the spikes and pulled a pipe out of his pocket. Sitting there, puffing at the stubby stem, he looked like a beardless Santa Claus. "I strip to the waist and roll around on it. After that, I make a jump and fall on it. As a climax I get three men from the audience to jump up and down on me."

"What do you do for an encore?"

"I'm trying to work out a routine with the five-legged horse. But they've got to take those shoes off her feet first. She keeps kicking me in the face."

Suddenly there was a noise outside the tent that sounded like someone beating on a gong with a lead pipe. Instantly old man Krinko slapped the brilliant green turban on his head and stumped toward the entrance.

Bally in front of Ten-in-One (sideshow).

On the bally platform of the Ten-in-One: (from left to right) Captain Billy, Cal, Bronko, Lu, Mountmorency and Krinko (leaning over).

"First bally! Come everybody!" he shouted over his shoulder.

Everyone began leaving the roped-off section in the middle of the tent where the performers had their stands. They were all carrying one or two props. Standing in the entrance was a thin man with a long horse face. He was holding a brass triangle and a metal rod. He clashed them together and called, "Bally, everybody!"

Captain Billy stopped as we went by him. "Mountmorency, this is Slim, he's with it. Learning to be a fire-eater. Slim, this is Mountmorency, our talented talker."

The talented talker and I shook hands. I remembered him from the evening before. He was what I would have called the show's barker, but I afterward learned that the term "barker" is never used in a carnival.

"You got your torches with you?" he asked. Mountmorency looked very well-dressed, but I noticed that his cuffs had been trimmed with a pair of scissors to keep down the fraying and his necktie was so worn that he wore a piece of bright cloth like a scarf to hide the worn part.

"I can't eat fire yet; I'm only learning," I explained.

"Well, light the torches and wave them around anyhow. There's nothing like a fire act to draw a tip." I remembered that the Impossible had told me that tip meant crowd. "You join us on the bally platform as soon as you can."

The Impossible had given me the torches and I had put them with my bedding. I ran back and soaked the heads in the gas. The rest of the performers were on the bally platform in front of the tent when I returned. Mountmorency was beating on the triangle and Krinko had produced his pot-bellied flute and was making it wail like a banshee with its tail caught in a trap. I climbed the steps and stood behind the others with my torches in my hand.

I'd never before seen a carnival from the vantage of a bally platform. We were well above the head of the crowd, and I could look over the big curve of the midway. The tents were bespangled with varicolored lights, so brilliant you could scarcely see the stars overhead. Like a forest of Christmas trees, the tents glimmered and sparkled in the night. The whole midway danced with sound—the chant of the gamblers, the shouts of the talkers, music from three bands, and the racket of the rides. In front of us the moon was rising between the spokes of the ferris wheel, silver-plating the brown tops of the tents. The midway was black with people. Most of the men were in shirt sleeves, carrying their coats, and nearly everyone was eating. May, the snake charmer, was walking up and down the front of the platform with her snake wrapped around her and a few people had stopped, but not many.

Mountmorency stopped beating the triangle to wipe the sweat off his face and saw me. "O.K., kid. Give 'em the fire," he said hurriedly.

I peeled off my shirt and stood naked to the waist. Captain Billy lit the torches for me. As the double flame sprang up, I heard a long "Ah!" from the crowd. From the black river of the midway, little streams of people began to flow toward our platform and formed a pool under us, their upturned faces yellow in the flare of my torches. Mountmorency whispered "All right, kid, drop back," but I didn't want to disappoint the crowd. Throwing back my head, I put in the first torch. I heard the gasp of the crowd as I withdrew it. Then I did the same with the other torch. In the excitement, I felt nothing.

When I turned around, the other side show people were all grinning at me. Mountmorency came forward, pulling the hand mike with him. He slapped me on the shoulder, and I saw a little flurry in the crowd directly below the platform. A woman had fainted when I did the fire-eating. Mountmorency whispered, "Kid, you're with it. Now let me turn this tip fast."

I stepped back and Lu slid her bare arm through mine. "How do you feel, Slim?" she asked anxiously.

"Fine!" I said. A couple of blisters had burst, but I didn't mind them. "What's 'turn the tip' mean?"

"Bring the crowd into the top. Any talker can get a tip together, but turning them is mighty hard. Watch Mountmorency."

The talker was standing on the front edge of the platform talking into the hand mike. "Step right up! Friends, you are now standing in front of the premier attraction of the midway, Krinko's Great Combined Circus Side Shows." His voice came booming back to us from two loud-speakers hung at both ends of the tent. "Inside here we have the greatest congregation of attractions ever to appear under one top. If you will look from one end of the banner line—" he leaned over the edge of the platform and waved the mike toward the long line of brightly colored canvas paintings in front of the tent—"right down to the other, you will see the acts which we present on the inside."

May stepped forward with her snake, and without looking around the talker put his hand on her shoulder. "This is Conchita, whose mother was frightened by a snake, thus giving her innocent child a strange power over reptiles. Over here, we have Bronko Billy, fresh from the plains of the Great West, with genuine cowboy feats to amaze and interest the kiddies." The cowboy, looking very fine in his buckskin suit, spun a loop with his rope, and then sent it shooting up into the air for a flashing second. "Captain Billy, the most tattooed man in the world, and his Bed of Pain!" Captain Billy shucked off his shirt for a moment and turned slowly around. "Madame Roberta, the gypsy queen, who will read your palms and tell your futures by the secret methods of the ancient gypsies combined with modern, scientific techniques!" The elderly lady in the gypsy costume stepped forward and bowed. "And finally, we have Krinko himself! The magician straight from Egypt, presenting mysteries of the Orient for your approval!" Old man Krinko waddled forward, bowing and waving.

"And don't forget folks, on the inside we also present Dot, the five-legged horse, with an almost human intelligence," shouted Mountmorency. "The performers are now leaving the platform and the show is about to start. The admission price is fifty cents to adults and twenty-five cents to kids. But wait!" A few of the people had begun to wander away now that the free show was over, but his shout stopped them. "I'm going to put away those fifty-cent tickets." The ticket seller held up a roll of big, red tickets. "And I'll make kids out of everyone here! Anyone who can get to the ticket box within two minutes by my watch," and he pulled out a large time-piece, "can go in for twenty-five cents! This is the first show of the evening, folks, so I'll make it an exception. Don't forget this is the premier attraction of the entire midway, so step right up, ladies and gentlemen!"

He began to beat the triangle and everyone shouted and filed off the platform, except old Krinko who began to play his flute again. He ran back and forth as if he were an old dog herding the people in. His flute sounded eager as though he were saying, "This is my show, folks. Please come in and like it. It's only a quarter." It seemed to me to be a pretty good show for a quarter.

May's python was so long she couldn't hold all of him, and the end of the big snake dragged on the platform. I followed her down the steps, holding the snake's tail up as though I were carrying her train. As soon as we were inside the tent, Bronko picked up two big black-snake whips and began cracking them, one in each hand. The cracks went off like gun shots, and the whole tent jumped with the reports. The people in the tip hurried in to see what the noise was.

"You better stay out of the pit, Slim, on account of your act's not smoothed out yet," said Captain Billy kindly. The pit was the roped-off section in the center of the tent where the performers put on their acts. Later, I realized that Captain Billy was afraid I'd try to do a regular fire act and hurt myself but at the time I thought he didn't want me to lower the tone of the show. Feeling snubbed, I wandered over to the inside platform and sat down.

Bronko opened the show by rope-spinning, guitar-playing and rapid-draw shooting at a bale of hay. Then he cut a cigarette out of Lu's mouth with the whip and lit a match she held in her fingers. Following him was Captain Billy. He did his Bed of Pain routine and then offered to tattoo various designs on anyone interested. While May was showing off her snakes, Mountmorency came to the entrance and shouted "Bally!" Instantly the two performers who had finished their acts went out again to draw a new tip. As soon as May had finished, she went out to join the others on the bally platform, while Krinko held the crowd inside with his fakir tricks. The old man deftly stretched his act, watching the bally platform through the tent entrance, until he saw Mountmorency was ready to turn the new tip.

Then he led the old crowd into the blow-off, the curtained-off section of the tent, to see Dot, the five-legged horse. Anyone wanting to see Dot had to pay an additional dime admission, but most people went. That left the top virtually empty as the new crowd streamed in. Bronko began his cowboy act over again, while Krinko went out to take the next bally. Because several of the show's acts were dangerous and put a heavy strain on the performers, the routine was so arranged that no one had to give his act more than two or three times an evening, although he might go out to give a dozen ballys.

I went out with Krinko and tried to do my fire-eating again, but both he and Mountmorency told me to take it easy. The talker had rigged up a wooden cross on the platform and a Negro canvasman, naked except for black trunks, dragged Lu, screaming and kicking, out of the tent and tied her to the cross while I illuminated the grisly scene with my torches. This promptly drew an expectant crowd. Krinko pretended to thrust some of his long hatpins into the struggling Lu, who screamed hysterically. The cries of the almost naked girl acted on the crowd like catnip on a mouse. I saw a shiver of delicious ecstasy go through the tip. I was afraid the tip would be disappointed when they found that Krinko wasn't actually going to impale the girl, but now that the tip had been attracted by the girl's screams, Krinko turned slowly and thrust the hatpins through his own cheeks. This was such a grisly spectacle that the crowd forgot about the girl and watched, fascinated, while the fakir plunged the long needles through each cheek and then through the flesh of his forearms. Then Mountmorency took over, quickly turning the tip into the tent. The Negro canvasman untied Lu, and we all went into the top together, Lu chattering cheerfully with her torturers.

I had almost forgotten about the Impossible until Krinko reminded me that I had to act as a stick. I went along the little gambling joints near the entrance to the carnival, but the Impossible's concession wasn't among them. I finally located him at the other end of the midway, set off by himself in a little booth hidden among the big tops of the Minstrel Show and Fun House. He had no bally and the booth was dimly lighted but somehow people found their way to the spot, for a small crowd had formed.

You could bet on any one state or any state east or west of the Mississippi. Also, the states were painted red, yellow, brown and blue, so you could bet on any color or combination of colors you wanted, the odds varying according to your choice. I put my dollar on the red and won four bucks. Then I bet on the western states and won again.

By this time I was attracting a little notice. I bet again, and lost. Then I split my bet, and laid down a dollar on the blue states and a quarter on Texas. I lost on the blue states, but won on Texas.

"And he's picked the state where the light stopped!" shouted the Impossible. "If he'd laid down a dollar, I'd

r Easler, of Lorraine, Ohio in 1933. Known as the hum shion because his nerves did not register pain. Never ng in his life. Could sit down on a hot stove and neve it. Shown with hot pins stuck through cheeks and lips.

The human pincushion routine (unknown performer with act similar to Krinko's).

now be owing him forty-eight dollars. But he only had a quarter and so I pay out twelve dollars."

He paid me, counting out the bills. I felt a little worried about taking the money, but when I came to examine it, I only had one dollar folded around some paper. How he made the switch I have no idea. The crowd began betting, and I headed back to the side show.

Mountmorency was having some trouble with the tip when I climbed up on the platform. A bunch of small-time toughs had mingled with the crowd. As in all such groups, there was a leader who caused the real trouble, while his followers stood around giggling and getting a vicarious thrill out of his antics. Tailed by his stooges, the head sport had forced his way into the tip, pretending to be absorbed by the performers on the platform, until he was behind a girl. Then, without taking his eyes from the platform, he caressed the girl's hips while his friends watched, snickering. At first the girl thought it was an accident and tried to move away. The head sport moved with her. I could tell Mountmorency was watching. He speeded up his bally and tried to turn the tip before there was any trouble.

Suddenly the girl swung around, slapping at the sport. Her escort turned on the tough and told him to lay off. The sport promptly offered to fight. Right away his stooges crowded in around the girl's boy friend, trying to intimidate him. No one in the tip was paying attention to Mountmorency. Everyone was watching the argument. The girl began to cry. Mountmorency signaled to the talker of the next show to start his bally. As the Oriental Dancing Girls went into their routine, the crowd drifted away and the sports went with them, leaving the sobbing girl to be led off the lot by her angry boy friend.

Mountmorency left the bally platform cursing. "Those damn hoods made me lose a good tip. After you've been with it for a while, Slim, you'll get to recognize bastards like that halfway across the midway. If you try to interfere they call the cops, and then the lawmen hand a fine on you for molesting local boys. I sure would like to see those sons of bitches get it in the tail."

I agreed with him, but it seemed to me that the gang of hoods played it so safe that they could never get what was coming to them. Of course, I didn't know then that the sports were going to tackle the Impossible Possible.

At eleven o'clock, everything on the midway stopped for the Free Act. We all gathered on the bally platform to watch it. Clear above even the ferris wheels rose up a big, hundred-foot scaffolding supporting a chute. Every night at eleven, a man and his wife rode a bicycle down the chute off into space and landed in a tank of water. During the evening there was a gentleman's agreement among the shows that one talker wouldn't start his bally until the man on his left had finished. But after the Free Act there was only time for one more show that night before the carnival closed down. All the shows got ready to fight for the homeward-bound crowd. While the Free Act couple

was getting ready on the chute with their bicycle, I could see all the different talkers mustering their performers on the bally platforms.

The Impossible had told me that this was tear-down night. Within an hour after the last show the carnival would be packed into trucks and started on its way toward the next town. Krinko and Captain Billy had already begun to loosen stakes and pile together odds and ends of equipment. Mountmorency watched anxiously until the Free Act was about to start and then shouted to the two men. They raced up the platform steps just as the Free Act couple started down the chute on their bicycle. The couple shot off the end, the bicycle dropping away from under them, and skimmed through the air, like skipped oyster shells, in their white crash suits. I couldn't see them hit the tank, but I could see the water fly up. They took their bows, and then every bally platform on the midway seemed to go crazy—yelling, beating on bells, and jumping.

As soon as Mountmorency had turned our tip and I wasn't needed in the bally, I headed over to give the Impossible a hand before helping with the tear-down. The bunch of sports was there, watching the map but not playing. There was also a group of tough-looking canvasmen watching the game. For some reason, they were all carrying umbrellas. I pushed through them to reach the counter. I had an idea the sports were going to start some trouble so I got close to the head sport, reasoning that if a riot started he was the one to knock out.

I won another twelve dollars on Texas, and then the head sport bet a quarter. I was disappointed because this seemed so little that the Impossible wouldn't even get back the dollar he'd paid me. The light flickered over the board and finally stopped. The sport had lost.

Before he could turn away, the Impossible called out impressively, "Stop! I don't want your money!" He motioned to the quarter that the sport had put on the counter. Then he tossed down two ten-dollar bills beside it. "To allow you to win your bet back, I'll spin the wheel again. This time, if the light stops on your state or any state bordering your state, you win your fifty cents back and twenty dollars in cash."

Naturally, the sport couldn't pass that up. He threw down another quarter and spun the wheel. This time I noticed that the Impossible was controlling the light with the push button.

The sport lost again, and the Impossible swore. "This young man has me trapped!" he announced. "I'm forced to lay down another ten dollars, and if the light stops on a state bordering any of the border states he wins!"

The sport was getting excited now. This time the Impossible made him bet a dollar, which seemed small compared to the thirty-odd dollars on the counter. The light missed him again and the Impossible got really mad.

"Again I'm forced to throw out a ten spot!" he shouted. "I've never had such hard luck in my life. If he

Mouse game.
The mouse is released in the middle of the circle. Each space on the wheel is numbered and has a hole; the hole the mouse runs into wins, like in roulette.

doesn't win this time, he'll stand to pull down a cool fifty dollars!"

The sport seemed really happy when the light stopped elsewhere, because now the Impossible had fifty dollars on the counter and if the light stopped anywhere west of the Mississippi, he stood to win.

He paid five bucks to win this time and lost. He seemed a little suspicious.

"What are you doin', feelin' under that counter?" he demanded.

The Impossible looked hurt. "After that crack, I'll move to the other end of the tent. I'll leave you in full control of the wheel and the map." He marched off very indignantly to where he could put one foot on the bar under the counter.

The sport played again, and when he lost the Impossible pulled out such a roll of bills people in the crowd whistled. The sport had to put down ten bucks to play this time, but he stood to win nearly a hundred dollars if the light stopped anywhere but in about ten states.

It kept up, with the sport having to put up more and more money and the Impossible flinging down greenbacks as if he hated the sight of them. After each spin the Impossible would curse and throw down more money, so it looked as though he were losing all the time. I know the sport felt he was winning. He must have thrown over a hundred dollars on the counter. Then he took his stooges' money and bet that. Finally, he put down his watch and tried to pull off his rings. When they wouldn't come he spit on his fingers and tore them off. He tore the skin, but he was so crazy drunk with the sight of that big pile of money lying there that he didn't care. At last he had every state covered except Rhode Island. Rhode Island is so small, I don't believe he knew it was there.

He spun the wheel. The light danced around and the sport leaned over the counter. His hands were shaking over the green heap of bills, ready to grab them when the light stopped. His eyes were tied onto that map. The light slowed down over New Mexico and the sport's fingers began to twitch. Then gradually the light flashed blimp-blimp-blimp on and over the Middle West and very slowly crawled up to New England. It hesitated on Connecticut and then finally stopped on Rhode Island.

"A very close finish!" shouted the Impossible, and swept away the money from under the sport's fingers. With the same movement he tried to pull down the canvas front of the joint, but the sport grabbed him.

"I been robbed!" he shouted. "Gimme back ma dough, ya lousy robber!"

I expected the tough canvasmen with the umbrellas to jump him, but they began to take his part, shaking their fists at the Impossible and crowding in. I got ready for a fight.

The Impossible suddenly leaned forward and held out his hand. "Hasn't it begun to rain?" he asked, looking up.

Instantly all the canvasmen opened their umbrellas. They formed a regular wall around the sport, hiding him from his friends. The sport hesitated and then glanced at the sky. Quick as a cat, the Impossible grabbed a hammer from under the counter and hit the sport over the head with it. The sport dropped like a sack of potatoes, but almost before he hit the ground, the Impossible had reached under the center drape, grabbed him by the feet, and dragged him under the counter flap. It all happened within a few seconds and before I could get my breath, the Impossible had pulled down the front flap of the joint which had a big clown's face painted on it and a sign that read:

COME BACK AGAIN SOON!
FUN FOR THE KIDDIES!
LAFFS! LAFFS! LAFFS!

All the canvasmen with their umbrellas folded them up and disappeared into the crowd. The sport's friends wandered around looking for him in a puzzled sort of way and finally disappeared. I went back to my show almost as dizzy as the sports must have been.

When I entered the top, Captain Billy was already knocking down the inside platform. I couldn't have believed a show could go so fast. Each performer just did the climax of his routine, and then waved the people on to the next act. Bronko cracked his whip and then pointed to Krinko, who ate a small electric light bulb. While he was still chewing it, he jumped up and down on Captain Billy, who was lying on his Bed of Pain. May held up a snake, and the gypsy queen read some palms while people were looking at the reptile. I don't think the audience knew what was going on, but before they could say anything the sidewalls began to collapse around them, and they had to get out.

I helped Bronko and Captain Billy drop the rest of the sidewalls. When we finished, the top looked strangely naked. Krinko and I loosened the stakes with a sledge until the top stood with nothing holding it but the four end poles and the double lines of centerpoles that made up the pit.

"Bronko, you and Captain Billy run the center line," called Krinko. "Slim and me'll throw out the end poles." The two men took their places. Krinko and I took down the four end poles, two at each end of the top. Our poles were secured to the canvas by lines in case of a heavy wind, but the double line of centerpoles only had six-inch rods sticking up at the top, which fitted through metal grommets in the canvas. When a pole was jerked away at the base, the rod fell easily out of the grommet.

We dropped the lines and pulled the end poles away. Immediately Bronko and Captain Billy began to run down the line of centerpoles, jerking out each pole as they passed, and throwing it out to one side so it would be clear of the falling top. The canvas fell flat, following right at the heels of the running men who always kept a few steps ahead of it. They reached the end of the pit line, and then breaking out to the side, pulled away the last two centerpoles. The top settled down like a gray cloud in the moonlight, talking gently to itself until it flattened out leaving little hillocks where pockets of air had gotten caught.

I had always thought that a big tent was all one piece, but it is really made up of many canvas strips laced together. Bronko and Captain Billy ran across the canvas, taking care to step only on the reinforcing strips. I found out later that if a man walks anywhere else on a top, it will leak there the next time it rains. They started unlacing the strips, and soon the hill of shaking canvas had turned into a pile of flat pieces like a heap of sheets from the laundry.

The whole carnival was melting away in the moonlight. Only the bones of the rides were left and half of the ferris wheel was gone. I could see the men crawling over the web of spokes like lanky spiders. Every now and then a slice of the wheel would suddenly tremble and be lowered down.

A canvasman from one of the other shows came over to tell Krinko that he was wanted on the phone in a restaurant near the lot. Krinko left us loading the truck while he went off to answer the call. In a few minutes he came stumping back through the fast disappearing carnival, looking disappointed.

"The fat lady no can make it," he told us sadly. "The carny she with folded last night. All the acts gone now but her, and she no can get away. She no can get into ordinary car so she has special car made for her. The manager of side show stole her car and sell it to farmer for moving cows."

"How are you going to get her then?" asked Captain Billy. Everyone looked worried. Apparently they had been looking forward to having a good freak with the show.

"I don't know." Krinko plunged his short fingers into his stubble of hair and pulled. This seemed to be a habit of his when he was puzzled. "She no can get in phone booth—too fat—but she sent girl friend to call me. Now girl friend gone too. Manager who took her car got her under contract. He away now, calling different carnies trying to sell her. She mad at him, but can't get off lot."

"Well, we'll have to go over there and kidnap her," said Captain Billy.

"But how we move her without special car?" asked Krinko. "She no get through door of ordinary car."

"Why not put her in one of the trucks?" I suggested.

Krinko and Captain Billy looked at each other. "That's an idea," said the captain.

"We do that," said Krinko decisively. "We pile double load in one truck. Captain Billy drive that truck. I take other truck and go get fat lady. We meet you at new lot."

We unloaded one of the trucks and put the extra equipment in the truck Captain Billy and I had been loading, tying it down with ropes as it rose above the truck's sides. Krinko and the ticket seller—an emaciated, deadpan man—departed in the empty truck for the kidnapping.

I shoved in the last armful of stakes, and stopped to wipe my face and look over the empty lot. We were the last to leave. Not a stick of the carnival remained. The yellow headlights of the truck shone over a flat expanse. The sawdust circle of the midway stood out in the white moonlight, as clear as an airplane ground marker, now that the tents were gone. Captain Billy honked his horn, and I swung up beside him in the front seat of the truck. The truck jolted over the lot's ruts, bumped on the curb, and then began to move smoothly over the deserted paved street. Captain Billy threw it into high gear and I felt that I was really beginning my life as a carny.

Paul, the canvasman.

Captain Billy and his Bed of Spikes.

CHAPTER 4

I didn't realize how tired I was until I stretched out on the seat of the truck. Paul, the show's Negro canvasman, had curled up on a sort of shelf behind us and had already fallen asleep with his legs tucked up almost against his chest. Captain Billy drove steadily, heading north. Although I'd traveled around the eastern seaboard states, being with the carnival made it seem completely different. I felt as though I were entering another country. The road was almost empty at that hour except for the big, night-driving Diesel trucks that occasionally swept by us with a sudden swish. I dozed off, waking every now and then as the undimmed headlights of a car struck me in the face. We hit a light drizzle of rain, and Captain Billy switched on the windshield wipers. The soft murmur of the wipers on the glass sent me off to sleep again.

I was awakened by the glare of purple neon lights in my face. Captain Billy had stopped by an open-all-night diner. The rain had settled down into a steady pour. I tried to stretch. My legs were so stiff I could hardly move them.

"We crossed the state line a mile or so back," said Captain Billy, switching off the motor. "The new lot is about forty-five miles from here. It'll be daylight soon, so let's break for a cup of coffee."

He leaned back and, reaching over his shoulder, shook Paul, who awoke and slid down between us, rubbing his legs and staring through the wet windshield at the restaurant.

"Maybe they won't let me in there," he said doubtfully. "You just bring me out a sandwich and a mug of coffee."

"They'll let you in all right," said Captain Billy. "You're in the North now, kid."

We ran through the rain, leaping over puddles, and ducked into the restaurant. While we were having ham and eggs and hot coffee, the dawn began to break in the east. It was Sunday morning. Captain Billy explained that we wouldn't open until Monday night so there were two days to get the carnival set-up on the new location. That was the standard routine; tear-down after the last show Saturday night, drive all night to the new lot, and set-up on Sunday morning. Then rest and sleep until the Monday night show.

"This is a good, average jump we're making," explained the captain. "In carny, they talk about a

'small jump' and a 'big jump.' A small jump is anything up to a hundred miles. A big jump may be two hundred miles or even four hundred. When you get a four-hundred-mile jump, you play hell getting the top set-up before the Monday night show."

Although the rain clouds held back the dawn, it was getting lighter every minute. We finished our coffee and cigarettes, and climbed back into the truck. Paul drove, and Captain Billy hoisted himself up onto the shelf to sleep. We had been driving through farming country, but now we started to hit more and more gas stations, tourist courts and cheap restaurants. The traffic got heavier and heavier. We were entering the city where the carny was going to show that week.

Ahead of us I could see the miles of grimy houses and crowded streets that mark an industrial town. The great highway we were on rose contemptuously on a magnificent ramp to shoot over the dirty congestion. Many a time I had sped over such ramps, glad to miss the traffic and dirt below me. Now Paul turned down one of the by-passes and swung out on a cobblestone street striped by trolley tracks belonging to an era fifty years before that of the elevated highway overhead.

There were no parks, no wide streets, no trees—nothing but block after block of little houses, all exactly alike. At regular intervals we passed giant factories that occupied several city blocks. Because it was Sunday, the factories were closed, but a layer of smoke seemed to hang in the atmosphere like stale cigar smoke in a closed room.

"You're seeing carny life at its worst right here, Slim," said Captain Billy from over my shoulder. He had evidently awakened when we hit the town. "We've got to set-up upon a city lot in the rain. But it ain't all like this. After we play these city spots, we get out in the country under the trees. It's a real pleasure to be under canvas then."

"Man, oh, man, I'd sure hate to live in this place," said Paul, shaking his head. "In a carny we can go anywhere and do anything, but these poor folk have got to live in this place and breathe smoke all their lives."

When we reached the new lot, most of the carnival was already set-up. In spite of being in the middle of a city, the lot was very large. The carnival occupied one half of it, the circle of tops surrounded as usual by the thinner, black, outside ring of cars and trailers belonging to the show people. A crowd of townies had already formed around the carnival and stood in a tightly packed mass regarding the circle of tents without a sound. At first they wouldn't open to let our truck through, although Paul honked and I shouted at them. Finally Paul put the truck into low gear and moved slowly forward while I leaned across him and kept one finger on the horn. The people nearest turned to stare, but didn't move until the bumper of the truck actually touched them. Then they sullenly shrugged themselves barely clear.

Twice Paul stopped when people seemed determined to let themselves be run down rather than step aside and admit defeat. Their attitude seemed to be, "I got my rights. I got as much right to stand here as you have to go through. And I'm going to stand up for my rights, too." In each of these cases I leaned out of the truck and called, "We've got to get through to the tents. Do you mind letting the truck by? You can move back again as soon as we're clear." After bitterly considering this, the defenders of their rights moved back as little as possible and we were able to keep going. The atmosphere was so malignant that I was surprised no one tried to jump on the running board and stop us.

Paul nosed the truck into the line of cars and I got out, followed stiffly by Captain Billy. The captain started to look for our lot stake. The day before the show arrives on a new lot a man called the "lot staker" measures out the positions of the different shows and concessions and marks the boundaries of each outfit by driving flat mark stakes into the ground. On one side of the stake is lettered the name of the show starting there and on the other side is the name of the neighboring outfit. This week we had been placed between the Minstrel Show and the Monkey Circus. The Octopus, one of the noisiest of the rides, was directly across the midway from us.

"Well, I guess we have to take our turn on the racket," said Captain Billy looking unenthusiastically at the looped, steel tracks of the Octopus. When the iron cars, full of screaming passengers, were raced around this circular track at full speed, the Octopus made so much noise that it drowned out the bally of the neighboring outfits.

We started to unpack the great folded sheets of canvas that made up the tent. As the sheets were laid out on the ground, they were overlapped slightly and sewed together with light lines called "lacers." For additional strength, other ropes called "seamers" were led around hooks above and below the overlap to strengthen the joining and hold the lacing tight. While we were working, Bronko and Lu arrived in their car and set-up their little living top. When they were finished, the cowboy came over to help us. It was slow work because Krinko, Mountmorency, and our ticket seller were away getting the fat lady and we were shorthanded.

We were almost the last show to complete setting-up. Looking around, I saw that the entire carnival had grown into place. Except for the rearranging of the various shows so that each one would "take its break on the noise" I was looking at a complete reproduction of the carnival I'd seen on the old lot the evening before. A community of several hundred people and dozens of structures had moved over a hundred miles and rebuilt itself in less than eight hours.

Setting up.

Later on I was to discover that this weekly miracle was accomplished without any of the discipline that generally holds together large bodies of people such as an army or even a circus. A carnival is composed of little units, each completely separate from the others. Krinko didn't even know the name of the man who owned the shows on either side of him. A performer could easily go through the whole summer without meeting anyone on the lot except the people in his own show. At any time a concessionaire might tell the carnival manager that he had decided to join another outfit and wasn't going to open at the next lot. And yet the format of the carnival never changed. If one show dropped out, another would mysteriously appear in time to take its place—brought in by a hurried ad in *The Billboard*, the outdoor showman's famous magazine. The performers were free to go and come as they pleased, and contracts were almost unknown. If a performer didn't like an outfit, he didn't show up on the next lot. The other acts would stretch their routines to fill the gap, and in a few days another man would come to fill the spot.

After the top was up, Lu brought her little portable gasoline stove into the pit and made us some hot coffee. Aunt Matty, the elderly lady in the gypsy outfit who read palms, contributed a batch of doughnuts she had cooked that morning in her tiny, immaculate trailer. We all sat around on the inside platform of the tent eating the doughnuts and drinking Lu's steaming coffee. Through the open flap of the tent I could see the sawdust truck going around the bare midway, dumping piles of golden sawdust at regular intervals. Two men followed the truck, spreading the sawdust with long-handled rakes. As the midway took shape and color, I could smell the rich sawdust odor. This was the last touch necessary to make the carnival complete.

We had finished setting-up just in time. A cold wind sprang up and a light drizzle began to fall. Captain Billy rose and dropped the tent flap. Although it was still early morning, the interior of the tent darkened to a soft twilight—lighted only by the dim radiance that soaked through the canvas walls. Lu shivered.

"Gee, I sure wish we was still playing down South," she complained.

"I don't," said Paul. Everyone laughed.

"No sir," said Paul decisively. "I was born and brought up in the South and it's no place for me. Seemed like everything I did down there was wrong. I tell you, it was a lucky day for me I joined with the carny and got away from all that."

As Paul talked I felt a real sympathy. It would be ridiculous to say that our situations were analogous, but the carnival seemed a lucky break for me too.

Bronko had taken one of his lariats out of a bag and was trying to spin a flat loop. The rope twisted up in his hands. "It's too damp here in the East for first-class rope work," he complained. "Your ropes all kink up. Now out on the prairies, we don't have this trouble. I

allow it rains, but the air's dry." He coiled up the rope and regarded it affectionately. "Now this here's the best rope you can get—genuine maguey rope made out o' cactus fibers. All the top hands use it. But I can't hardly do a thing with it here."

"Your wife's freezin' to death and you worry about your damn rope!" squeaked Lu indignantly. "Give it here." She snatched the rope from the cowboy and with great care hung it on a center pole near her gasoline stove to dry. I saw Aunt Matty smiling at the girl. As the elderly woman looked back again, she caught my eye. We grinned at each other. I saw that Matty, like myself, knew that Lu's bad temper was as big a fake as her husband's cowboy pose.

May, the snake charmer, came staggering with an enormous box through the back flap of the tent. Two sections of the sidewall met at the back of the tent and, instead of being joined with a lacer, were left loose as a sort of rear entrance. Paul and I jumped to help May. When I took hold of the box, I couldn't believe the slender woman with her pipestem arms had been able to carry it. The thing must have weighed over a hundred pounds. Paul and I carried it to her platform in the pit.

"Be careful, Sultan's in there and he's sleeping," said May. She sat down exhausted on a camp chair that Captain Billy offered her. Sultan was her big python. "It's terribly cold in my living top so I brought him in here. I thought it might be warmer."

"O.K., give the God-damned snake my place by the stove," shrilled Lu furiously, moving over. "What with the damn rope and the damn snakes I guess I'll just get neemonia. Why we ever came north so soon, I don't know."

"Anyhow, no one can call you a forty-miler after this season," said Captain Billy grinning. Turning to me, the captain explained, "A forty-miler is the kind of carny who never gets more than forty miles from his home town."

"I ain't no forty-miler," called Lu resentfully over her shoulder. She was helping May drag the snake box over to the stove. May opened the box, revealing great masses of coils, each coil nearly as big around as May's thigh, and a beautiful light tan color. May patted one of the coils. Instantly it swelled up like a firehose with the pressure suddenly turned on. A hiss louder than the exhaust of a steam engine came from the mass. Lu jumped a foot. "If that bastard bites me, I'll brain him with the stove—so help me God," she said earnestly to May. Then, turning back to Captain Billy, she went on, "Listen, I been on jumps up to Canada and played Cuba and Mexico, too. You can ask Bronko. But if I was runnin' this opry, I'd never come to this town. This is a bloomer if I ever seen one. Look at the way them townies is actin'. There's going to be a clem here, sure as Christ."

"What's a clem?" I asked.

"A clem is fight with the town people," said Captain Billy. He had lighted his pipe and was smoking comfortably, leaning back in his camp chair.

Aunt Matty shook her head. "I hate them," she said in her gentle voice. "There's really never any reason for them."

"Well, it's years since I've seen a real, old-fashioned clem," said the captain. It seemed to me he spoke almost regretfully. "All I look for on this lot are some ordinary hecklers in the tip tomorrow night. Slim can easily handle them with his fire-eating."

"Who, me?" I said, suddenly alarmed. "Why, I can't even do my act yet."

"You don't have to do your complete act to handle hecklers," explained the captain. "After you swallow a couple of torches, some gee is bound to yell out that it isn't real fire. This gives you a fine chance for some audience participation. Call him up and give him one of the torches to examine. While he's looking at it, quietly set his hair on fire with the other torch. The stunts people will pull trying to put their hair out, especially if they're a little drunk, always gives the tip a big laugh. From then on, the tip is on your side."

While we were finishing the coffee, a truck pulled up behind the tent and we heard the motor shut off. The backflap of the tent was pushed up and Mountmorency, the show's talker, came in. He looked tired. "Christ, we had a hell of a time," he said. "Is that coffee? Give me a cup."

"Did you get the fat lady?" asked Bronko.

"Yes, she's out in the truck." Mountmorency poured himself a cup of almost boiling coffee. "Krinko and Jake are laying planks against the tailboard so she can get down. I don't know if she can make it in here. She'll have to walk a couple of hundred feet."

"What's the matter with her?" demanded Lu.

"She's just so damned big it's hard for her to walk."

The backflap was lifted from outside and Jake, the ticket seller, slipped in. He tied the canvas up to a side-pole, leaving a triangular-shaped opening. Through this came the fat lady, gripping the staggering Krinko to steady herself. She weighed almost seven hundred pounds, nearly half a ton, and was dressed in a fantastic imitation of a little girl to exaggerate her huge size. Her fluffy pink dress was soaked through with sweat and her thick legs, only partially covered by her socks, were barely able to support the great mass of her body swaying uncertainly above them. Her fat baby's face looked around despairingly as if seeking some place to drop her vast bulk.

"Where's a bed?" she gasped, her breath wheezing in her over-taxed lungs. "For God's sake, leave me lay down!"

"Right here, lady!" called Captain Billy. He had produced a folding iron bed from somewhere and was opening it up. The fat lady stared toward him vaguely through short-sighted eyes, running a spongy hand

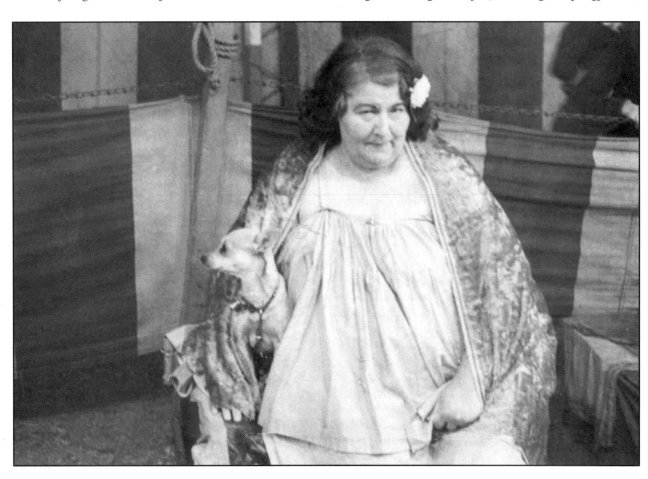

Jolly Daisy.

through her blonde hair and automatically adjusting her blue hair ribbon. Supported by Krinko and the wiry ticket seller, she staggered across the tent and collapsed on the iron cot. Instantly all four legs disappeared into the ground. The woman lay there, a mountain of exhausted flesh covered with pink silk.

"Oh God, I think I'm dying!" she moaned. Perspiration was trickling off her nose and the ends of her fingers. She had only lain on the bed a few seconds and already it was wringing wet. "I'm dying this time for sure. Oh, I wish I was dead!"

"Give me some help with this bed, Slim," gasped Captain Billy.

I went to his aid. Krinko was completely worn out and had sat down on one end of the cot. We moved him and tried to lift the bed's legs out of the ground. We did manage to get one leg high enough to slip a board under it but while we were struggling with the other side, the board cracked across and the leg plunged into the earth again.

"To hell with it," said Krinko, who had been watching us sweat and strain to lift the seven hundred pounds of bed. "Let the damned bed sink. Put some boards under it when she gets up."

Bronko brought in a bucket of water and put it by the cot. "You can start giving her drinks of this, but take it easy or she'll flounder herself."

Lu crouched down by the woman's side and rinsing out a coffee cup, gave her a few mouthfuls of water. Then she wrung out a cloth and put it on the fat woman's head. The woman sighed a few times and then fell asleep.

"I guess we'd all better get some sleep," said Captain Billy, stretching. "Thank God it's Sunday so we can sleep the rest of the day."

I suddenly realized that I was dead tired. I spread my sleeping bag out on the inside platform, blew up the air mattress, and crawled into the sack. In spite of the snores of the fat lady, I was asleep in a few minutes.

When I awoke, I could tell by the soft light that filtered through the canvas that it must be late afternoon. The fat lady was sitting up, swoshing the cloth around in the bucket of water and mopping her face. I crawled out of my bag and sat up scratching myself. The fat lady looked up and smiled at me. She seemed to be completely recovered.

"Hello," she said cheerfully. "My name's Daisy . . . Jolly Daisy they call me. Who are you?"

I told her they called me Slim.

"I guess you're the kid Krinko told me about who's learning fire-eating," said Jolly Daisy. She finished wiping her face with the wet cloth and started to adjust the ribbon in her hair. "You must have the makings of a real carny to want to learn a dangerous act like that. Boy, I'm glad I don't have to do nothing like that. My act is jest to set still and have people look at me." She laughed heartily.

Aunt Matty came hurrying through the backflap into the tent. I introduced her to Jolly Daisy. The two women smiled and shook hands.

"I'm so glad you're awake," said Aunt Matty to the fat lady. "We've set-up a little living top for you, just on the other side of the backflap. You'll only have to walk a few feet from there to reach the blow-off for the shows."

"Now that's real thoughtful," said Jolly Daisy gratefully. "Maybe Slim will get my stuff and put it in there for me. My things are in the front end of the truck."

I went out to the truck. After a little trouble I managed to slide the fat lady's bags over the tailgate and carried them into the little living top. Lu was inside, making up Jolly Daisy's special bed. Lu must have carried the bed in herself, section by section. The living top looked quite comfortable. While I was wrestling the bags into a corner, Jolly Daisy came in with Aunt Matty helping her. The fat woman was walking uncertainly but managed to reach the bed. She sat down with a sigh.

With the four of us inside, the top was crowded. Aunt Matty was rather plump and kept bumping into Lu or me every time she turned around.

"Gracious, I'll have to go on a diet or I'll be doing a fat woman act myself," she said with a little laugh.

Jolly Daisy apparently took her seriously. "You can't be a real fat woman jest by eatin' too much," she explained solemnly. "It's my glands make me so fat. There's nothing the doctors can do about it neither. When I was a little kid and started to get fat, my folks called a doctor who give me injections. Them injections made me so darned jittery I near jumped out of my skin and they didn't do no good. But my folks was bound and determined I was going to be normal even if they half killed me."

"Jeez, I guess all parents want their kids to be normal," said Lu, beginning to unpack Jolly Daisy's clothes.

"Well, if the kid is a freak, it's awful hard on him," said Jolly Daisy seriously. "I've met lots o' freaks in show business and they all tell the same story. No matter what's wrong with a child, the parents won't ever admit he's a freak. I guess it hurts their pride to admit a child of theirs could be deformed. When the kid is little, the parents maybe admit he's a little funny-looking, but they always claim he'll outgrow it. Then when he's bigger and there ain't no doubt, they start taking him to doctors. Don't matter what the doctor's tell them, they keep insisting the kid can be cured. They drag him around from one clinic to another all over the place. Don't tell me, I been through it."

"It must be terribly hard on the child," said Aunt Matty sympathetically.

"It sure is. Why, my Ma even made me go to dances with my brothers and sisters 'cause she wouldn't admit I wasn't an ordinary girl. O' course, none of the little boys wanted to dance with me but their folks made them, so as not to make my folks mad. The boys would whine and complain and then the other little girls would laugh at me. Oh my, was I miserable! I wanted to run off and hide where no one could find me."

"How did you get into show business?" I asked. Jolly Daisy's story reminded me of the hard times I'd had as a kid because I was so tall.

"At one of the clinics Ma took me to, the doctor there told her straight out that there wasn't anything he could do and I'd keep on getting fatter and fatter. It ain't often a doctor will tell the parent of a freak the truth right out like that and Ma was half-crazy. She said I'd be better off dead. Imagine how that made me feel. Then a man came over to us. He worked in carnivals as an India Rubber man because he could dislocate any part of his body. Doctors used to hire him to show medical students where the different dislocations was at. He told Ma I was real lucky. I could travel all over the country with carnivals, make a good living and only have to sit in a chair and have people look at me because a freak is always a big attraction."

"I'm surprised your mother didn't think of that herself," suggested Aunt Matty.

Jolly Daisy gave her hearty laugh. "Oh, Ma thought the whole idea was awful. But I sure didn't. When I heard there was a place where folks wouldn't feel I was something awful just because I was different from other people, I was all for it. So I talked Ma into letting me join a Ten-in-One. I guess at that she was glad to get me out of the house."

Ten-in-One is the carny term for a side show because there are several acts under one top. "Then you're happy?" I asked.

"Oh, sure. On a carny lot, everybody is different from ordinary people, so I'm all right. And I guess you get a kick out of doing anything you can do real well. I'm a real good freak and I know every night there's hundreds of people willing to pay money to see me. I bring in more people than any ordinary act and I know it. The other carnies appreciate it. Instead of just being a freak, I'm somebody important. That's a good feeling."

Both Aunt Matty and Lu nodded understandingly. "Yes, many people have a special gift for something, but usually they don't have enough confidence in themselves to go ahead and do it," said Aunt Matty thoughtfully. "I've often noticed that in my study of palms."

"Well, if you're different from other people you might as well admit it and not go hankering to be normal," said the fat lady. "Now you take my case. After I got to be as fat as I am now, I was famous. Ripley wrote me up in 'Believe It or Not.' I was in a couple of motion pictures about circuses and they paid me good. I had plenty of money. My pa lost his job about then, so I supported the family. I sent my brother and sister through college and bought the folks a new car and an electric dishwasher and lots of things. I'm making more money than any of those kids that used to laugh at me in school and living a better life. The way I see it, I'm a very lucky woman."

Captain Billy looked through the tent's door flap and asked if anyone wanted to go down to the cook shack with him to get some lunch. There wasn't anything more I could do to help, so I said I'd go along. The newly laid sawdust on the midway hadn't been trodden down yet, and it was as soft as moss. While we walked, I was thinking of Jolly Daisy. I wondered if all freaks were as proud and content as she seemed to be. Finally, I asked Captain Billy.

"I don't see why freaks wouldn't be happy," said the captain in some surprise. "They're always top attractions with any show. I tried to make a freak out of myself with my tattooing, but I never made the grade."

I'd never thought of a tattooed man in exactly that way, but what the captain said was true enough.

"Did you deliberately start out to make a freak out of yourself?" I asked.

The captain thought for a moment. "Well, I wouldn't say that. I was serving on a freighter and there was a man on board who had a tattooing outfit. Those long trips get pretty dull, so about everybody on board had some tattooing done. The next ship I signed up on, this same tattoo artist happened to be aboard. By the time we hit port again, I was pretty well tattooed. I figured I might as well get a complete job done and then I could earn my living as a tattooed man."

"Do you ever regret it?" I asked.

The captain gave a short laugh. "Hell no. If I had my way, I'd have only one eye and that'd be right in the middle of my forehead. I'd have my arms growing out of my chest and be walking around on three legs. With a setup like that, I could live better than Clark Gable and the president of the United States combined. And I'd never have to do a lick of work. But there's a lot of tattooed men in show business. It's an easy act . . . don't require no practice and no brains. So to have a real performance I had to learn my Bed of Pain routine. That's hard work. But if I was a freak you can bet I wouldn't be laying on no bed of spikes."

"Then you think Daisy is lucky to be a fat woman?" I asked. Somehow, I couldn't get used to the idea that freaks were something to be regarded with envy.

"Why, sure she is," said the captain a little bitterly. "The whole blow-off depends on her. The blow-off is the most important part of a Ten-in-One. Before Daisy we only had Dot, the five-legged horse, in there. Dot was all right but people like to see a human freak. They'll pay a quarter to see Daisy and that's as much as they'll pay to see the whole seven acts in the pit. And don't forget the money they pay for the blow-off is on top of their regular admission. A good blow-off can carry a whole side show."

"I wonder why people want to see freaks so much," I said thoughtfully.

"Well, it's natural," said the captain casually. "When you was a kid, didn't you get a big kick out of reading books about giants with two heads and octopus men and stuff like that? Sure you did. Everybody's interested in freaks, whether they'll admit it or not. Just you get a collection of pictures of famous freaks and start passing them around in a group of people. The people who start off by saying they don't want to see the pictures are the ones who won't let go of them. Look at how people went for Ripley's 'Believe It or Not' business. Most of his stuff was about freaks in one way or another."

As we walked along, Captain Billy explained the layout of the carnival to me. There were five big shows: our side show, the Minstrel Show, the Girl Show, the Monkey Circus and the Motordrome. The Motordrome was the only one of the shows that wasn't under canvas. It was a circular wooden structure about thirty feet tall that looked like an oil reservoir. Inside this giant well, daredevil motorcyclists performed. The cyclists would build up enough speed so they could rush up the sides of the tank and then keep whirling around it as though they were on a race track.

The smaller shows were called concessions. There were about ten of these, such as the Waxwork Exhibit, the Wild Animal Exhibit, the Crazy House, and the Model Show. The Model Show was a smaller organization than the Girl Show, and employed only six girls. The Girl Show gave half an hour of burlesque, had a small band and a couple of male comedians, but in the Model Show the girls did nothing but take statuesque poses in the nude. There was a gauze curtain between the girls and the audience. The girls could see through the curtain but the audiences couldn't see them. The girls would take their poses and then a light would be switched on behind them so the audience could see through the veil. Captain Billy explained that if the show's advance man

could work out a good deal with the local cops, the girls would be completely nude. Otherwise, they wore G-strings. "And in some places in New England, they even got to wear bras," added the captain.

The Model Show was the only concession that had a talker. The rest had to be content with "grind men." The grind man was often the ticket seller and he continually ground out the same memorized spiels such as "It's never up and never over, folks. Oh, come and see those genuine waxwork figures of famous murderers. See the bullet holes where the cops shot them down. It's only a dime, folks, the tenth part of a dollar. It's never up and never over, etc."

"Most grind men would like to be talkers," the captain told me as we walked along. "But they don't have the talent for it. Sometimes you'll hear people say of a poor talker, 'That gee's a grind man who thinks he's a talker.' But being a good grind man isn't as easy as it looks. He has to pick up a sort of singsong chant that takes time to learn. There's always a demand for good grind men."

Still smaller than the concession shows were the gambling joints—usually one man setups like the Impossible's outfit. In the joints, you could bet on a spinning wheel, roll a ball down an inclined board into a cluster of numbered pockets, throw a dart at balloons, or toss rings over little blocks having a prize tied to them. There were about fifteen of these gambling games, usually designed to look like a sure thing, but for some tricky reason almost impossible to beat.

Motordrome.

"In some places, the crabbers raise too much of a beef with the town clowns and the word is passed to lay off the grift," remarked Captain Billy. "Then the joint men don't pay off in cash but with slum. Slum means prizes—kewpie dolls, canes, plaster statues, and stuff. Then if the marks do win, the joints can pay them off in slum which is only worth a few cents."

I noticed that some of the booths were exhibiting slum that looked fairly expensive—such as chrome-plated electric clocks and six-tube radio sets. I mentioned this to the captain. He grinned.

"Some of that slum has been traveling around the country for years. Look at that tenpin joint." We were passing a booth with a big tenpin on the counter. A bowling ball hung down beside it, suspended from a scaffolding overhead by a long chain. To win, the mark had to swing the ball past the pin and then have the ball knock down the tenpin as it swung out again. If the mark won, he received a handsome, pure wool blanket. "I know the man who runs that joint. He's had those same blankets for the last three years. They've been dry-cleaned so much that they're coming apart. With a lousy flash like that, no joint can do any business. But a lot of these joint men will carry the same old slum around with them until the stuff falls to pieces."

The rides were the bread and butter of the carnival, always bringing in a comparatively small but steady return. The biggest were the two great ferris wheels and the merry-go-round. There were also the Chairaplane, Boatswing, Ridee-O, and a couple of others. Captain Billy told me that the closer a ride came to murdering the people who got into it, the more popular it was. The best-liked ride on the lot was a devilish apparatus that shot you up to the top of a thirty-foot pole in an open car and then turned the car upside down while an ingenious mechanism tried to shake you out. Captain Billy assured me that people stood in line for hours to get in that one.

Carnivals are probably the only form of live entertainment that caters personally and frankly to the great mass of the American people. Circuses are mainly attended by "respectable" people, and as a result their side shows don't dare to exhibit a really shockingly deformed freak or put on such routines as Krinko's torture act in which the old fakir runs needles through his arms and cheeks. Gambling is barred on most circus lots and so are exhibitions of nude girls. But in carnivals, anything goes that the public wants—from merry-go-rounds for the kiddies to strip shows for their daddies.

The cook shack was hidden away behind the other tops, but as it was the only concession that had lights on at that hour in the afternoon, Captain Billy and I finally located it. The place was about half-full of carnies. It smelled wonderfully of hot coffee, frying bacon, and sizzling pork chops. I saw the Impossible sitting at one of the two long benches that ran down the center of the concession. He waved us over, and we sat down beside him.

"I've got a present for you, Slim—something left over from my own Human Salamander days," said the Impossible, producing a much-battered red metal ball from his pocket. "This is a 'hot ball,' very useful in fire-eating."

Captain Billy nodded as if he recognized the piece of apparatus. I accepted it gratefully, but without any idea how it could be used. While I was looking the ball over, it suddenly began to get warm. I was so surprised that instead of dropping it, I tried to juggle the ball from hand to hand like a hot potato. Then the ball actually began to burn me and I had to drop it. The Impossible grinned through his beard at my puzzled expression and Captain Billy chuckled. Obviously they both had known what was going to happen.

"A hot ball is great for getting a little comedy into your routine," explained the Impossible. He turned the ball over with a fork and showed me a secret button set into the side of the ball. "Once you press this button, the ball becomes red hot in a few seconds."

"It's good to use on crabbers," explained Captain Billy.

"Exactly," agreed the Impossible, shutting off the ball so it could cool down. "When you start your act, announce that because your mother was frightened by a lighted match, you have a strange control over this terrible element—fire. Explain that there is nothing supernatural about your powers, but just as homing pigeons have a weird ability that science can't explain, you have a control over flame. In the country districts, people will often believe you. But around cities there are usually some young sports who'll give you the razz."

Captain Billy grinned. He knew what was coming.

"As though you were deeply offended, call a sport up and let him examine the ball. Then explain that you will hypnotize him into thinking the ball is red hot. Press the button and tell the sport to put the ball in his trouser pocket."

"A lot of times the sport will figure that you're going to make the ball vanish," put in Captain Billy. "So he stuffs it way down in his pocket with maybe a handkerchief over it. Then he stands grinning at his friends while you make passes and ask him if he doesn't feel the ball getting hotter and hotter."

"Then comes the fun," went on the Impossible happily. "After a few seconds, a worried look comes across his face. He usually suffers as long as he can and then tries to get the ball out. By this time it's too hot to touch and he'll have to tear off his pants. Sometimes the ball will even burn right through his pocket."

"Isn't he pretty sore after he's gotten his pants off?" I asked.

"Ah, then it's always well to have a stake within easy reach. Those stakes are wonderful things. They are strong enough so you can smash a table with them, but light enough to handle easily. For work like this, they're indispensable."

Our orders arrived and I had just begun on my ham and eggs when there was a little commotion behind me. An enormous man entered the tent followed by six girls with red and gold kimonos wrapped tightly around them. The Impossible told me that they were the Model Show and had been giving an off-the-lot performance at a men's smoker that afternoon. I'd had a vague idea that carnival show girls would be fat, peroxided old broads, but these girls looked pretty good to me. The man who led the procession was as tall as I and must have weighed at least a hundred pounds more. In spite of his heavy jowls and protruding belly, he gave the impression of great strength. The jowls couldn't hide his powerful jaw or the belly detract from a chest as big as a pork barrel. He was splendidly dressed in an electric-blue suit, a white Panama hat and snowy spats. The girls' faces were so covered with make-up that they seemed to be wearing masks.

The big man addressed the cook in a voice of calm authority. "See these girls get anything they want to eat. The bill's on me today. It don't make any difference what they want to order. I'm paying for it."

"Sure, Frisco," said the cook, wiping his pink hands on his white apron. "I'll see they get treated right."

Frisco turned to his harem. "Order what you want, girls. Anything you see is O.K."

As there were only six girls and the most elaborate full course dinner the cook house afforded was seventy-five cents, I didn't see how Frisco's treat could amount to more than five bucks. This didn't seem worth making such a ceremony about, but the girls obviously felt differently. They looked at the big man respectfully and chorused, "Oh thank you, Frisco. Gee, this is swell of you. You sure are thoughtful." They sat down happily and started giving orders to the cook with great pride. As far as I could see, it wasn't the prospect of a free meal that appealed to them as much as the delicious feeling that their beloved boss was treating them.

One of the girls came over and spoke to the Impossible. He introduced her as Billie Callihan. Billie seemed to be a few years younger than I was and, as well as I could tell from her grotesque make-up, fairly attractive. She was very excited about Frisco's buying the girls a free meal.

"He's always doing nice little things like that," she told us. She spoke in an affected, mincing way that broke down every now and then, revealing a hard, Middle-Western twang which Billie was evidently trying to eliminate from her speech. "I've been with shows where the man was mean—always bossing the girls around and never doing anything for them. Frisco's real kind to us, but if we ever start scrapping, he can stop it just like that." She snapped her plump fingers.

"I sure wish I could handle women like Frisco can," remarked Captain Billy, shaking his head sadly. "I got three wives but I have to keep 'em in different states."

"Well, it's Frisco's business to handle women," explained the Impossible. "It's just a knack—like lion-taming or mule-driving." He turned to Billie. "Sit down, kid, and join us."

"No, thanks, I just came over to see if any of you guys could do me a favor," said Billie, swiping a piece of bacon from the Impossible's plate. "A girl friend of mine married a sword swallower. Maybe you've heard of him—he's the Human Electric Light Bulb. Swallows neon tubes. He's playing in a dime museum in town here. If one of you has a car, maybe you'd drive me over so I could see them. I'll pay for the gas."

"I've heard about the Bulb," said the Impossible. "Works stripped down to the waist and after he swallows a tube he turns it on so the light shines through his chest. Must be a very nice effect."

"That I'd like to see," I said skeptically. I was sure that no one could swallow a sword unless the blade folded up into the handle and the idea of swallowing a neon tube, lighted or not, was ridiculous. I remember reading that Robert Houdin, the famous French magician, who was sent by the French government to Algeria toward the end of the last century to expose the Arab conjurers, was able to explain all their tricks except sword swallowing. When he returned to France, he questioned the leading physicians and was told that it was a biological impossibility to swallow a sword. Houdin knew that he hadn't been fooled by sleight-of-hand and finally decided that the Arab he saw perform the effect must have had some abnormal development. I had talked to several doctors since then about sword swallowing, and they assured me the swords must fold up in some fashion. As one doctor said, "If you knew how much trouble it is to swallow the soft rubber tubing of a stomach pump, you wouldn't ask if anyone could swallow a hard steel blade."

But everybody took me seriously. "Well, if you want to see the Bulb's act, you can borrow one of the show's trucks and drive Billie over to see her friend," said Captain Billy.

"Sword swallowing's one act I never tried," remarked the Impossible, leaning back on the bench and sipping his coffee as though it were rare, old wine. "I worked in a show where we had a sword swallower who used to swallow an umbrella for a flourish. One day it opened up inside him. What a mess that was! Fire-eating is a nice, clean routine, but sword swallowers don't know where to stop. First they swallow swords, then bayonets, then giant scissors, then neon tubes. No sir, not for me."

Billie said to me, "I'm staying with the other girls in a hotel near here." She told me the address. "We don't sleep on the lot like you fellows do. It's too rough. You can pick me up any time after eleven o'clock. Don't forget I'm paying for gas."

"A very nice young girl," said the Impossible approvingly after Billie had left. "Of course, you can't appreciate her with her clothes on. You ought to catch her act some evening, Slim."

Looking at Billie's well-rounded little figure as she walked away, I wondered what had ever made the girl go in for posing naked in public. She seemed reasonably intelligent and was certainly more than ordinarily attractive.

Captain Billy was looking into his coffee and swishing the grounds around thoughtfully. "Think there's going to be a clem on this lot?" he said suddenly, addressing the Impossible.

"The townies are building up for one now," said the Impossible casually. "It'll probably break around sunset."

Both men seemed to take the possibility very calmly. I looked from one to the other. "Any chance of stopping it?"

The Impossible gulped down the last of his coffee, skillfully straining it through his whiskers. "There's only one way to handle a mob, Slim. That's not to give them any argument. You've got to remember a mob is always fighting for the highest ideals. Sometimes they don't know that the ideals are, but they're fighting for them anyway."

Captain Billy grinned a little. "That's right. They're either saving the country from the jiggs or Jews or protecting the chastity of American womanhood or something. In this case, they've got a moral duty to run a lot of foreigners like us out of town."

"The smart thing to do is go right along with the crowd," continued the Impossible. "If you give 'em any back talk you're attacking some sacred ideal, and the leads to trouble."

"Suppose you've got a mob that's bigger than the other bunch," I suggested. "What do you do then?"

"That's different," said the Impossible mildly.

Captain Billy and the Impossible ordered more coffee while I started back to the side show tent. Advance skirmishers from the crowd had begun to spread through the carnival. They were mostly young men, followed by convoys of scampering little boys. Women, almost always with babies in their arms or on their hips, stood in the forefront of the encircling mob. The would occasionally shout to the men and receive terse answers. The men were obviously examining the setup with an eye for attack. They had the bearing of scouts for an advancing army. I realized that they must have a local tradition of enmity toward "outsiders" and the men vaguely felt that they were morally sworn to uphold it. They were clearly as proud of this tradition as a Balkan country would be of its independence, and were determined to acquit themselves well before each other and their girls.

I entered Bronko's top and found him and Lu virtually in a state of siege. None of us spoke. Bronko was silently plaiting a silk snapper on the end of his whip lash, while his wife, her usual shrill voice hushed, was trying to cook supper. Every now and then the tent flap would be jerked back and one of the scouts would stick his head in. "Two men and a girl here, Bill," he would call out, his voice artificially brisk and efficient. "Got that, Bill? Two men and a girl." Once Lu screamed, "Get out of here, damn you! People are living in this top. How'd you like it if I come in your house and looked at you?" Bronko said nothing, silently continuing to plait his silk snapper.

Then a stone struck the tent. Lu shivered a little and Bronko silently raised his head and gazed at the spot the stone had struck. I could tell by the way his jaw set he was thinking, "Well there's going to be trouble sure now. In a few minutes. Just a few minutes." Another stone struck the top and then a little shower of them. I couldn't bear sitting there motionless. I got up and went outside.

A crowd of boys were slashing the sidewall with their pocket knives. I shouted, "All right, clear out of there." The boys ran at once, much to my surprise. A gang of young men about my age were sitting and standing on the running board of the truck. I strode up to them and said, "Get off that." Again to my surprise, I was instantly obeyed. I stood wondering at my own authority.

Our ticket taker came toward me. His lean face was as expressionless as a pot of paint. "Go down to the saloon on the corner and phone the cops," he said briefly. "I gotta stay here. These townies are getting ready to wreck the place. We paid the city for this lot. They oughta help us."

"You'd better watch the cars," I told him and forced my way through the mob. They opened a path for me that closed at once.

I found the saloon and put in the call. The police sergeant at the desk was more sympathetic than I expected him to be. "We got two radio cars down there now," he told me. "We're going to send a couple more as soon as they get in." I found out afterward that our advance man had fixed the police so heavily to be allowed to put on the Model Show that they felt obligated to us.

When I returned to the lot, the air was trembling with the coming fight. I pushed through the crowd and came out to face a line of ride men and canvasmen surrounding the cars and the tents. None of them were armed with anything but their fists. Still they seemed able to stop the crowd.

A bunch of small boys were stoning them as calmly as if the men were bottles on a wall. I walked over to one boy who was just about to throw a stone and grabbed his wrist. "What's the idea?" I asked him. He looked up in astonishment, wriggling frantically to get loose, his eyes bulging. Then he began to scream with fright. A man standing near said to me, "Let the kid alone." I released the boy and answered, "Didn't you ever think it might be wrong for him to throw stones at people?" "That's all right," said the man. "Pick on someone your own size." The crowd began to form around us. I was growing shaky with anger. "Pick up that stone," I told him, "and I'll smash in your face with it." "I ain't got nothing to do with this," said the man. "I ain't going to see a kid hurt, that's all." The man obviously considered himself a noble character, defending the rights of women and children. It was impossible to argue with him.

I went through the line of carnies who ignored me, never taking their eyes from the crowd. I ducked through the back flap of the side show top. Jolly Daisy was gone and Krinko sat on the edge of his platform in the pit eating half a grapefruit. He nodded to me.

"Hello, son," he said cheerfully spitting out seeds.

I walked over to him. "Looks like you got some trouble on this lot," I told him.

"Crazy," he said, digging into the grapefruit with his teeth as though it were an orange. "Crazy suckers who want to play. If you want to play with them, sure they'll play. If you leave them alone, the quit."

This sounded like the Impossible's comments on mob psychology.

Then a patter of stones came from the tent top. We both looked up. "That doesn't sound like play," I said.

Krinko swore. He stumped over to the sidewall and pulled the canvas taut to reveal the knife slits made by the boys. "Look at that!" he shouted, twisting the canvas back and forth. "My top! Look at that, the damned suckers!"

Suddenly from somewhere outside came a cry "Stakes!" Instantly shouts and screams sprang up like the crackle of artillery fire. I turned and bolted for the flap. "Get a stake!" yelled Krinko. "Get a stake, son. Hey, wait for me!" I looked around hurriedly but I couldn't see a stake. I thought Krinko was worried that I might get hurt. "You wait here, I'll get a stake somewheres," I shouted as I ducked through the flap.

It was almost dark outside, the evening light having almost disappeared while I was talking to Krinko. I could see the men charging the crowd which was breaking and scattering in all directions. Some of the townies were throwing stones, rushing forward a few steps and snapping the stones out with an accuracy learned on many a sand lot. I saw one of the canvasmen's head suddenly jerk back and he ducked around, shielding his face with his shoulders and clapping both hands to his temple. He walked back towards the tents, swaying his body with pain and cursing.

Suddenly Bronko burst out of his top cracking his long whip with the new snapper on the end. The reports sounded like a rapid volley from a machine gun. He rushed the crowd and the section he attacked began to run in good earnest. I shouted and picking up a board form an old packing case, followed him. Just then the street lamps on the edges of the lot all came on together. The whole scene was suddenly lighted up and filigreed with long, twisting shadows. "Stakes!" came the yell again. More canvasmen came pouring out of the spaces between the tents. I saw the ticket seller and Captain Billy with them, both carrying iron tent stakes. Then the whole line of carnies which had been formed around the tents swept forward and the fight was on.

Bumper cars. The cars have rubber rings around them and the drivers amuse themselves by hitting each other.

Police on the lot after the fight.

CHAPTER 5

The rush was so sudden that the town people were not prepared to meet it. We were on top of the first line before many of the townies could turn to run. People were knocked down and we passed over them. I saw a man and a girl running hand in hand. The girl tripped and fell, and the man, still running, tried to jerk her to her feet. Then the crowd swept around them and I could hear the girl screaming. A terrified little boy rushed by me, blood pouring from a cut on his forehead. Just behind him, came a fat man running in blind panic. He overtook the boy and ran him down apparently without seeing him. The child fell on his face and lay there shrieking in terror. One of the canvasmen pulled him up and gave him a spank toward the rest of the crowd.

A gang of local toughs tried to form a ring. They broke again before the carnies even reached them. The toughs tore through the crowd savagely, striking right and left to get away from the pursuing stakes. A plump, elderly woman, unable to run farther stood clutching two weeping children to her ample breast and screaming hysterically, "Don't you touch me!" I passed several girls crouching on the ground, covering their heads with their arms, sobbing in fear. A tiny boy who couldn't have been more than six stood yelling at every carny who passed, "You want the names of them kids who cut your tents, mister? I'll tell you who they was." He had obviously been deserted by the older children and was expecting a fearful fate.

The wailing scream of a siren swept up above the tumult and a red police car rushed across the lot, plowing through the retreating crowd so recklessly it seemed a miracle that no one was killed. Its siren was instantly answered from the other side and I could see a second red car whirl to a stop. From both cars blue-coated men leaped, carrying night sticks. Knowing the hatred there is between the "lawmen" and carny people I thought they would take the side of the crowd, but instead they joined forces with the canvasmen. Two of them walked back and forth on the flank of the retreating mob, hurrying them off the lot while their comrades followed a few steps in the rear, holding their sticks suggestively. The carnies stopped at once and stood as a back wall to the police, watching the retreat.

Captain Billy came swiftly up to me. "Drop that stick, kid," he said briefly. I threw it away and then noticed with the advent of the police all the stakes and clubs had mysteriously disappeared.

We wandered back toward the dark tops. Everyone was silent. There were no chortlings of victory. I was wondering how we could possibly hope to give a show in this town. If the people felt such bitterness toward us, they certainly would not patronize the carny. An air of depression overhung the lot. There were no lights. The wheels and rides were still draped funereally in their oilcloth covers. The banner lines were not up. The only light on the entire lot came from a single kerosene lamp hung from a nail in the center of the cook house. It was a single spot of dirty light but the carnies drifted toward it like moths.

I joined the silent figures walking across the midway. At the cook house there were some bursts of liveliness. Occasionally someone would laugh and although the laugh was almost instantly smothered by the gloom, it helped to break the thick atmosphere. I saw Bronko, Lu and Captain Billy drinking coffee together and I joined them.

"Now you can say you've been to a clem, Slim," said Captain Billy, grinning at me.

"How are we ever going to open on this lot?" I asked. The cook handed me a cup of coffee without even asking what I wanted and I gulped down half the hot liquid.

"Why shouldn't we open?" asked Bronko. "They didn't do no real damage. Maybe a few sidewalls slit. That's all."

"Why sure," said Captain Billy with quiet confidence as he sat nursing his coffee cup between his big, thick-fingered hands. "A little clem will just make them curious about the carny. They'll all be around tomorrow night to see what we're like."

I began to realize that the crowd might patronize the carnival tomorrow night as casually as they had attacked us this afternoon. The town girls, who had been screaming hysterically at the canvasmen during the clem, would be impressed by the rough efficiency with which the carnies handled the mob and try to make dates with the same men they had cursed so bitterly the day before.

Captain Billy was right. The carnival opened the next evening and we had a good turnout, although there were only a few lights on the midway. During the clem, the townies had cut the cable line running to the juice truck. The carnival didn't carry its own generator and the juice truck had to plug into the main city line and then step it down and distribute the current to the various shows. The juice crew had worked all Monday to repair the damage but only a few shows had any electricity. The merry-go-round and most of the rides were silent, and there were plenty of blackouts among the tent shows, including our side show. The Model Show and the Girl Show got their lights first of all and for most of the evening they practically had an exclusive on the entire midway. By ten o'clock, the juice man came around to say we had current and we gave our first bally.

When the tip collected, I could see townies in it with black eyes and strips of adhesive tape pasted on their faces. But they didn't seem to have any hard feelings and Mountmorency turned the tip easily. We had a good crowd for our first show. On the next bally, I swallowed a couple of torches and got a round of applause. When I stepped back to let May, the snake charmer, exhibit her python, I saw a girl in the tip standing with her boy friend watching me. The girl winked and then jerked her head toward the black shadows surrounding the tent. Her boy friend saw that I was watching, and turned to look at her. The girl instantly assumed a demure expression and seemed fascinated by May's snake.

Lu, who was standing behind me on the platform, giggled and nudged me.

I was all set to do some fire-eating in the pit, but Krinko passed me over while the other acts performed. Although I knew I couldn't do a real fire-eating routine as yet, I felt humiliated. I realized that except for our canvasman, I was the only person with the show who didn't have an act. Everyone had been so nice to me that I'd thought of myself as a real member of the troupe. Now I realized that they were just carrying me. I wasn't "with it." I was a young punk traveling with the show but not part of it. I determined to get started on my fire-eating routine no matter how many blisters I developed.

Early the next morning I left the lot and went into town. I needed a metal bowl to hold the gasoline I used in my act. A fire-eater generally starts his act by pouring a few ounces of gas into a bowl and soaking up the fluid with the heads of his torches. Then the performer drops a lighted match into the bowl and lets it flare up. The burning bowl serves as a "flash" to add color to the routine and also acts as a constant source of fire so the man can light his torches from it at any time during the performance.

I found some ornamental Chinese brass bowls in a hock shop that were flashy and about the right size. I got two of them so I could have both a "burning bowl" and a "soaking bowl" in case I needed to put more gas on my torches during the act. You can't pour gasoline over a torch's head because you'd spill a lot and it's not a good idea to be standing near a puddle of gasoline while you're waving burning torches around. Instead, you pour a little gas into a bowl and touch it with the cotton head of your torch. The cotton draws up the gas like a wick and you're ready to go.

After buying my bowls, I went back to the carnival lot. There was no one in the side show top during the day so I spread out my props on the inside platform and got ready to practice my act. Without the Impossible there to encourage me, I felt a little nervous. In the still air of the tent, the torch flames shot up red as blood and straight as columns. Their twisting streamers of black smoke writhed upward until they reached the tent's roof and there flattened out, feeling along the canvas for some hole through which they could escape.

Lu after the fight.

A typical "tip."

The flaming torch heads looked much larger and more dangerous than when I was working with them outside the day before. I turned the torches back and forth, hoping they'd die down a little. The sight of the burning torches throwing scarlet light against the canvas made me think of Flamo for the first time. These same torches had lighted up the outside of the top just this way the night he'd had his terrible accident.

If something happened to me, while I was practicing, I'd be alone in the top. Still carrying my burning torches, I went to the tent entrance and looked around. I'd never seen the midway so deserted. Gloomily, I climbed back on the bally platform and eyed the torches. Instead of dying down, they seemed to be burning brighter every minute.

While I was wondering if there wasn't some other side show stunt I could learn instead of fire-eating, the entrance flap shook and the Impossible Possible strolled in with his hands in his pockets.

"I just happened to be passing and smelled gasoline," he explained easily. "At first, I thought somebody's car might be on fire and then I remembered you. I see you're practicing. How are those blisters from yesterday?"

"I don't mind the ones on the outside," I told him. "It's the ones on the inside that bother me." I opened my mouth wide. "Uk, hee?"

"Yes sir, they're really beauties," said the Impossible, climbing up on the platform and bending over to look inside my mouth. "But the ones on the outside are very

fine specimens too. Oh well, they'll heal up in a few weeks and only leave a slight scar."

"I hope gasoline is a good disinfectant," I said ruefully. Several of the blisters inside my mouth had burst leaving little spots of raw flesh.

"The very best," the Impossible assured me. He picked up a couple of my unlit torches and examined them. "I'd tie the heads of these torches in place if I was you. Sometimes the burning head of a torch falls off and you swallow it by mistake. Of course, it goes out after a few seconds, but I always hate those few seconds. Well, let's see what you can do."

With the Impossible there, I felt more confident. I'd learned the day before to throw my head back until I could feel my collar pressing into the back of my neck. Then I'd insert the flaming torch at an angle of about seventy-five degrees. When I did it correctly, the flame would rush out of my open mouth instead of going down into my lungs. I had to breathe out at the same time. The trick was to keep a steady, almost imperceptible current of air coming out of my mouth that prevented the torch's flame from hitting my lips and yet didn't make the fire jump around and singe my cheeks.

"I'm glad to see you're learning how to breathe," the Impossible went on, revolving around me like a tailor fitting a suit as he watched my handling of the flame. "Don't let the gas fumes get down your lungs. They've got a habit of exploding in there. Gas fumes are always

The Impossible Possible.

getting caught in a cross-draft inside of you and they're apt to go wandering around."

I'd thought fire-eating simply consisted of learning how to swallow the torches. But the Impossible explained that for a complete act, there were many variations to the routine that I would have to learn. "Get a torch with plenty of gasoline on the head and when you put it in your mouth, wipe off some of the burning gas on your tongue," he told me. "While this gas is still burning, take another torch and light it from the flames coming out of your mouth. Makes a very pretty effect. I've also seen fire-eaters deliberately swallow gas fumes, puff them out and then set fire to them as they hit the air. That's called 'The Human Candelabra.' You can also lay two torches together and put both in your mouth at the same time."

The Impossible also told me that after I'd finished my flourishes with the torches, I'd have to do some other fire effects. He suggested that I soak a piece of wood in gasoline to make it burn better, set fire to the wood, and lay it on my tongue with a pair of long-handled forceps. Members of the audience could light their cigarettes from it. I should also set fire to my "soaking" bowl of gasoline and then drink the burning gas with a spoon. A wooden spoon has to be used for this effect, because a metal spoon becomes so hot that it burns your lips.

"So much of the gas we get nowadays has lead in it, you've got to be careful when you do this stunt," the Impossible explained. "Leaded gas will poison you. I think a little deception is permissible here. After you dip up a spoonful of the gas, talk for a few seconds until most of the gas is burned away. The spoon will keep on burning for quite some time after the gasoline is gone and by putting the spoon into your mouth while it is flaming and then closing your lips, you can put out the fire and give the impression of having swallowed the burning gas. Of course, if some hecklers in your audience discover that you aren't doing anything but sticking a blazing spoon down your throat, they'll complain. Then you really have to drink the gas."

I've never actually understood the physical principles that make fire-eating possible. I have talked to several doctors about it and they all had conflicting theories. Apparently the extreme heat of the flame coming suddenly in contact with the moisture inside the mouth creates a thin layer of steam which acts as insulation. The inside of your mouth and lips must be wet before you can swallow a torch. The flame will burn your skin if it touches any other part of the body except the inside of the mouth and the red part of the lips. Of course, sometimes it burns you there too if you aren't breathing correctly or if you're holding the torch at the wrong angle.

Although my mouth felt like the inside of a carburetor, I didn't experience any pain while I was practicing. I thought I was at last getting onto the trick. But a few hours later, blisters formed all over the inside of my cheeks and the skin on the roof of my mouth began to peel off in thin strips. I was too sick to appear on the bally platform that evening and the pain kept getting steadily worse. Everyone with the show was very sympathetic but no one suggested that I see a doctor. Their unspoken attitude seemed to be that this was just one of the things you go through learning an act. Curiously, it never occurred to me to go to a doctor, either. I tried to keep down the burning in my mouth by making periodic trips to an open-all-night diner and filling my mouth with ice cream. About three o'clock in the morning, the diner ran out of ice cream, so I started buying the cracked ice the proprietor kept his ice cream cartons in. The man began to look at me rather curiously after that, although I was paying him as much for his darned cracked ice as I had for the ice cream, and the ice was full of salt that stung. Finally he quietly closed down between two of my trips. I really suffered after that until the drugstores opened in the morning. Then I bought several commercial ointments sold to relieve burns, but they all tasted horrible and didn't do any good. Finally, I went back to ice cream.

I was all right again in a few days, but during that time I didn't feel like eating anything but soup. The soup at the cook shack wasn't very good and one morning Bronko came to me and explained that he and Lu needed some extra money and would I eat with them? I agreed. Lu cooked excellent thick soup, which was almost a stew, on her little camp stove and they charged me ten cents a bowl. It didn't occur to me until long afterward that this kindly couple had become worried about me, and hit on this trick to make sure I was getting decent meals. I think Lu probably lost about a quarter on every bowl of soup she sold me.

While I was waiting for my mouth to heal, I hung around the side show top doing odd jobs and currying Dot, the five-legged horse. By the end of the week I was feeling all right again. I was even able to do some fire-eating on the bally. But for a long time I was afraid that I'd never be able to do fire-eating as a regular act. I'd taken so much punishment during my practice sessions that even swallowing a couple of torches and putting a few hot coals on my tongue would make my whole mouth ache. But later I realized that not even a hardened professional Human Salamander could have stood the steady, six-hour bouts of fire-eating that I'd inflicted on myself while practicing. In a carnival, a fire-eater only gives his complete show three times in an evening and in addition he may swallow a torch or two on the bally platform to draw a tip. Once you've learned how to handle the torches, this isn't too much of a strain. By the end of a couple of weeks, I was able to open in the pit as a regular member of the company.

On the morning of the last day we were on that lot, I was stretched out with Paul on the bally platform taking a sunbath when Billie Callihan came over with another girl from the Model Show. They were dressed in street clothes and didn't have any make-up on, not even lipstick.

"Say, Slim, how about taking me over to see my girl friend that's married to the sword swallower," Billie suggested. "You promised you would and this is the last day."

I'd forgotten about Billie. I put on my shirt and looked up Krinko. He told me I could borrow the smaller truck and a few minutes later, Billie and I started for the city.

We drove through the factory town, hit the main highway and started over the ramp. Billie was sitting beside me, humming to herself. Finally she said, "You know, in spite of the clem, this hasn't been a bad spot. The guys sure appreciated our Model Show. We topped the Girl Show every night. Frisco had it fixed with the cops, so we didn't need to work behind the curtain all the time. First, we'd put on our regular show and then Frisco would tell the tip that anyone who wanted to pay fifty cents extra could stay and he'd pull up the curtain. Of course everyone stayed and we really made money."

Billie.

"When you first started out in the Model Show, didn't you feel funny about standing up in front of a lot of men without any clothes on?" I asked her. Without her make-up, Billie didn't look tough and although no one would have confused her with a Vassar graduate, she was a pleasant kid and very pretty.

Billie smiled. "With all the other girls doing it too, you don't mind so much. The men in the tip can't touch you or nothing. I guess it makes you proud, too, that all those men are willing to pay money to look at you. Aren't you proud that people are willing to pay money to see your act, Slim?"

I did get a kick out of it, but somehow I felt that a different principle was involved.

"How did you first join up with the Model Show?"

"I got a real rough deal back home where I come from," said Billie. She spoke vehemently. "I used to run around with a bunch of young people we called 'The Gang' and in the evenings we'd stop in at a roadhouse and play the juke box and dance. Sometimes some of the fellows got a little tight and sometimes we'd go out in the cars and do some pretty heavy necking, but we never did anybody any harm. Well, one evening the cops raided the roadhouse where we was. A bunch of old women who ran some sort of purity club put in a complaint about us and kept after the cops until they had to do something. The cops didn't have anything on us but they put us in jail for forty-eight hours anyhow. After that I left home."

The sword swallower lived in a district that Billie described as "the hobos' main stem." It was the business section of the downtown slums. I parked the truck and we walked under the shadow of an elevated train, past hock shops, tattooing parlors, hash houses, ten-cent movie theaters, and flop houses advertising beds for twenty-five cents per night. The sword swallower was performing at a local dime museum. We inquired at the box office and the ticket seller told us that the sword swallower wasn't working that week due to a slight accident. He gave us the man's home address and we went there.

The couple lived on the third floor of a walk-up apartment. We mounted the dingy stairs. When we reached the third floor, Billie yelled "Mayme!" A door opened and Mayme looked out suspiciously. When she saw Billie, she gave a squeal of delight and rushed out to meet us. Mayme was about the same age as Billie but considerably plumper. Her hair, a dirty blond, showed signs of having been touched up and she was already developing a middle-aged spread. After the girls had kissed, Mayme led us into the room and announced importantly, "Folks, I want you to meet my husband, Rafael, better known as the Human Electric Light Bulb."

The Bulb was in bed with an old blanket pulled over him reading a comic magazine. He must have been twice as old as his wife: a slender, dark Italian with a narrow pleasant face. He tried to get up to greet us, but Mayme pushed him back.

"He doesn't feel so well," she explained apologetically. "He swallowed a sword with engraved work on the blade. The engraving caught on the lining of his stomach. There he was standing with the sword sticking out of his mouth and couldn't get it out again. Well, he finally worked it loose but he don't feel so well now."

"I think I eat the big plate of spaghetti," said her husband grinning broadly. "I take big gulp—bang!—sword stick in my stomach and won't come out. Ha ha ha!"

We all laughed heartily. "I thought you just swallowed neon tubes," said Billie.

Rafael pointed to a collection of long glass tubes partly wrapped in old towels, lying on the table. "I no swalla da swords no more," he said, waving a long finger at us. "I swalla only da neon tubes—all lighted. See here."

In spite of Mayme's shrill protests, Rafael got out of bed and began excitedly plugging in the neon tubes to a step-up transformer so the tubes could be run from the house current. One after another, the tubes flashed on, filling the tiny room with their eerie, jewel-like light. They were all different colors. Rafael grabbed one tube and brandished it as though he were going to swallow it and Mayme yelped, "You swallow that thing and I'll never speak to you again. Your insides ain't ready for it yet."

"In my new act, she all neons," Rafael explained eagerly, waving the tube while he talked. "Other men swalla one neon tube. I only man do all tubes—no swords, no bayonets, no corkscrews."

"He's got a beautiful set of swords, too," complained Mayme. "Look here." She pulled a sheet off a stand that had been shoved into one corner of the room. The stand was a big heart-shaped affair about a yard wide. The heart had been covered with shining scarlet paper, and arranged on it were a series of swords, held in place by little brass brackets.

The smallest of the swords was about eight inches and the largest nearly two feet. There was also a bayonet in the collection and a huge, nickel-plated pair of scissors measuring about a foot.

I went over to examine the collection. Rafael, obviously very pleased by my interest, slid the swords out of their brackets one after another, wiping them off with a cloth, and explained their fine points. He showed the one with the engraving that had nearly killed him—a short weapon with a red handle, the blade completely covered with elaborate scroll work.

In my studies of magic, I'd read quite a bit about sword swallowing, so I examined the instruments with great interest. Sword swallowing is very old. No one knows who was the first man to discover that he could swallow a sword, but he certainly must have been an unusual personality with a flair for experimentation. Traveling jugglers performed the trick for the Pharaohs, and Agrippa mentions seeing the trick in ancient Rome. He was somewhat drunk at the time and later ascribed what he saw to the wine, but Remy, the great fifteenth-century philosopher, also saw the stunt

This is the man I call Rafael. I bought his swords from him.

and decided it was done by the aid of demons. "Any other explanation is unreasonable," he pointed out in his treatise on witchcraft. In my reading, I had never been able to find out if the performers actually did swallow the swords or if the illusion was due to some trick. I asked Rafael.

The girls were sitting on the bed, chatting, and with a quick glance at his wife to make sure she wasn't watching, Rafael took one of the swords, wiped it carefully, flung back his head, and swallowed it up to the hilt. He stood there for a moment and then withdrew the blade. He wiped it again and returned the sword to the stand. I was convinced. There was no doubt that Rafael had really swallowed the twenty-inch blade.

Rafael explained that swallowing a sword was simply a matter of practice. You shoved the blade down your throat until your throat muscles became accustomed to the touch of the cold steel and you stopped retching. He always wiped a sword before swallowing it because even the smallest particles of dust adhering to the blade could make you retch. After withdrawing the sword, he wiped the blade again to remove the stomach fluids. These fluids corrode the nickel-plate on the blades and nickel-plate is expensive.

Rafael told me that he had gotten most of his swords from hock shops. They were old cavalry sabers and lodge swords. He had the blades nickel-plated to make them smooth. He always made sure that the blades were firmly fitted in the hilts. Sometimes after swallowing a sword, the blade falls out of the hilt and the performer really swallows it. Unless he can reach the broken end of the blade with his thumb and forefinger, he is indeed in a predicament. Rafael had had the giant scissors made up specially as a flash item. The bayonet was a standard one he had gotten at an army surplus store.

I asked Rafael how he had happened to take up sword swallowing for a living. He told me that he was born in Italy and was the youngest of ten children, all big, healthy kids except himself. He was the runt. The family came to America when Rafael was seventeen and immediately the other boys were able to get jobs as ditch diggers or railroad track layers. Rafael couldn't do heavy work and this preyed on his mind. One day, he left home and joined a carnival as a "carny punk"—a young boy who hangs around the lot running errands for the performers, sleeping where he can, traveling from city to city curled up like a puppy on top of the canvas, helping the joint men set up their concessions.

Rafael had no act. In the evenings when the carnival lighted up, and the bands began to play, no one came to see him. He had no newspaper clippings about himself. He could not boast that he had introduced some little wrinkle into a routine that no one ever thought of before. He was just a punk, but he didn't want to leave carny life.

So he decided to learn an act. Unfortunately, he wasn't a freak. He couldn't afford the elaborate apparatus for an aerial act and his faulty English kept him from becoming either a talker or a joint man. So he became a sword swallower. His swords only cost him twenty dollars and he made the stand himself.

I asked Rafael what he was going to do with his swords now that he was specializing in neon tubes. He shrugged.

Mayme looked up from her conversation with Billie. "I sure wish we could sell the things," she said wistfully. "But who'd want to buy them? Sword swallowers have their own outfits and we'd only get a few bucks from a hock shop."

Suddenly I had an idea. Probably no one in show business had ever put on a combined fire-eating and sword swallowing act. If I learned to swallow neon tubes, I could work in the dark, my act illuminated only by the flicker of the torches and the glow of the variously colored tubes. It would be a hell of a routine.

"How much do you want for the swords and the stand?" I asked Rafael.

They all stared at me. Billie said, "Gee, Slim, you're a fire-eater. What do you want with two acts?" I didn't explain. I was afraid someone might steal my great idea. Rafael sold me the swords and stand for ten dollars. He showed me how to break down the stand for traveling and gave me the scabbards for the swords. The swords were always carried in scabbards when not on the stand to keep the blades from being scratched or chipped.

On the way back to the lot, Billie was very quiet. I finally asked her if there was anything wrong. She sighed.

"No, I guess not. But I sort of wish I was a man. Here you're going to have two acts and all I can do is pose. It must be great to want to do something and then go right ahead and do it like a man does."

"You could learn to be a sword swallower if you wanted to," I said lamely.

The little stripper sniffed. "I certainly could not. Sword swallowing isn't lady-like."

When we reached the hotel where Billie was staying with the other Model Show girls, I let her out. "Say, Billie, how about having supper with me some night?" I asked.

Billie looked surprised and then said gently, "Well, I guess not, Slim. You see, I got a regular fellow on the lot."

"Oh. Well, then, so long," I said regretfully.

"So long, Slim, and thanks for the lift." Billie ran up the hotel steps and paused at the door to wave. I drove away, sorry to think that I probably wouldn't be seeing her again. It isn't often that performers from different shows meet on a carny lot, but I was too much interested in my idea for a combined sword-swallowing-and-fire act to think much about Billie. Inside the side show top, I assembled the sword rack and slid the swords out of the scabbards. I put the shining weapons in their brackets on the stand, then I got out my torches and brass bowls and arranged them beside the swords. It made quite an impressive display. I sat there for a long time in front of my apparatus, gloating over it.

Lu and Bronko.

CHAPTER 6

I was awakened the next morning by Lu's shrill voice. She was fighting with Bronko. Lying on the inside platform of the side show top, I could hear Lu's angry tones clearly through the thin canvas walls. I listened, grinning to myself, and luxuriating in the warmth of the top as the hot morning sun soaked through the translucent canvas. Then the odor of frying bacon began to wander in through the open front flap and I decided to get up and investigate.

Lu had set up her camp stove on a folding table outside their little living top and was frying bacon, pouring coffee, helping Bronko on with his fringed buckskin jacket, and denouncing the world in general, all at the same time. The Bronkos had invited Aunt Matty for breakfast and the old lady was sitting quietly in a chair she'd brought from her trailer. She was knitting a sweater and listening to Lu's complaints as quietly as though the girl's high-pitched voice were a babbling brook.

When Lu caught sight of me she screamed, "Here comes another one to feed. Well, he's got to do the dishes then."

The day before I'd bought a paper bag full of bread, eggs, bacon and a quart of milk. I turned the bag over to Lu without comment and after investigating the contents, she remarked, "Well, this is real nice of you, Slim. There's enough to keep us a couple of days, if you don't eat too much."

"I'll do the dishes, too," I offered and reached for the coffee. After a cup of Lu's extra-strong brew and a dish of bacon and eggs, I lay back on the grass with my eyes closed and felt that life had nothing more to offer.

I began to think about Billie. As we talked I gradually worked the conversation around to the girl with what I considered consummate tact. Suddenly I heard Lu giggle. I rolled over and opened my eyes. Lu was bent over the stove, red in the face from suppressed emotion. Bronko wore a broad grin as he sat picking out chords on his guitar and even Aunt Matty was looking out over the midway with a benevolent smile.

When they saw me look up, everybody laughed. "Gee, it didn't take Slim long to find himself a girl," said Lu cheerfully.

"Wait a minute!" I protested. "I only gave Billie a lift out to her girl friend's place."

"Well, how long does it take you to make up your mind whether you like a girl?" shrilled Lu. "Gee, the first time I saw Bronko I fell in love with him."

"What happened?" I asked.

Bronko and Lu grinned at each other. "Well, I useta do piece-work in a factory way down South," explained Lu. "Our union hired some fellers from a carny to play at the spring dance. One of the fellers was Bronko. He played the guitter and he had a girl with him that sang."

"She was a good-looking girl, too," said the cowboy with his ear against the guitar while he tested the strings. "She had a bad temper, but she was mighty pretty."

"Aw, she wasn't so pretty," Lu said disdainfully. "Well, while I was dancin' with this guy what brung me, I noticed Bronko followin' me around with his eyes. O' course, I didn't let on I seen it, but this girl that Bronko had with him took notice of it and kept pullin' his hair every time he looked at me. So after a spell I got sore and jest walked up to her in the middle of the dance floor and I says 'You let him alone,' I says, 'Don't you go pullin' his hair.' 'Well, I got a right to!' she says, real snippy-like to me. 'I'm his wife and I got a right to.'"

"She wasn't my wife. I was just living with her," said Bronko casually. "I guess I lived with her for a couple of years."

"'Course I didn't know that," continued Lu. "But jest the same I says, 'I don't care who you is. You leave him alone!' So then she and me get in a fight and they have to pull us apart, but I'll bet she won't forget some of the slaps I give her in a hurry. Then Bronko takes me outside for a drink and I'm cryin' somethin' awful. He says, 'Why don't you and me get married?' and I says, 'Ain't you married to her?' and he says 'Oh no, I'm jest livin' with her.' So I says, 'All right, I'll marry you!' jest to see what he says. And he says 'All right,' and damned if we didn't go off and get married!" Lu laughed happily.

This was whirlwind courtship that really whirled. "What happened to the other girl?" I asked.

Lu instantly became serious. "You know what that girl done?" she asked in a shocked voice. "She took on somethin' awful! When she went up to Bronko's room to get her clothes, she stole a lot of his things. A whole Ingin suit worth easy fifty dollars and a lot of his shirts and good socks. Then she took them some place and got 'em all covered with tar and grease so they was ruined. Can you imagine anyone like that? She was awful mean kind of woman!"

Although I liked Lu, my sympathies were all with the other girl. She seemed to have had a rough deal— Ingin suit or no Ingin suit.

Aunt Matty said mildly, as though desirous of changing the subject, "It would be a good thing if Billie took up with some nice boy on the lot . . . although I don't think Slim is exactly her type. But Billie should do something to get rid of that awful Steve."

I was instantly interested. "Who's Steve?"

Lu sniffed. "Aw, he's jest a guy who's supposed to be Billie's boy friend."

"What's he like?"

Bronko laid his guitar across his knees and said with a good deal of feeling, "That Steve is what I'd call a typical carny bum. He ain't got no act, he don't do nothing, and he's a pain in the tail. He hangs around the lot picking up odd jobs and living off Billie."

"What does she see in him?" I asked wonderingly.

No one said anything. Aunt Matty continued to work on her sweater with an enigmatic, Mona Lisa smile on her face. Lu shrugged and began to collect the breakfast dishes.

"Aw, he's supposed to be a great lover or somethin'. I wouldn't touch the guy with a centerpole, myself. I think Billie's nuts."

It sounded to me like a good deal not to get mixed up in. As I helped Lu with the dishes, I decided to keep clear of Billie Callihan.

After the show that evening, I exhibited my set of swords and told the troupe that I intended to become a sword swallower as well as a fire-eater. They were surprised and a little doubtful. Usually a performer has only one act. Once a side show worker has learned a certain routine, he generally sticks to it for the rest of his life. There's no real reason for him to develop a repertoire. Every week the carnival moves on to a new lot so the show is constantly opening in a fresh locality and the acts never have a chance to grow stale. There is no point in giving one routine in Hoboken and a new one next week in Rochester. But I was interested in the carnival acts themselves and hoped to be able to do them all. Also, I intended to combine sword swallowing and fire-eating into one routine and call it "Fire and Swords."

Captain Billy shook his head sadly when I explained my idea and even old man Krinko, who could do several acts himself, told me to take it easy. "You get your insides used to fire and then all of a sudden you shove a sword into them. It's not good to surprise your insides like that. They not like it," he assured me. The only encouragement I got was from the Impossible Possible when he dropped around after closing up his gambling joint. He said he thought it was a very fine idea.

"I was like Slim myself when I was a young man," he told the troupe who had gathered around my sword stand and were doubtfully examining Rafael's weapons. "I was ambitious. Used to have an act where I drank a bottle of any kind of ink the audience brought in. Very unusual and made a sensation. Never seemed to do me any harm except to make my teeth fall out. I was making twenty dollars a week in those days and coining money. But I spent it all foolishly. Invested it in training alligators and did they turn out to be a flop!"

"What happened to them?" asked Jolly Daisy suspiciously. I'd been explaining to the fat lady how Rafael tore his stomach with the sword that had engraving on the blade and she'd been thanking providence that she'd been lucky enough to be born a freak.

"The star of my show was a ten-foot bull 'gator that I'd caught myself in Florida," said the Impossible, hoisting his lean hips up on the inside platform and bumming a cigarette from Captain Billy. "I don't trust the ordinary run-of-the-mill 'gators you get from dealers. They're liable to be spoiled."

"How in hell do you spoil an alligator?" demanded Lu.

"'Gators are very high-strung," explained the Impossible, fitting the cigarette into a holder so it wouldn't singe his whiskers. "The first thing to do when you're confronted by a vicious 'gator is to turn him over on his back and tickle his stomach. Then he knows you're his friend. Otherwise, his actions are unpredictable."

May, the snake charmer, nodded eagerly. "I hate to get poisonous snakes that have been mishandled by dealers. A lot of these professional snake hunters use a noose on the end of a long pole to catch rattlesnakes. Then the poor rattlers thrash around and hurt themselves. The correct way to collect rattlesnakes is to talk to them quietly and then pick them up with your hands. Of course, sometime they bite you, but if you're going to be afraid of a thing like that, why go into the snake-collecting business?"

The Impossible nodded. "My point exactly. Anyhow, this big bull 'gator of mine had a den way up in the Okeechobee swamp. I hired a couple of Seminole Indians to help me dig him out and tie him up. It was hard work and the 'gator didn't like it much either. I taught him to roll over, play dead, hold an American flag while the band played 'Rule, Columbia' and wrestle any member of the audience for a ten-dollar purse. Teaching an infuriated bull 'gator a routine like that isn't as easy as it sounds. Then damned if the scaly son of a bitch didn't let me down."

"What did he do, eat the mark he was supposed to wrestle?" asked Captain Billy.

"Worse than that," said the Impossible sadly. "He bit me. And I'd been a second father to him. I had him up on the stage one night and I was tapping him on the nose to get him to open his mouth and hiss for the tip. An easy thing for any 'gator to do. All of a sudden he grabbed me by the hand. The instant his jaws snapped together my whole arm went numb. I thought 'there goes my arm.' I expected him to roll—you know, as soon as a 'gator grabs your hand he generally starts rolling to twist the arm off at the shoulder. So I fell down on the platform and decided to fool the bastard and roll with him. Fortunately, my assistant ran out with a fish and when the 'gator saw that he opened his mouth. While his mouth was still open I lifted my hand off his teeth and got it out."

"I don't think it was really the 'gator's fault," said May reprovingly. "He probably mistook your white hand for the belly of a fish and thought you were trying to feed him."

The Impossible shook his head. "I don't like 'gators that are that short-sighted. Fortunately, I was able to unload the ungrateful brute on a woman who had just come up from Florida and wanted a baby 'gator as a pet for her little girl. She wrote me asking if I had anything suitable and I charged her twenty bucks for the old bull and sent him to her C.O.D. for the express charges. I'd have liked to been around when they opened the crate. They say excitement is good for your liver and I'll bet that woman didn't have to take any liver pills for the next fifty years."

I started practicing with my new set of swords the next morning. Sword swallowing turned out to be much harder to learn than fire-eating. The first time I tried to swallow a sword I was promptly taken sick. This kept up for several days until my throat gradually became accustomed to the touch of the cold steel. I made it a point to practice an hour every day before each meal. If I practiced after eating, I simply lost the meal. Finally I stopped gagging only to find that my throat had closed up so tight that I couldn't get the sword down. There seemed to be no opening there at all. Apparently an involuntary muscle in my throat had snapped shut and there was nothing I could do to open it. This was very discouraging. I might have given up if the other members of the troupe hadn't shown so much interest and sympathy in my struggles.

At first the other acts had tried to persuade me not to attempt two routines. But once they saw I was really serious about learning sword swallowing, everyone tried to help me out. About all they could do was to keep away from me while I was practicing and tactfully make no mention about the gagging noises that came from inside the side show top while I was trying to get the swords down. Jolly Daisy was particularly anxious about me. As Daisy couldn't walk about herself, she'd send Paul scouting around the top to see how I was doing. When Daisy decided from Paul's reports that I'd practiced enough for one morning she'd stagger to the entrance of her little living top and bellow, "You, Slim! You come here!" If I didn't come at once, Daisy would roar loud enough to shake the ferris wheels. When I finally wiped off the swords and went over to the fat lady's top, Daisy always had a pot of coffee ready for me and some sandwiches. She knew that once I'd eaten I'd have to stop practicing until the food digested. So Daisy would stand guard over me until I'd gotten the meal down.

While I was waiting for the food to settle, Daisy and I would light cigarettes, put our feet up on her over-sized camp cot, and talk about life. The fat lady was a curious combination of conflicting traits, brought about by her freakishness. Jolly Daisy had traveled widely, both in this country and South America, but because of her great bulk she had seldom been outside of a side show tent. She had met thousands of people and yet was lonely. Daisy was a comparatively wealthy woman with no responsibilities, but she couldn't spend her money on clothes, night clubs, automobiles, or parties. She had all the instincts of a normal woman, but ties. She had all the instincts of a normal woman, but

for her marriage was practically impossible, or, at least, so I thought until one afternoon Daisy casually mentioned to me that she was thinking of marrying again.

I must have looked surprised for Daisy said with a touch of irritation, "Yes sir, I can get all the men I want any time. I been married five or six times already and lived with plenty of men on top of that."

She inhaled deeply on her cigarette and then sighed wistfully. "But to tell you the truth, Slim, I ain't got much use for most men. I figure a man oughta support himself some of the time."

"Most husbands earn all the money and support their wives," I remarked.

Jolly Daisy looked a little puzzled. Of course, she must have known that this was true. She'd probably read about it in magazines and heard rumors. But in carnival life most women work and a surprising number of them are supporting some man. As far as Jolly Daisy was concerned, my statement might have been a comment on the curious marital habits prevalent among Hottentots.

"Well, I guess that's right," she said vaguely. "It sure would be nice if you could get a husband who could support himself. That was the big trouble with my last man—he was real good-looking but he always wanted money. Finally we had a fight and he blew." She said this somewhat regretfully. "He's the father of my little girl."

"Have you a child?" I asked surprised. "Is she . . ." I hesitated, not knowing how to put it.

"Oh, no," said Daisy without anger. "She isn't a freak like me. She's perfectly normal." Taking her feet off the cot with a groan, she fumbled in a box on her dressing table and produced the picture of a very pretty, curly-headed girl. "This is her," she said showing it to me proudly. "She's at a Catholic convent. She doesn't know I'm her mother. It ain't wise she should know. But the sisters send me pictures of her all the time. This is the latest one."

"You must miss her," I said handing the picture back.

"I sure do," said Daisy, regarding the picture affectionately. "It's funny how you can miss somebody you ain't never hardly seen, but I miss her. Sometimes I think about getting married again so I could have her with me. I figure if one of her parents was normal, she wouldn't mind so much about me being a freak." Daisy sighed and put the picture away. "But that's just a fool idea. My place is with the carnies and I'm happy here. You can't be a side show fat woman and a mother. Slim, any time you see me show signs of forgetting I'm a freak and trying to be a normal woman, you got my permission to heave off and kick me right in the tail."

I wanted to say something to make Daisy feel better. But I felt the fat woman was wise in leaving the child in a convent. Daisy's men had obviously been bums who'd only lived with the fat lady for what they could get out of her. Such people certainly wouldn't make good stepfathers for a little girl. The fat woman was happy in the carnival, but she was probably right when she said you can't be a Ten-in-One freak and a housewife at the same time.

Jolly Daisy usually lived up to her name, but now she seemed so depressed that I was glad to say good-bye and get back to my sword swallowing.

To an ambitious young sword swallower, there is nothing more discouraging than trying day after day to force a sword into your insides when your throat has closed up so tightly that the whole business seems useless. For the last week I'd been feeling around the bottom of my throat with the point of a blunt sword, hoping that eventually something would open up. I'd long ago given up gagging, but there didn't seem to be anything I could do about this involuntary throat muscle that refused to relax. But as I climbed up on the inside platform of the side show top that afternoon, I wasn't thinking about my throat. I was thinking about Jolly Daisy and her problems. I automatically selected one of my swords and started to swallow it, forgetting to worry about that damned throat muscle. Instead of meeting resistance, the sword suddenly slid down inside of me up to the hilt.

Instantly I was sick. The blade was now passing over a new set of nerves that hadn't become accustomed to the touch of the steel. But I was too excited to stop. I swallowed the sword again, vomited again, and kept it up until it was almost time for the evening show.

When the troupe came in to set up their props, I exhibited my new art. Everybody seemed as proud and pleased as if they'd learned the routine themselves. Captain Billy confessed that he never thought I'd make it. Krinko said he'd been forty years under canvas and never heard of a combined sword swallowing and fire-eating act before. I think I was happier with their applause than I've ever been about anything else in my life.

After two more weeks of constant practice, I was finally able to swallow a sword in public. For a long time I wasn't able to let the sword go straight down my throat. I first had to let the blade go down until it touched the back of my throat. Then I would bend forward, still keeping the sword straight out in front of me, and slide it in another couple of inches. This would take it over a little hump in the throat just back of the Adam's apple. Then I could straighten up again and let it go straight down.

Rafael had told me that because I was so tall I ought to be able to establish a world's record for sword swallowing. The length of a sword that a man can swallow is determined by the distance from his lips to the pit of his stomach. Rafael, being short, had never been able to swallow a sword more than eighteen inches long, although he tried to give the illusion of swallowing a much longer sword by running his lips as far up the blade as possible. To find out how long a sword I could swallow, I purchased a very long saber and then swallowed it gingerly until I could feel the tip of the blade touch the pit of my stomach. This is a very curious sensation to describe. I didn't feel a definite impact, but a sort of thrill ran all through my body. Then I marked the blade with a grease pencil just above my teeth. I withdrew the blade, had it cut off at the mark and refitted into the hilt. The blade was just twenty-six inches long.

Although learning sword swallowing wasn't as painful as learning fire-eating, it was considerably more dangerous. The lining of the stomach is almost paper-thin and if a sword penetrates this lining, the performer is almost certain to die of peritonitis. The edges of the swords are not sharp because they must push the sides of the throat apart as they go down. But you can swallow a sword that has a sharp point—as long as the sword isn't long enough to touch the pit of your stomach. Captain Billy told me that most carny sword swallowers keep a couple of swords with dagger-sharp tips to use on hecklers.

"Every now and then you get some hoods in the tip who start hollering that the swords are faked," the captain explained. "The best way to handle those gees is to swallow a sword with a sharp point on it. Then you bring the sword up and throw it at the hoods. When they jump out of the way, the sword hits the spot where they were standing and sinks into the ground half-way up to the hilt. Makes a very good effect."

"Suppose they don't jump in time?" I wanted to know.

"Then they get hit," said the captain simply.

During the next few months, there were plenty of times I was tempted to try this stunt. In every tip we drew there were half a dozen smart guys who had read an exposé of sword swallowing in some Sunday supplement and claimed that the swords folded up into handles. It didn't do any good to give them the swords. They claimed I must press a secret button that made the solid steel blade collapse like a telescope. I finally decided to fool these hecklers. So I got a straight blade without a hilt so there was nothing for the blade to fold up into. This instrument was finally broken by a young man in his efforts to find something wrong with it. Later I heard him say to a friend, "That thing folded up. I could'a found out how but it busted on me."

The one effect in sword swallowing that hecklers usually can't question is swallowing a lighted neon tube. When the skeptics see the light shine right through your chest, there isn't much they can say. After my hiltless blade didn't succeed in convincing the hecklers, I decided to take up neon swallowing.

I was a little apprehensive about working with the tubes. I'd recently read in *The Billboard* about the death of Prince Neon, a performer who claimed to have invented neon swallowing. One of the prince's tubes had broken inside of him and he'd died before they could get him to the hospital. I'd also gotten a letter from Mayme saying that during a recent show, Rafael had gotten a short circuit in a tube while he was swallowing it. It hadn't hurt him, but as Mayme said, "It sure as hell made him jump." Sometimes being able to swallow a tube hardly seemed worth the danger.

But when performers from other carnivals dropped in to catch our show, I hated to have them look over my sword rack and not see any neon tubes there. Our gang would try to cover up for me and explain that I was just learning the business, but it was still pretty humiliating. After all, Bronko was the best whip-cracker in the business, Captain Billy was the only Bed of Pain man who'd let people jump on his chest, and nobody but Krinko could sew buttons on his eyelids. We had a high standard to keep up and if I were going to put on a sword act, I wanted it to be good. So I decided to shoot the works and get some tubes.

This turned out not to be too easy. Most electrical companies won't sell you a neon tube if they know you intend to use it for swallowing purposes. Every time a tube breaks inside a sword swallower, there are headlines in the papers and the companies feel this is bad publicity for their product. So the tubes have to be bootlegged.

Neon tubes designed for swallowing have to be specially made. With neons, you must have an electrical connection at both ends of the tube before the gas inside will light. If you have just swallowed two-thirds of the tube, this is naturally hard to arrange. For swallowing, the tube has to be made U-shaped so the ends can stick out of you mouth. This means swallowing a double tube which is naturally much harder than swallowing a thin sword blade and so the tubing has to be made as thin as possible. The thin tubes are very brittle and therefore likely to break inside of you.

After several companies had refused to make me any swallowing tubes, I took my problem to the Impossible Possible. As usual, he had the answer.

"I know of a little electrical shop that's only a couple of hours' drive from the next lot," he told me. "The man there will be glad to fix you up a couple of tubes. He once made me a very serviceable machine. I used to give electromagnetic treatments to old men to restore their lost virility."

"Did it work?" I asked.

"Yes, many of my patients reported that it greatly increased their powers. Of course, I had a few squawkers. For them, I had a special attachment on the machine that stepped up the amperage. I called it my 'Big Bertha.' I'd attach the wires to a certain part of the squawker's body and then pull the switch. I don't know if it cured them or not but they never came back for another treatment."

When we hit the new lot, I drove the Impossible to the electrical appliance store and he explained to the man what I wanted. I decided to get two tubes, one full of red neon gas and one full of yellow. The man did a rush job on them, and the Impossible and I were able to pick up the tubes before the carny made its next jump. We packed the precious things very carefully in a suitcase full of crinkled newspapers so they wouldn't break, and headed back to the carnival.

It was late at night by the time we got back to the carny and everyone was asleep except for the lot watchman, but I wanted to try out the tubes right away. Neons can't be run off an ordinary power line unless you have a transformer like the one Rafael used. I'd forgotten about the transformer, so the Impossible went out and hooked us onto the main city power line. I waited for him inside the side show top. It was a frightening feeling to see those two tubes beside me suddenly glow red and yellow with their uncanny witch light.

"I'm getting scared," I told the Impossible when he came back. I was thinking about Prince Neon and Rafael.

"If you're scared, I wouldn't swallow 'em, m'boy," said the Impossible matter-of-factly. "Your throat'll tighten up and snap the tube."

I knew if I was going to swallow them, I'd have to do it at once before they got too warm. If you swallow a hot tube, it will stick to your insides and you can't withdraw it. So I picked up the red tube, and, while the Impossible watched me with deep interest, I wiped it with a cloth as I would a sword I was about to swallow. This had become an instinctive reaction. I still had an instant's nervousness before swallowing a sword, and wiping it gave me a couple of seconds to get up my confidence.

I stood with my head thrown back and the tube held straight up from my lips. I held it by the electrical connections with my right hand and with my cupped left I guided it down my throat. The basic principle of sword swallowing is to establish a straight line from the throat to the stomach and with the delicate glass tube I made a special effort to hold myself as straight as possible. As the tube slid down, it was pleasantly warm, unlike the chill of steel, but terribly wide. I had to force it a little as it began its descent.

I felt the tube hit my breast bone. I'd had this happen with swords. It's always a creepy feeling, for it sends a shudder all through you. Very often even a slight blow will bruise the bone so it aches afterward. I can only describe the feeling as similar to a sharp blow on the solar plexus in boxing, but you'd have to experience the sensation yourself to understand it. The tip of the tube slipped off the bone and glided down smoothly until my right hand, holding the electrical connections of the tube, touched my lips.

I withdrew the tube and turned around to the Impossible. "Did it shine through my chest?" I asked anxiously.

"M'boy, you shone up like a jack-o'-lantern," he assured me respectfully. "It's a lovely act. I was very nearly taken sick myself."

The next day I purchased a transformer so I could work the tubes in the tent. I presented the neons as the climax of my sword swallowing routine. The act was a sensation. Captain Billy turned out the tent lights and I worked stripped to the waist. Paul stood behind me holding the burning torches for dramatic effect. The pit was completely dark except for the scarlet flame of the torches and the red and gold light of the neons. As my chest lit up, two women had to be carried out and a child was frightened into such hysterics that his parents later sued the carnival. Everybody agreed that the act was a great success and Krinko raised me to seventy-five dollars a week.

The Impossible assured me that I was made for life. "A good neon swallower can always get a job," he told me. "They are always having tubes break inside of them and this keeps the supply of performers down so there's always a demand for that type of act."

Mountmorency began advertising me on the bally platform as the "King of Sword Swallowers—the Man Who Swallows the World's Longest Sword and Giant, Lighted Neon Tubes!" Because of my height I was able to swallow the twenty-six-inch saber which is three or four inches longer than the average performer can handle. I began to be famous. People on the lot went out of their way to speak to me, and I got letters from other side show managers offering contracts. I left some of these letters around where Krinko could see them and he raised my salary another ten dollars a week. Krinko added two extra banners to his banner line; one showing the Human Salamander eating fire and the other depicting the King of Swords holding a sword as long as he was. The banners didn't explain that both personalities were the same man, but the crowds never complained and I did both acts every night.

As the carnival left the Middle Atlantic States and began to move north through New England, we stopped setting-up on city lots. The advance man was able to get locations in the suburbs that were much pleasanter. Everybody was happy over the change. City lots are nearly always used as dumps and we'd often had to spend half the night cleaning the places before we could set-up the tops. We were crowded in by houses and streets and there was no such thing as privacy. On a city lot, the canvasmen can't dig donikers (as the carnies call latrines), so you have to use public washrooms which are usually filthy and crowded. Getting water for washing is a problem, and the dirt and dust from the city traffic makes things worse.

On country lots, we sometimes had a few trees around the midway to give shade and nearly always an acre or so of grass where we could set-up the living tops and park the cars. Everybody took sunbaths during the day and the canvasmen were often able to rig a makeshift shower so we could wash. In the afternoons, I'd take Dot, the five-legged horse, and stake her out where she could graze. Then I'd light my pipe and lie in the grass beside her, listening to the noise of the traffic on the highways and dreaming. That was the way I'd always pictured life under canvas. It was perpetually camping out. On good nights I'd lay my sleeping bag in the tall grass and sleep under the stars.

When I first joined the show, Captain Billy had told me comfortably, "Carny is a lazy man's life." The captain was pretty much right. Our last show was at eleven o'clock, right after the Free Act. Then we'd put away our props, have some coffee and sandwiches, talk awhile, and go to bed. No one got up before ten or eleven o'clock the next morning. The hour of rising depended solely on when you began to feel hungry. After waking up and dozing off again a few times, you'd crawl out of your blankets and either cook up some breakfast on a camp stove or stroll over to the cook shack for coffee and conversation. Then, unless it was Saturday and you had a matinee, the rest of the day was yours to do with as you liked. You could stroll around town and see the sights. Or you could stay on the lot and chat with the other carnies. Mostly, you just did nothing. Occasionally a card game would get going or some of the women would get together for an impromptu sewing bee. But usually the carnies simply loafed around in the sun, fooling with their props, or reading pulp magazines.

The show began to open at dusk. Then the midway would gradually wake into life. The concessions catering to children like the merry-go-round and the Fun House started first. There was no set hour for our show to open. It depended on when Mountmorency decided there was enough of a crowd on the midway to form a good tip. If it rained, we didn't open at all. Everybody went in town, had supper and drank beer until we felt like going to bed.

Saturday night and Sunday morning were hard work. We tore-down after the last show on Saturday, packed the top into our trucks, and drove all night to the next lot. We generally had the top set-up again before noon on Sunday. As there was no show on Sunday, we could sleep until Monday night if we wanted to.

I'd picked up a little publicity in local papers over my Fire and Sword act and had started a scrapbook of clippings. I was close to being "top salary" with the Ten-in-One—that is, I was getting more money than any other act except the Bronkos who drew double pay because Lu worked with her husband and, of course, Jolly Daisy who was a genuine freak. That made me feel pretty good. It wasn't the money but the feeling that in a little over two months I'd come up from being nothing but a young carny punk to a top act. Instead of being jealous, the other acts seemed to be proud at the way I'd taken hold. The troupe regarded me as their protégé and when I did my routine, everyone stopped whatever he was doing to see how I was coming along. They were too tactful to offer suggestions, even when I made a slip in timing or presentation, but afterward Captain Billy or Krinko would casually drop a hint and I had enough sense to take their advice.

One afternoon in midsummer when the sun was baking down on the midway like a magnifying glass, I came back from drinking lemonade at the cook shack to find a little group sitting on our bally platform. The Bronkos were there and Krinko. The old fakir was smoking his pipe, a luxury he never allowed himself except when things were going particularly well. May had a couple of her snakes out on the platform and was washing off

Cook shack.

Ticket seller at cook joint.

their bellies with a mild disinfectant to kill the tiny mites that get under the snakes' scales and cause sores. Altogether, it was a very pleasant and domestic scene but I had eyes for only one member of the group. Billie Callihan was there, looking very neat in shorts and a halter which showed off her full little figure.

I said hello to everybody and sat down beside Billie. The little stripper looked at me curiously as though trying to find something in me that she'd been missing.

"Well, I hear you're getting to be famous," she said rather incredulously. "I can't pick up a paper without reading something about your fire or swords. Gee, I sure never thought when I asked you to run me over to Mayme and Rafael's place that I was starting a top act."

"There was a piece about Slim in *The Billboard* last week," said May as she curried down her snakes.

"Looks like Slim is really going places," agreed Lu proudly.

"What's new with you?" I asked Billie.

She shrugged. "Oh, the same old thing. I'm getting a little tired of carny. I may give it up and go on the stage and be a real actress. When we played New York I was talking to a talent scout for a big Broadway show and he said I had lots of talent."

No one said anything to this bit of fiction. After a pause, Billie turned abruptly to Krinko and asked with irritation and eagerness in her tone, "Well, what about it?"

Krinko removed the pipe. "What about what?" he said, not looking at her.

"Will you give Steve that job?"

Krinko stuck the pipe back in his mouth and continued smoking. One of the characteristics of carny people seemed to be that when they didn't want to give a direct answer they kept quiet.

Billie waited awhile and then said again, "What about it?"

Krinko pulled the pipe out and turned to her angrily. "What you want me to say? Sure, if Steve want to clean out top and carry water for acts I give him job. I pay him forty cents an hour. I do that for anyone."

"You don't need to be unpleasant about it," said Billie uncomfortably. She got ready to slide off the platform.

I said hurriedly, "How about going in town and have a beer with me, Billie?"

Billie shrugged. "Sure, I'll go with anybody for a free beer."

We started down the midway, leaving behind us a disapproving silence you could have hacked pieces out of with a knife. I found a little bar. We went out of the hot sun and into the cool, half light.

"People just don't understand Steve in this org," Billie told me as we slid into a little booth and I ordered the beer. "Steve doesn't want to be just a carny act all his life like these other gees. He's got big ideas for himself."

"What does he want to be?" I asked. I was getting curious about Steve.

The waitress brought beer. Billie stuck one finger in the foam on her glass and began to play with it. "Well, he doesn't know. Oh, gee, he's really a wonderful guy, Slim. He's so masterful. When he tells you to do something, you feel you just gotta do it. He oughta be a big executive and give people orders. But I don't know how you start out being an executive. I guess you need a lot of money first."

I remembered that Bronko had once said that Steve was living off Billie. "Don't you give him money?" I asked unwisely.

Billie looked up angrily. "I most certainly do not. Steve's not the type of guy to take money from a woman. I guess some of those bums with the Ten-in-One told you that. Well, you can tell 'em from me that it's not so." She took a drink of beer. "Steve is just borrowing that money. He's going to pay me back every cent."

I didn't know what to say to that. I drank my beer slowly while Billie stared into her glass as though it were a crystal-gazing ball. Then she said plaintively: "It's awful hard for a man to get a start in something. That's what I can't understand—a kid like you getting to be a top act in just a couple of months while somebody who's got real ability like Steve don't seem to be able to get anywheres. Of course," she went on hurriedly, "I don't mean you're not a nice guy, Slim. Everybody on the lot likes you. But Steve—oh, gee, he's just so grand." She sighed.

"If he's that good, I suppose he'll find something," I said encouragingly. Billie's remarks didn't hurt my feelings particularly, but she did make me feel inadequate. I don't think Billie even knew I was there. She seemed to be talking to herself.

"Steve does drink a good deal," Billie said slowly, making a ring on the table with her damp finger. Then with a sudden flash of irritation she went on. "I can't understand why if a guy is in love with a girl he's always drunk when he comes to take her out. Steve oughtn't to hit the booze like he does. He's too fine a guy for that. Drink makes him mean and he's not really mean."

I didn't know what to say. Billie swallowed her beer in one gulp. "Steve's going to be all right. Now that Krinko has given him a regular job, he'll have some money of his own. It gives a man a lot of confidence in himself to have his own money. That's just what Steve needs."

I saw Steve the next day when he came in to clean up our top. He was a heavy-set young man, a few years older than myself, with a thick neck and a handsome, sullen face. He went around the top picking up cigarette butts and candy wrappers in a gloomy silence. He didn't speak to anyone and nobody spoke to him. When I passed close to him on my way to the pit, I got a whiff of alcohol that made me jump. He smelled like a gallon of antifreeze solution. After the show, I could hear him arguing with Krinko over his pay in a voice that managed to be both deep and querulous at the same time.

A couple of day later, Krinko fired him. Everyone felt relieved to see him go.

Krinko, Captain Billy and I were all sleeping in the side show top that week. Krinko had turned his living top over to Jolly Daisy, and Captain Billy was having his repaired. The other two men used camp cots. I slept on the inside platform in my sleeping bag.

The night after Krinko fired Steve, I had hardly dozed off when I was awakened by a blaze of light in my eyes. I looked up and saw Steve standing on a chair screwing one of the hundred watt bulbs into place. I cursed him silently and began to understand why a drunk is not popular on a carnival lot.

It was obvious from the cautious way that Steve got off the chair that he was tight. Captain Billy raised himself on one elbow and asked wearily, "Now what in hell is the matter with you?"

"Where's that old bastard Krinko?" Steve demanded belligerently. "He ain't goin' to fire me without paying what he owes me."

Krinko threw his ponderous weight out of his cot. "Here, shut up and get out!" he bellowed.

"Oh, there you are, you old devil," said Steve, turning around. "I been waiting for you. I got it in for you."

"Can't you wait until tomorrow to start something?" I asked wearily from the platform.

"I ain't talking to you. I'm after this old son of a bitch," said Steve approaching Krinko threateningly.

The old fakir sat forlornly on the edge of his cot, staring dully at the oncoming Steve. Like most old men, Krinko's face seemed to go to pieces when he first woke up. It took a few minutes for his facial muscles to start operating and pull his sagging cheeks into shape. Krinko looked like a tired old bull waiting for the butcher to come and cut his throat. He was so obviously incapable of defending himself that I began desperately to kick my way out of my sleeping bag to help him.

Suddenly Krinko bounced off the cot as though he had springs in his tail and hit Steve in the face with a fist like a pile driver. Steve staggered back across the top so fast he looked as though he was running backward. He'd have gone into the sidewall if Captain Billy hadn't grabbed him from behind. The captain threw a short, muscle-knotted arm around the drunk's throat and clamped down. Steve kicked and thrashed wildly. Krinko jumped off his cot and stumping across the sawdust, hit Steve four or five heavy blows to the face. Then he tore him out of Captain Billy's grip and started frog-walking the drunk out of the top.

Steve managed to twist around. He sank his teeth into the fat of Krinko's left hand. Krinko flung the drunk back and forth, trying to make him relax his grip, but Steve hung on. Then Krinko threw him down on the sawdust. With Steve still biting him on the hand, Krinko began methodically to kick the man in the body. Krinko never took off his heavy boots when he went to bed and Steve could only take so much of that punishment. He let go. Krinko and Captain Billy dragged him out of the top. I could hear the drunk's screams as the two men finished beating him up.

They came back in a few minutes. Krinko waddled over to a bucket of water by his cot he used for drinking purposes and began to wash his bitten hand.

It may seem hard to believe, but I regarded the business as more of a nuisance than anything else. After spending a couple of months on the road, I was pretty well used to rough stuff.

"Are you badly hurt?" I called to Krinko.

Krinko snorted. "Hurt?" he said, without looking up. "Sure I'm hurt. I hurt like hell. What the devil you think, I don't hurt?" He went on with his washing.

"What happened to Steve?" I asked. Captain Billy answered me. "I don't know and I don't give a damn," he said, preparing to go back to sleep. "Steve could walk. That's all I know."

He unscrewed the bulb that Steve had turned on and we all went back to sleep. The next morning Krinko had a terrible-looking hand. It was so swollen that it looked like an inflated rubber glove with tiny fingers sticking out of the end of it. But that evening he put on his regular act in the pit.

Steve vanished off the lot. Nobody ever saw him again. He probably rode the rails to the nearest tent show and started hanging around the lot there. I saw Billie the next day in the cook shack, her eyes puffy and red from crying. I tried to talk to her, but she only answered in monosyllables. Her manner was so cold that I thought she connected me with Steve's beating. But for the next few weeks, Billie avoided everyone with the carny. She never came on the lot except to do her posing act. She even rented a separate hotel room for herself in the different towns where we played so she wouldn't have to associate with the other girls in her show.

The evening performances settled down to a smooth routine. My Fire and Sword demonstration was the most spectacular act with the show and Mountmorency always gave it a big play in the bally. I added a big, nickel-plated corkscrew to my sword swallowing routine. I had the corkscrew specially made. It wasn't particularly hard to swallow but it was a dangerous-looking thing and added a nice flash. Whenever we hit a new lot, the carny's publicity man called in the newspaper reporters to talk to me. I had worked out a standard interview, always delivered deadpan, in which I pretended that the reporters hoped to be fire-eaters and sword swallowers themselves and wanted me to give them lessons. It was a new angle and the reporters enjoyed it. With all this publicity, I began to get a very swelled head. I decided that I was not only the finest act with our show, but probably the finest act in all carnival history. I unconsciously started to adopt a condescending attitude toward the other performers and even began to advise them on how to build up the dramatic suspense in their acts. Nobody told me to go to hell, but after a few days I noticed that I wasn't asked to the late evening parties when everybody went to the nearest bar for a couple of glasses of beer. When I dropped in at the cook shack, no one shouted, "Here's old Slim. Sit down, damn it, and have some coffee." When I joined a group, everyone was perfectly pleasant to me, so I didn't notice the change for some time. When I finally realized something was wrong, I decided it was nothing but professional jealousy.

But somehow I wasn't having so much fun. I got a little sullen. But I still liked Jolly Daisy, the Bronkos and Captain Billy. I liked the traveling outdoor life of the carny. I decided that there was nothing wrong with me; the trouble all lay with the other performers. I hung around waiting for them to change their attitudes.

One afternoon while I was sitting outside Bronko's living top listening to him playing "The Strawberry Roan" on his guitar and feeling sorry for myself, I saw the Impossible Possible coming across the midway toward me. I was always glad to see the Impossible, so I got up eagerly to greet him.

"Slim, I've cooked up a little scheme that'll either kill you or make you famous," said the Impossible putting his long arm on my shoulder. "There's a movie running in town here that's got a sword swallower in it who's playing a bit part. He's some kind of a Hindu called Mohammed Ali and advertises himself as the King of Swords like you do. This gee is making a personal appearance with the movie in town here."

"Is he good?" I asked anxiously.

"Nothing compared to you, m'boy. He does have a few unusual little stunts. At one point in his routine he swallows a sword with a tin blade and then twists himself around until the sword is bent inside him. He straightens it out again by constriction of his stomach muscles so he can withdraw it. Another wrinkle he has is to partly swallow a sword mounted on the butt of a rifle. Then he fires off the rifle and the kick drives the sword the rest of the way down him. I understand he also swallows red-hot swords. But I'm sure you can beat him in the contest I've arranged."

"What do you mean, contest?" I asked in horror. I had heard Mountmorency call me the "World's Champion Sword Swallower" so often on the bally platform that I'd begun to believe it myself. But compared to this Mohammed Ali, I might as well never have seen a sword. I realized what a fool I'd been making out of myself these last few weeks, posing as a top carny act when I was still a raw amateur.

The Impossible said soothingly, "You haven't a thing to worry about, m'boy. I've made all the arrangements. I talked to the manager of the theater where this Ali is appearing and he's agreed to put on a sword swallowing contest between you for the Sword Swallowing Championship of the World. The winner gets the title and a sum of money out of which I'll keep a small percentage as my commission. It'll be fine publicity for you when you win."

"I'd make a fool out of myself, trying to compete with that guy," I admitted. After the way I'd been behaving, as though I were the premier attraction of the entire midway, I hated to make the admission. "I'm still nothing but a First-of-Mayer."

A First-of-Mayer is a carny who never comes out until after the first of May when the cold, wet spring is over and nothing but the pleasant summer months lie ahead. Carnies use the expression as a term of contempt for an amateur.

Although I was feeling very humble, I was still a little taken back when the Impossible nodded his head as though he completely agreed with me.

"However, you've got one good stunt with that long sword," he pointed out. "Can't you swallow a longer sword than anyone else?"

I explained that I probably could. Swallowing a long sword doesn't require any skill. The performer just has to be tall.

"That's what I thought," agreed the Impossible. "Now the manager of this theater is going to get some prominent local businessmen to judge this contest. Fortunately, none of them happens to be a professional sword swallower. I've talked to several of these gentlemen and explained that the only way you can judge a sword swallower's ability is by the length of the sword he can swallow. I have them convinced. Mohammed Ali can't talk much English so he won't know what's going on. This contest will be what we sporting men refer to as a boat race and you're sure to win. It'll be a wonderful ad for the carny and give you plenty of publicity. What do you say?"

I felt sorry for poor Mohammed Ali, but I told the Impossible to go ahead.

When the write-ups of the contest broke in the local papers there was more excitement on the lot than the day of the clem. Everyone came around to wish me luck. I tried hard to think up some new sword swallowing stunt, but there wasn't time. But I was sure of one thing; if Mohammed Ali was shorter than I was, I could swallow a longer sword.

The contest was to take place on the stage of the motion picture theater. Bronko and Lu drove me in with my collection of swords and tubes. I was scared stiff. My stomach felt as though I'd swallowed a cold weight and my legs tingled unpleasantly. Worst of all, I could feel my throat muscles tightening. I was afraid that when I got on the stage I wouldn't be able to swallow as much as a jackknife. Lu and Bronko were talking together and tried to draw me into the conversation, but I didn't feel much like talking. Lu was sitting beside me in the back seat while Bronko drove. Suddenly she slid her arm under mine and crowded closer.

"Don't you go lookin' back, now, Bronko," she called warningly. "You know I always figured old Slim was the best-lookin' man on the lot and this here's my first chance to be alone with him."

"Don't you two forget I got a rear-view mirror here," shouted Bronko in a threatening tone. "I can drive and keep an eye on you two."

Working hard, the good-natured couple managed to pull me out of my nervous tension so when we arrived at the stage door, I could walk in without having my knees knocking together. The feature was still on and we came in behind the screen. The picture showed through the screen and we stood for a few minutes watching the show from this unusual angle until the Impossible joined us.

"M'boy, the whole contest is in the bag," he assured me. "This Hindu has a crazy idea that he can swallow the world's longest sword although he's several inches shorter than you are. You're both to do some flourishes and then swallow your longest swords. That decides the contest." He clapped me on the shoulder. "The whole audience is full of carnies so you haven't a thing to worry about. You'll win by fair means or foul."

"And with you handlin' things, I know which it'll be," said Lu cheerfully. "O.K., Slim, want us to help you with the sword stand?"

I preferred to assemble the props myself. I hooked up my portable transformer so I could run the neon tubes from it and we waited.

When the picture was over, the house lights went on and the theater manager announced the contest. The judges came on the stage, prosperous-looking citizens who obviously considered the affair a great joke. When I was introduced and came on with my swords, there were shouts, whistles, and mad clapping from the carnies in the audience. Then my rival was presented. He was a slender, dark, fine-featured man wearing a rather soiled turban and a business suit. He bowed and smiled to the audience and instantly a storm of boos and abuse burst from my claque. The Impossible had obviously instructed the carnies to play rough in the hope of scaring the Hindu so his throat would close up and he couldn't compete. Unfortunately, Mohammed Ali obviously considered this merely a typical American welcome and stood bowing and smiling in front of the howling crowd until the theater manager had to remove him. I was relieved to see that the Hindu was much shorter than I was.

Mohammed started the contest. He brought out a highly ornamented table. On top of the table was a sword supported at either end by metal stands. Behind the sword was a lighted blow torch, the long feather of red flame playing steadily on the steel blade. Mohammed touched the blade with bits of paper which instantly burst into fire. Having shown that the sword was really hot, Mohammed mysteriously walked off stage for a few seconds. He returned walking in a curiously stiff, unnatural manner. He lifted the sword by the hilt and actually swallowed the red hot blade. He stood for a minute with puffs of steam coming out of his mouth and then withdrew the sword. Without taking a bow, he left the stage again but returned in a moment to acknowledge the applause.

I knew perfectly well what Mohammed must have done, although I'd never heard of such a stunt before.

When he left the stage for the first time, he had swallowed an asbestos scabbard. He had then returned and slid the sword into that. Afterward he had to make another exit to get rid of the scabbard. It was a remarkable feat but not particularly impressive. The presence of the scabbard was supposed to be a secret and it is very difficult to walk around naturally with a scabbard inside of you. The audience seemed to sense that somehow they'd been tricked. Mohammed would probably have done better to handle the whole thing openly instead of trying to turn a remarkable feat into a miracle.

I prepared to swallow my giant corkscrew. I explained to the audience that my corkscrew, unlike Mohammed's sword, had no hilt into which it could fold. I also said knowingly that I didn't have to leave the stage before performing my act. I could see this made an impression on the judges although they didn't have any idea how Mohammed had faked his stunt. The corkscrew made my Adam's apple leap around like a flea on a hot griddle as it went down and this gave a particularly horrible effect that went over big. The carnies shouted themselves hoarse and even though Mohammed Ali had performed a far more difficult feat I felt I was ahead.

Mohammed seemed to specialize in scabbards. For his next effect, he came out with a very thick sword which he tried to present as an ordinary weapon but was really a sword in a scabbard. The scabbard was metal and had been painted with aluminum paint to make it resemble a sword blade. Mohammed swallowed both the sword and the scabbard, and then pulled out the sword, leaving the scabbard inside of him. The sword was obviously several inches shorter than the scabbard had been and while I was wondering about this, Mohammed reached into the open mouth of the scabbard and produced a handful of folding paper flowers. Then he pulled out a large silk American flag and held it outstretched while the orchestra broke into "The Star Spangled Banner."

It was unquestionably the damnedest effect I've ever seen. But like Mohammed's previous stunt, it didn't go over very well. The audience didn't fully realize what was going on. Mohammed retired to disgorge the scabbard and I did my neon routine. Most of the audience had never seen anyone swallow neon tubes before and were more impressed by my routine act than Mohammed's remarkable feat. So far I was well ahead of the Hindu on points. Now we had to see who could swallow the longest sword. Here I was positive I had the edge on him. This feat would decide the outcome of the contest. I selected my twenty-six-inch sword and waited confidently to see what Mohammed would produce.

To my astonishment, Mohammed came back with a sword three inches longer than mine. I was positive he couldn't swallow the thing. His only solution would be to run his lip as far up the blade as possible to give the effect of swallowing the entire sword as Rafael had done. I swallowed my sword, making sure the hilt

Swords Are Always Wiped before and after swallowing.
Lucky Ball, who appears with Shirley Temple in Twentieth
tury-Fox's "Wee Willie Winkie," makes sure his sword is
n . . . Because the weight of food in the stomach lengthens
passage (called the esophagus) which leads to it, he has eaten
meal to prepare for his performance.

Sword Swallower Shows
HOW IT'S DONE

2 Lucky Bends the Sword to prove it doesn't fold up. He says it's easy to
low a flat sword like this one. Corkscrew swords are difficult . . . Lucky
only man in the country who can swallow one, For flat swords, his record is
lowing 16 all at once, varying in length from 16 to 23 inches.

Down. When the sword enters his
ucky throws his head far back so
rom his mouth to his stomach is a
The next step is to control his
s not to disturb this passage.

4 All Gone But the Hilt. Going down, the
sword does not prick him. X-ray pictures
show no scars or abnormalities of any kind.
Once learned, the trick requires little practice.
After a vacation, he is as good at it as ever.

5 He Flips It Out with his finger. Lucky
nine out of 10 persons, with practice, co
learn to swallow swords. The only drawbac
a sword swallower can't eat chocolate. It rem
in the esophagus and sticks to the sword.

Mohammed Ali.

rang against my teeth, and then waited to see what Mohammed would do.

Mohammed bowed to the audience, assumed the traditional sword swallower's stance and then swallowed the sword right up to the hilt. I couldn't believe my eyes. Instantly the Impossible was up on the stage screaming fake.

"That sword must fold back into the hilt," he howled. "You can't trust these foreigners."

When Mohammed understood what the trouble was, he cheerfully explained his stunt. Before the contest, he had eaten a heavy meal. This weighed down his stomach the few extra inches he needed to win.

The Impossible shouted foul. The carnies took up the cry. The theater manager tried to restore order while the puzzled judges were talking anxiously among themselves. Finally they announced that Mohammed had won. That did it. I grabbed my precious neon tubes and ran while the furious carnies started another clem and the distracted manager telephoned the police.

Everyone on the lot was very sympathetic with me the next day, and spoke very harshly of Mohammed and his tricks. Personally, I was willing to admit that he had won. If you have to swallow red hot swords to be the world's champion sword swallower, I was willing to concede defeat. But the carnies didn't see it that way. The publicity man issued a statement saying that I had won on a technical foul and was still the King of Swords. The carnies congratulated me and I was back in everybody's good graces. But my swelled head had diminished considerably and after that when Mountmorency shouted "Bally!" I was the first one out of the top.

On tear-down night, Billie came to the Ten-in-One top looking for me. I was surprised and flattered.

"You haven't forgotten about me, have you, Slim?" she asked gaily.

I assured her I hadn't.

"Then will you drive me over to the next lot in your car?" I'd bought a second-hand car a short time before to travel between lots. "I been riding with a couple of the other girls in our ticket seller's car, but it's kind of crowded."

I couldn't see why the car had suddenly gotten overcrowded, but I didn't ask any questions. I told Billie I'd be glad to take her.

She was waiting for me after tear-down. We stopped at a truckers' restaurant for coffee and then started the hundred-mile drive to the new location. Billie started talking about Steve almost at once.

"I've decided to forget him," she told me. "I was pretty mad at you guys in the Ten-in-One for beating him up that night, but I guess you had to do it. He didn't say a word to me when he took off. If a fellow really loves a girl, he'd at least say good-bye to her when he gets run off a lot."

"Sure he would," I said comfortingly. "I don't think Steve really loved you."

"He loved me once," said Billie with determination and a little sadness. "We were going to get married and everything. But I guess Steve never really grew up enough to take responsibilities. Well, if I was a fellow I wouldn't want to get married. I'd run around and make love to all the pretty girls and have a good time. Only," she went on in a small voice, "when you're one of the girls that makes it awful tough."

I reached over and took her hand. Billie leaned her head against my arm and for a few miles we watched the black road with its gleaming white stripe running down the middle in silence. Then Billie began to talk. She told me about her home town and the boys she used to know and her family and how she hoped some day to marry a man who "wasn't rich but who really loves me" and maybe go on the stage in New York where "the guys that date you are a higher type of guys." But eventually the conversation always drifted back to Steve. Although she kept repeating, "I was much too good for a guy like Steve—all the girls at our show told me that," she left no doubt that if Steve had suddenly stepped out of the shadows along the road and whistled to her, she would have gone to him without a moment's hesitation. I listened, marveling, to a way of thinking I knew nothing about.

The next day Billie came over to the Ten-in-One to see if I'd take her out to lunch. In return, she mended my socks, polished my swords, and put fresh cotton heads on my torches. The other carnies casually took for granted that Billie and I had teamed up. By the time we moved on to the next lot, I found somewhat to my astonishment, that I'd gotten myself a girl.

Billie with the ticket seller from the Ten-in-One (sideshow).

CHAPTER 7

As the carny moved north through New England, we began to run into some of the problems that make the outdoor show business a tough racket. Our biggest headache was finding lots well away from other carnivals playing the same district. This wasn't always possible. One week we set-up on a corner lot where two main highways intersected. It was a fine location . . . and two other carnies must have agreed with us. They moved in on adjacent corners. There we were, like three gas stations working in competition with each other. As a result, our crowds were cut by two-thirds.

Like most of the three hundred carnivals in America, we were a "truck show." We moved from one lot to another in our trucks. If our advance man happened to hear of a good locality, we'd run over and play it. Our mobility gave us certain advantages over the big "rail shows" like John J. Jones or Royal American. These outfits employ over five thousand people and move from one location to another by railroad, loading all their equipment on special flat cars. As a result, they can only set up on lots near railroad tracks. We could go anywhere there were roads. But these midway giants don't have to worry about competition. When they start out in the spring, their routes are booked straight through to winter. All the smaller shows keep out of their way.

We were seldom booked for more than two or three weeks in advance and our schedule was subject to change without notice. Because of this "hopscotching," we often found ourselves running up against little semi-local "rag shows." Rag shows are tiny outfits consisting of half a dozen rides and perhaps three or four gambling concessions. They can't afford to carry any big concessions like our Ten-in-One or the Model Show. They can stay a month in one locality because they pull such small crowds, then when they want to move they have to rent transportation from some local company. But they often grab the best lot in a district and if we had to play near one, we did lose some of our crowd.

Occasionally we'd find that the lots ahead of us had all been booked, either for some local event or by a rag show that had appeared out of nowhere. Then we either had to spend another week on the same location or try "backtracking": go back and play a district where we'd been before. Nothing is so discouraging to a carny

as backtracking. It's even worse than a long spell of rainy weather. In carnival life you must always keep moving ahead, opening new territory and leaving mistakes and failures behind like your old tin cans and broken props. To go crawling back again to the same location makes you feel like a failure and the crowds are never as good a second time.

The carnies reacted strongly to a run of backtracking. They became sullen, irritable and complaining, although they seldom jumped the show and never considered going into a less hazardous profession. Billie always reacted to a spell of bad luck by announcing that she was going to get married. Although Billie often spoke confidently of someday going on the stage or into the motion pictures, I think she knew in her heart there was no real future for her in show business. When the weather and business were good, Billie could forget about the years ahead when she would become too old for the posing racket. But when times were bad, the shadows of apprehension that were always in the dark corners of her mind moved in and took over. Then Billie longed desperately for the security of marriage.

Unlike more fortunate girls who have mothers to do their conniving for them, poor Billie was on her own. The little stripper wasn't much of a conniver. She was too open. When she was fond of a man, she let him see it. This is usually poor feminine strategy. While we were playing Bridgeport, Connecticut, the Model Show lost its talker. Frisco, the big, overdressed bull of a man who ran the show, sent for another talker. The new man had the reputation of being one of the best in show business. He was a square-faced, light-haired young fellow, very confident of himself. Like all talkers, he made a point of keeping himself natty. He had a pleasant word for everyone on the midway, but he kept off the lot except when he had to take the evening ballies. He spent most of the day in town hanging around the hotel cocktail lounges picking up unattached girls. Billie considered the new talker the ultimate in sophistication and fell hard for him.

One rainy evening, I took Billie out to supper in a town restaurant. Billie spent all evening telling me that the new talker was the most wonderful thing who had ever hit a carnival midway. "All the girls are crazy about him, but he'll only kid around with them," she confided in me. "When a man like that comes to get married, he wants a girl who can dress good and he can take around to fashionable parties."

Billie obviously considered that this was a perfect description of herself. "Did he ever show any special interest in you?" I asked.

"Oh sure," said Billie easily. "I was teasing him yesterday and he got mad and said 'I'd like to turn you over my knee and spank you.'"

The new talker caused a good deal of trouble on the lot—especially for Mountmorency, who handled the ballies for our Ten-in-One. Before the new man appeared, there had been an unspoken agreement among the talkers that no show would start a bally until the outfit on its left had finished turning its tip. The new talker with the Model Show paid no attention to this gentleman's agreement. He'd start his ballies whenever he felt like it. As soon as Mountmorency had collected a tip, the Model Show talker would bring out his girls and Mountmorency had a hard time holding the crowd. It's hard to surpass sex as an attraction, but Mountmorency did his best.

Next to pretty girls, the American public likes children and animals. After collecting a tip with my fire-eating, Mountmorency would tell May to bring out Sultan, her big Indian rock python. Then, carrying the mike with him, Mountmorency would walk to the edge of the platform and announce,

"I wonder if any little boy out there would like to see the show free? If so, just hold up your hand." A forest of hands always shot up. Mountmorency would continue, "There's a boy right there. Just come a little closer, sonny. A little closer yet. Say, I want to congratulate you on getting a free pass. Let me shake your hand."

Dropping the mike, he'd reach over the edge of the platform and take the boy's hand. But instead of shaking hands, the talker would swing the boy up on the platform. Of course, the kid got a big kick out of being on a carny platform, but Mountmorency always whispered to him to pretend to be scared. Most kids have a lot of ham in them, so the boy would put on a good act.

"Now, sonny, will you tell us your name?" Mountmorency would shout, holding the mike down so the boy could talk into it. "Bill Smith," the kid might answer, his shrill voice sounding very funny over the amplifying system. "Say, aren't you Mr. Smith's son?" the talker would ask in great astonishment. "Yes, I am." "Well, well, I'm sure glad to hear that. Never heard of your father in my life. Shake hands." Then Mountmorency and the kid would solemnly shake hands.

This may sound corny, but the crowds loved it. There's nothing as appealing as a kid. People who won't laugh at the highest paid comedian in the business will unbend at the sight of a boy or a girl. When Mountmorency felt he had the tip with him, he'd ask,

"Bill . . . do you mind if I call you Bill?" The kid would holler over the mike that he didn't mind and Mountmorency would explain, "Well, Bill, do you see that big snake the little lady has there? Now that snake is very hungry and it's time for him to eat." Here Mountmorency would look expressively at Bill and Bill would look equally expressively back at him. "I know you wouldn't want a poor snake to go hungry, Bill. But I'll tell you a funny thing about snakes. They can't digest pants." Another dramatic pause. "Do you mind slipping off your pants for a minute, Bill?"

This kept up for some time, with Bill insisting he didn't like big ole snakes anyhow and the talker explaining that all Bill needed to do was to shut his eyes and it would be over in a few minutes. The shouts of laughter caused by Bill's comments on the subject of

Mountmorency and boy.

snakes could be heard all over the lot and people started hurrying from different parts of the midway to get in on the fun. Nothing attracts a tip like laughter. When Mountmorency had extracted the last drop of humor he could from Bill, the snake and Bill's pants, he suddenly grew serious.

"Friends, on the inside here we have ten big acts—the biggest money's worth you ever saw in your life—including Jolly Daisy, the world's fattest lady. I'm going to send Bill in first with his free ticket and who's next?" Then Krinko would snatch up his pipe and start blowing while the rest of us shouted and filed back into the tent.

It was a hard bally to top but the Model Show talker did a good job. He started bringing out the girls with red cloaks wrapped close around their bodies as though they had nothing else on. Then the talker would address the crowd in a low, confidential tone from his big loudspeakers.

"Now folks, just a word about the beautiful girls we have here whose purpose is to teach the public something about sex. Naturally, in a small, backward village like Higgin's Corners, where we played last week, we couldn't show lovely girls in a complete state of nature. But here in a forward, modern community like Ground Hog Springs, we can throw conventions to the winds."

Then he'd reach over and pull Billie forward. As she moved up, the wrapper would slip back, disclosing her long slim legs. There was no sign of a skirt or dress under the cloak, although the girls did wear tights on the bally platform.

"Now boys, I don't want you to think you're going to see an old-type hoochy-coochy. This is an educational demonstration of Oriental muscle dancing. Also, it begins where the hoochy-coochy leaves off. Every muscle, every fiber of those beautiful bodies are kept in constant motion. It's a dance that makes the old feel young and the young feel worried. You owe it to your future wives to see this show! Hurry, boys, and watch the fugitives from a harem do the dance that broke the sultan's thermometer!"

Inside the tent, a four-piece orchestra instantly struck up. The girls would shout, wave their hands and mince back into the tent. All the lights in the top were suddenly turned on and the show's sticks would rush up to the ticket box to "buy" tickets and start the crowd moving. If the Model Show talker hit his spiel while Mountmorency was still trying to turn our tip, we usually lost half our crowd.

Krinko wanted to kick to the carny's manager, but Mountmorency's professional pride wouldn't let him admit defeat. Then one day while we were playing within a few miles of the Canadian border, our talker got a real inspiration.

We were sitting around drinking beer one Sunday evening when suddenly the talker jumped up.

"I've got it!" he announced.

We looked at him doubtfully.

"I'll be a mechanical man," said the talker. "All the time that Model Show talker is giving his ballies, I'll be standing on our platform doing a mechanical man routine. It'll be murder. Every now and then my machinery'll run down and Slim can come tearing out with a big key and wind me up. Nobody will look at those girls. They'll all be watching me."

We tried it the next night. Mountmorency mounted the bally platform with stiff, robot-like movements, his face completely covered with heavy make-up. I followed behind, guiding him with a couple of electrical wires hooked to a small battery. When he reached the platform, I unhooked the wires and wound him up with the key. Mountmorency swayed back and forth and nearly toppled over until I put one of his feet a little forward of the other to give him balance. Then he stood there, turning his head with quick, jerky movements and raising and lowering his hand like a semaphore.

He kept it up all evening. Whenever the acts came out, Bronko did the talking while Mountmorency just stood there, going through his automatic movements. When we went back into the top, Mountmorency stayed on the platform. It drove the Model Show talker wild. All the time he was trying to collect a tip, our talker was standing there going through his clockwork motions. People were fascinated. They collected around our platform, making bets on whether or not Mountmorency was alive. They were far more interested in the silent figure than in the girls' bumps and grinds.

This kept up for a few evenings. Then one night a bunch of little kids about ten years old collected in front of our bally platform to watch Mountmorency. Like everyone else, the kids were arguing whether the talker was alive. One hatchet-faced, gum-chewing little devil didn't take any part in the discussion. He just stood regarding Mountmorency with an evil eye.

Suddenly the kid announced, "I'll find out if he's alive or not," and produced an enormous slingshot from his hip pocket. He fitted a buckshot into the pocket and drawing back the sling he let Mountmorency have the buckshot in the seat of the pants.

The talker leaped a foot. Then with a howl of rage he jumped off the platform and started after the kid who fled like a rag on the wind. Mountmorency came puffing back, swearing under his breath, and resumed his stance. But he was finished as a mechanical man in that locality. Every time a tip collected, the kid would reappear and say eagerly to the crowd, "You want to find out if that man's alive? I'll show you for a quarter."

Billie was making a big play for the Model Show talker, so I didn't see much of her. Now that my Fire and Sword act was running smoothly, I didn't have to practice and during the long afternoons I sometimes felt a little lonely. Most of our troupe was busy during the day on their own affairs, but the Impossible was usually available for a talk. One afternoon after I'd finished helping May take her snakes down to the lake for a swim, I started back toward the carnival grounds and found the Impossible sitting outside Aunt Matty's trailer having a decorous cup of tea with the palmist. They called me over and I was only too glad to join them.

"I understand that Billie has gone overboard for that new talker, m'boy," said the Impossible cheerfully as I accepted a cup of tea from Aunt Matty. "However, with a little effort you can find another girl just as good. It's not true that all women are the same, but the difference between them is so slight that it's not worth worrying about."

"I'm sure Slim is too sensible a boy to get emotionally involved with Billie," said Aunt Matty comfortably.

"You're taking a lot for granted there," remarked the Impossible, helping himself to one of Aunt Matty's doughnuts. "It's very easy to become emotionally involved with a girl—even if you're only seeing her for recreational purposes, so to speak. I always feel a sentimental twinge when the time comes to leave one of my women, no matter how much trouble she may have given me. Have you ever been in love, Slim?"

"No, thank God," I assured him.

"Ah, it's a noble emotion. I have only experienced it once. I was little more than a boy at the time. The girl was a very stunning blonde who had a cat act— by that I mean she was a female lion tamer. Her name was Gertrude and she specialized in working with Bengal tigers."

"I should think you would have worried about her," remarked Aunt Matty.

"Gertrude had big, appealing blue eyes and a soft mouth that seemed to have been made for kissing," said the Impossible with a sigh. "However, I've often seen her hoist a two-hundred-pound traveling cage on top of a truck without apparent effort and she could knock down a half-grown lion with one crack of her fist."

"Gertrude seems to have had everything," I remarked. "I don't see how you ever managed to part with her."

"I became emotionally involved, as Aunt Matty would say. I was in love with the girl, but she could never love anything but her tigers. At first, I didn't believe such a state of affairs could exist. I'm frank to admit that a Bengal tiger is superior to me in many respects, but there are certain things I can do for a woman that a tiger would find impractical. I didn't admit defeat until one afternoon while I was watching Gertrude training a new tiger named Rajah in the big cage. It was a practice session so we were alone in the top. I pulled open the shute gate for her and the cat poured himself out of the run and into the cage. Rajah was a big fellow, part Siberian, with a ruff that stood out so far you could have sunk your hand in it up to the wrist. He glided across the sawdust toward her, making about as much noise as a ghost wearing gumshoes. Gertrude was standing there with her whip and chair. I happened to see her face. She was looking at that cat the way I'd always dreamed she might someday look at me. I helped her finish the training period and then

caught a fast freight out of town. She was killed a year later by that same cat. Her last words in the hospital were 'Don't let them kill Rajah. He was wonderful.' "

No one said anything for a minute. Then Aunt Matty remarked gently, "May feels that same way about her snakes. When one of her rattlers rears up, I've seen May kneel down and hold out her arms to him like a girl going to meet her lover. It's a very frightening sight. I can't imagine why she feels as she does, but I know no man could hope to mean anything to her."

I must have looked thoughtful for Aunt Matty went on mildly, "But I don't think Slim will have that trouble with Billie. She doesn't strike me as the kind of a girl who'd be particularly interested in either tigers or snakes."

The Impossible nodded in complete agreement. "No, Slim need fear no competition from the animal kingdom. But that's about the only kind of competition he doesn't need to worry about. Billie has made a business out of her body and she's certainly devoted to her work."

The Impossible was right and, although I missed Billie, I felt it was a good thing for me in the long run that the little stripper had attached herself to the Model Show talker. For a couple of weeks everything went smoothly. Then I got sick.

We had had a week of rain and the side show top began to leak. I was sleeping on the inside platform and one morning I woke to find puddles of water on my sleeping bag from the dripping top. The inside of the bag was damp and without sun there was no way to dry it. I had to sleep in the wet bag again that night and by morning I had a bad sore throat. Ever since I joined the carnival I'd been subject to a series of these attacks of laryngitis, but this case was really a dilly. By evening I was running a temperature and couldn't put on my act. I crawled into my damp bag again after the last show, hoping I'd be better in the morning. Instead, my fever became worse and by morning I was delirious.

I was lying on the platform, half sobbing with the ache in my throat and the burning of the fever, when I felt someone touch me. I looked up and saw Billie and the Impossible bending over me.

"What's the matter?" I asked stupidly.

"You're out of your head, m'boy," said the Impossible. "We could hear you yelling halfway across the midway." He put his hand on the damp sleeping bag. "This thing feels as though it had been underwater for a week. You can't sleep here."

"I haven't anywhere else to go."

"We'll put you in one of the trucks."

With both of them lifting me, I managed to stagger to my feet. I stood for a moment alone but would have fallen if the Impossible hadn't grabbed me. "I think I'm pretty sick," I managed to gasp.

"I think you are," said the Impossible. Billie looked so worried that I tried to smile at her. "What are you doing here?" I asked.

"Jolly Daisy sent one of the canvasmen over to get me when you started going out of your head this morning," said Billie, trying to get my arm around her shoulder to support me. "We'll get you out of this leaky old top into somewhere nice and dry."

The three of us staggered through the rain to the tailgate of one of the closed trucks. They hoisted me up and I stood inside, shivering in the cold and dark. The place was crowded with wooden boxes, extra curtains for the blow-off, and flashily painted props. The Impossible ran in a light stringer and started to screw the big bulbs into place. "These will make the place a little warmer," he remarked.

The dead-white glare of the bulbs flashed up in the little room. The bulbs became so hot that in a confined space half a dozen of them generate as much warmth as an electric heater. Billie climbed into the truck and closed the tailgate.

"You'll feel much better when you get warm and get some hot food into you," said the Impossible cheerfully. He was busy pumping the plunger on an extra gasoline stove we carried in the truck. He lit the blowtorch flame and turned it on high while the burners roared and hissed. Billie emptied one of the great coffin-like packing boxes and made a bed in the bottom of the soft, bally curtain stuff. Some of the cloth was wet and this part she carefully turned under.

"Take off your clothes and get in here," she ordered. I obeyed automatically, and half fell into the box. Billie covered me with part of the drapes.

The Impossible was examining some cans of food we kept in the truck. He selected one containing soup, opened it and poured the contents into a tin saucepan. "You warm this up for him," he said, handing the saucepan to Billie. "I'll get a doctor. I don't believe in spending money for luxuries ordinarily, but this is a special case."

Billie heated the soup over the little stove and then fed it to me with a spoon. While I was still drinking it, I fell asleep.

The doctor arrived late that afternoon. After sending Billie off for a prescription, he listened while I told him about the recurrent attacks of laryngitis I'd had during the summer.

"Sleeping in that damp bag undoubtedly augmented your condition," he said finally. "But I think the basic trouble comes from your fire-eating. The fire probably dries up the mucus membrane of your throat and makes you very susceptible to colds. Of course, the best thing would be to give up fire-eating. If you don't want to do that, I'd suggest you try gargling with olive oil after each performance."

When I was well again, I took the doctor's advice. The olive oil did the trick. I didn't have another cold for the rest of the time I was with the carny. The oil became as important a prop in my fire-eating routine as the gasoline. I always made sure I had some oil before doing my act and this once led to the most dramatic exhibition of fire-eating I ever gave . . . although it was completely impromptu.

I was trying to learn a very old form of fire-eating which is really smoke-eating. In this routine, the performer takes a small nut and hollows it out. Then he makes a small hole in each end and puts a piece of glowing punk inside. On the road, you're more likely to use a piece of twisted sacking than the punk. For the act, you begin to eat cotton or paper and secretly slip the nut in your mouth with the cotton. Then you begin to blow out through the nut. The smoldering punk begins to burn and soon you are puffing out clouds of smoke and sparks.

The hardest part of this effect is carrying a nut full of burning punk around in your mouth without showing it. I used to slip the nut in after breakfast and carry it all day long like a quid of tobacco, blowing out sparks and smoke every now and then to keep it lighted.

One night I was driving with Billie between lots. I was running short on olive oil and decided to stop at a drugstore and get a bottle. We were driving at the time through the darkened slums of a big city and stopped at a drugstore with a few late customers sitting by a single weak light. I happened to have the nut in my mouth when I went to buy the oil.

The clerk looked at me a little curiously. I don't suppose that store was used to having people drop in at two in the morning to get olive oil and although I wasn't in costume, I suppose I looked a little unusual. I was leaning on the counter, thoughtlessly rolling the nut around in my mouth. Suddenly I gave a little burp. A tongue of smoke and sparks leaped out of my mouth and some of the sparks fell on the hands of the clerk who was wrapping up the oil. The clerk stopped wrapping and looked at me in a puzzled way.

I was still easily embarrassed. I clapped my hand over my mouth and said, unhappily, "I beg your pardon," and hurried out with the oil. As we drove off, I happened to glance back at the store. The clerk and his few customers were standing around staring at each other as though suddenly paralyzed.

Since I'd recovered from my attack of laryngitis, Billie spent all her spare time with me. I was very touched that she was willing to give up her campaign for the talker in order to be my girl. Now that I was up and around again I took Billie out to supper regularly and gave her lifts in my car between lots just as we'd done before.

It wasn't until some time later that I found out the Model Show talker had jumped the carnival a couple of days before I was taken sick.

Ticket seller putting up our banner line.

CHAPTER 8

After making a great loop through New England, the carnival began to move southward toward the Middle West. As we hit the industrial cities of northern New York, the organization began to pick up new concessions—crummy little joints for the most part that would stay with us only as long as we played the fringes of the big manufacturing centers.

A carnival has a hard job refusing to take these little outfits because they are often good money-getters. A carnival has to carry a number of big shows like our Ten-in-One to add tone to the midway and keep the carny from being simply a clip-joint. But the big shows have a high overhead. They take up a lot of midway space and the carnival has to provide them with electricity and trucks for transportation. The little joints don't ask the carnival management for anything. All they want is a chance to get at the public. The joints usually feature some sure-fire attraction such as gambling, a hideously deformed freak, or sex. A good joint man can make enough money in a few months to keep him in comfort for the rest of the year, even though he must turn in nearly half of what he makes to the carny management in return for the privilege of playing on the lot.

These new outfits would join up with us so unexpectedly that often the advance man hadn't allowed for them when picking the lot. If the lot were big enough, it only meant readjusting the lot markers. But if the lot were small, there were always hard feelings between the different shows because everyone was fighting for every additional foot of space for his outfit.

Sometimes the midway was so crowded that the Ten-in-One had to "crescent" its banner line inward to make it fit. Occasionally we almost came to blows with the adjacent concession over the space necessary between the tops for stakes and guy lines. Usually both shows compromised by dropping off some of their banners to make room.

Other shows weren't always so lucky in adjusting their difficulties. Several fights broke out on the lots and when the carnival opened in the evening, there were occasional blackouts on the midway—caused by shows that were still arguing over space requirements. Then the other shows hurried to turn as many tips as possible before the combatants could adjust their difficulties and open in competition.

One night while we were playing near Buffalo, New York, we set-up the side show top in the rain and to save time, neglected to rig the banner line. The next morning I was awakened by angry voices. I was still sleeping in the truck and when I opened my eyes, I saw the cracks in the truck's side were glowing with sunshine. I guessed it must be nearly noon. From the sound of the voices, I figured that some of our bunch had started to frame the banner line scaffolding and had run into trouble with the next concessionaire.

I heard Bronko say, "Now listen. You jumped the line and you gotta slough your joint and move it back. There ain't no use talking about it."

A strange voice answered, "Those damn cutaway tops squeeze in every other outfit on the midway. I ain't going to stand for it. You crescent your banner line if you want more room."

"Listen, mister." Bronko's voice was deceptively sweet. "Our front looks like a snake now. I had to cripple this banner line already to make room for that two-bit sex show of yours. We got four drop-offs laying on the inside platform now."

When there isn't enough room in the line for all the banners, the extras are called drop-offs. I heard Captain Billy say quietly, "Mister, right there is where the mark stake went. You line up from that or you're liable to get hurt." I crawled out of my sleeping bag, pulled on my shoes, and climbed out of the truck. From the sound of things, I thought I might be needed.

Captain Billy was leaning on a sledge while Bronko argued with the new concessionaire. The newcomer's appearance was not actually unpleasant in spite of the harelip which couldn't quite cover his upper teeth. He was a young man, but there was an oily grossness about his thick-set body that suggested rich foods and city life rather than the rigors of living under canvas. I couldn't quite make him out. One moment he would seem to be talking with the honest indignation of a man deprived of his rights. Then his face would suddenly narrow to a foxy craftiness. His clothes, too, looked strange on a carny lot. Although he had apparently been driving stakes and was in his shirt sleeves, he was wearing ruby cuff links and red suspenders, while the shirt itself was a striking polka-dot pattern.

"I gotta put up my banners too, you know," he was protesting as I came up. He kept gesticulating with his hands and shifting around as though terrified of a fight and yet fearful of losing some of his footage. At one moment he would be aggressively plucking at Bronko's shirt and the next, dodging around his banner line as though the cowboy had taken a swing at him. "Don't you think I got rights too?" he kept urging with a disarming eagerness. "I just joined this outfit. I want to do the square thing by everybody, but I don't feel it's fair for anyone to bluff me out of anything."

"I ain't trying to bluff you out of anything," said Bronko. "But your line is too far over. You musta moved it since yesterday."

"You don't think I'd do a cheap, mean trick like that, do you?" the stranger cried indignantly. "Look, the mark stake's over there. But I guess I don't stand much of a chance. There's only one of me and a lot of you and I'm a newcomer. If you want to make me cripple my banner line, there isn't anything I can do about it."

"Aw, I don't want you to feel like that," said the cowboy good-naturedly. "I guess you're right about that mark stake. You let your line stand and we'll drop a couple more of our banners off."

"Say, that's damn square of you!" exclaimed the newcomer, grabbing Bronko's hand. "It means a good deal to a stranger to feel new friends will treat him right. Oh, what the hell, I'd be glad to say I made the mistake if it wasn't for that marker!"

"You didn't make any mistake," remarked Captain Billy coldly. "I was up early this morning and I seen you changing the mark stake after the lot marker went through."

"What!" yelled Bronko. Turning to the stranger he shouted, "You son of a bitch!" and made a grab for him. The concessionaire hurriedly ducked under a guy rope.

"Don't hit me!" he squalled. "I got a bad nose and it's easy broken."

"I wasn't going to hit you," said Bronko contemptuously. "I was going to kick you and it wasn't your nose I was going to kick, either."

"Now we've had our little bit of good-natured kidding, so let's all be friends," said the stranger coming cheerfully forward with his hand out. "Shake all around, what do you say? Two best outfits on the midway, eh? My name's Ben. What's yours?"

Bronko disdained to answer and turned to Captain Billy who was still leaning on his sledge.

"Let's set 'em up," he said. Then speaking over his shoulder to Ben, "Get your line clear of our front 'fore I pull it down."

"Sure, and if there's anything else I can ever do for you, just let me know," said Ben cordially. He went to work moving the cheap sepia banners of his own concession, whistling cheerily and occasionally throwing an encouraging word to us while we ran our own banner line back to the original mark.

When the banner line was framed, Ben came over and offered me a nickel cigar. Evidently he had decided to ingratiate himself with his new neighbors and selected me as the most gullible of the group. I didn't like to hurt Ben's feelings—although I later found that was an impossibility—so I accepted the cigar. Captain Billy and Bronko walked off silently.

As soon as Ben realized I wasn't mad any more, he began criticizing our side show.

"You can't make any money running a Ten-in-One nowadays," he told me contemptuously, lighting a

Bronko and Lu with whips.

much better cigar than he'd given me. "Fire-eating, sword swallowing, a fat woman—that's all old stuff. Costs too much to run, too. Now I can pack my whole show in the back of my car and I'm renting my top from the carny manager. If I don't make any money, he don't get paid. That's the way to run a business."

"What kind of a show have you got?" I asked.

"Seeing as you're 'with it,' I'll take you in free. Naturally, you won't give away my show if anyone asks?"

I agreed and we started off toward the entrance of his top.

"It's a nice, clean show—even if it's mostly about sex," explained Ben as we entered the warm darkness of the top. "Nothing in it to offend anybody. You can tell by looking at me I'm not the kind of man who'd stand for anything immoral being shown."

"That's obvious," I agreed.

Inside the top was a pit very like ours except it ran along the back of the tent instead of being in the center. The show was a "walk-through"; there were no regular acts and the tip simply walked through the top and looked at the exhibits. The only exhibits seemed to be a cage of guinea pigs and several dozen jars, each containing a pasty-white, shriveled object. The jars were arranged on a series of rough boards held up by sawhorses.

"What are those things in the bottles?" I asked, disgusted.

"They're human embryos in different stages of development," said Ben proudly. "Very fine collection. They show the growth of a child from the time it's conceived to the time it's born. There're a few chicken and dog embryos in there too, just for variety. And here's a two-headed baby."

He pulled a velvet drape off a large, ten-gallon jar. Swishing around in the amber colored preservatory fluid was a tiny, wrinkled, dull gray body with two heads. The membranous skulls were covered with silky red hair which floated upward like the hair of mermaids in paintings.

"What are the guinea pigs for?" I queried.

"To illustrate sex. I don't think anything illustrates the fundamental purpose of sex better than guinea pigs. Besides, people get tired of looking at dead things. They want to see something alive."

"You mean people actually pay money to see this junk?" I asked in astonishment.

"Sure they do," said Ben, equally surprised. "But I don't make my real dough from the admission fees. I make it on the after-catch."

The after-catch are objects sold to the top after the show, like souvenir postcards or cheap magic tricks. Jolly Daisy had an after-catch with our show. She sold pictures of herself for a dime. I didn't see any chance for an after-catch with this outfit and told Ben so.

Ben explained: "After the tip has looked around, I tell them, 'Frankly, folks, I've only brought you in here

so I could talk to you privately off the midway. I've got some genuine French postcards here—the kind you hear about but seldom see. The set of six sells for one dollar. But I am going to ask you to do me one favor. Don't take these cards out of their envelopes or start passing them around among your friends until you're well away from my concession. There're policemen around the lot so you can understand why I have to ask you this.' Then as the tip starts filing out, I sell them postcards. That's where I really make my b.r."

"B.r." is an abbreviation for bank roll. "I'd like to see some of those postcards," I said.

"Sure," said Ben with a grin. He pulled an envelope out of his pocket and handed it to me. It contained six postcards. They were French postcards all right. They showed views of the Eiffel Tower, Versailles, the Louvre, and other famous monuments.

"I should think you'd get some squawks on these," I said, handing them back.

"Sure I do," said Ben easily. "But what can the squawkers do about it? They can't have me jailed for not selling them dirty pictures. I don't misrepresent the pictures in any way. Some of the tip do get a little tough at times. So I have to hire a couple of canvasmen to hang around my concession with stakes. I also have a cop near by to protect my rights. The canvasmen run me about fifty bucks a week and the cop generally comes a little higher. But that's my only nut . . . except the sixty-forty split I have with the carnival to be able to show here."

The nut with the Ten-in-One was high because Krinko had to pay the acts regardless of rain or poor crowds. As Ben's acts were all in jars, he didn't have to worry about paying them and he took in sixty per cent of the admission fees plus the money he got for the French postcards. I could see that Ben had a very good racket.

That evening Ben gave his first bally. Ben was his own talker, ticket collector and bally all rolled into one. His manner of collecting a tip was to rush frantically up on his bally platform and start taking off his pants. When a sufficient tip had collected, Ben would stop suddenly and glare out at them wildly.

"No!" he's shout. "I can't do it, folks. I gotta control myself! It's that hot, spicy show inside here that drives me into a frenzy. Friends, within this tent there is an educational exhibit on sex that no one oughta miss. It's especially for men, but if your girl is the broad-minded type, take her along. You know the biggest factor in divorce today? It's the ignorance of young men about women. I have a mission in life, friends, and my mission is to correct that lack of knowledge!"

Ben always dressed for his bally in the white operating coat of a surgeon. At this moment he struck the coat for emphasis.

"I've been sent out by the Medical Society of America to correct this terrible state of affairs," he proclaimed. "Doctors and scientists all over the country

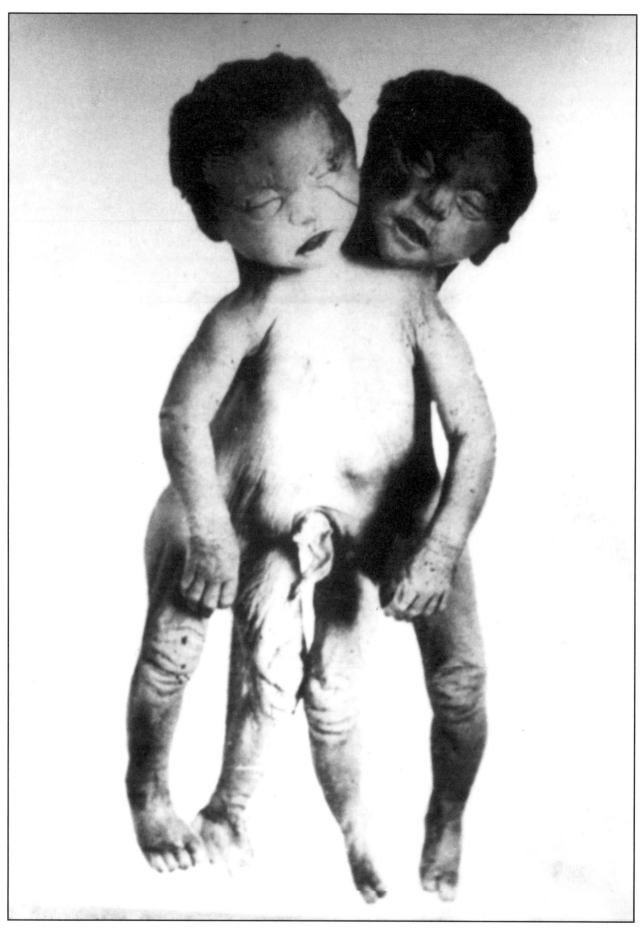

Two-headed baby: "This baby with one body but two separate heads was
born in Alliance, Nebraska in 1935 and died with a minimum of pain."

are worried about it. That's why I've been asked to run this show. That's why I've been allowed to adopt that remarkable two-headed baby which you'll see inside at no extra charge."

He pointed to a banner with the legend, TWO-HEADED BABY. BORN ALIVE! and showing a curly-haired, laughing baby with two heads playing with a rattle while an admiring circle of doctors and trained nurses stood in the background.

"That baby was positively born alive!" Ben assured the tip. "Right now she's . . ." he paused and, bending down, shouted into the tent at some invisible person. "Hey, you get away from there! Don't tease that baby! Don't annoy that little child!"

"Now folks," Ben continued, straightening up and lowering his voice to a whisper that could be heard halfway across the midway. "Just a word about the beautiful living models that illustrate our talk on sex." Apparently, Ben was referring to the guinea pigs. "Now gentlemen, this is the twentieth century and we can show things to an intelligent group of people that would have been impossible a few years ago. But if you are easily shocked, please let me ask you to pass right on down the midway because these models are absolutely nude. Now they are not pictures, they are not behind any sort of screen or veil. They are in the flesh! And they stand as close to you as I am! I will give you a dollar for every thread of clothing you can find on them!"

He pulled out a roll of stage money and flourished it impressively.

"Now I know there is a type of man who is not interested in normal sexual activity. You all know the type I'm referring to. I'm not here to criticize them, but if there are any such among you, I'll just ask them to stay outside while the rest of you pass in to see the show."

Naturally after that, everyone was afraid to stay outside, so Ben did a roaring business. What the tip thought when they found the beautiful models were guinea pigs, I never found out. But I suppose Ben went into his French postcard pitch so fast they didn't have time to get sore. Then before the marks had a chance to examine the postcards, they were back on the midway again. In case of trouble, Ben always had his two canvasmen and the bribed cop.

A few weeks later, an incident occurred that made me feel considerably more friendly toward Ben. Before swallowing a torch, I usually flicked it a few minutes to throw off the excess gas after lifting the head out of the soaking bowl. This had the bad effect of sprinkling the platform with gasoline but I'd grown careless. One night on the bally platform, I flicked one of my torches while I had another lighted torch on the rack. Instantly the gas on the platform blazed up, setting fire to the soaking bowl. Then the large glass preserve jar where I kept the extra gasoline suddenly exploded. I was so dazed by the explosion that I couldn't move for a second or two. Everything near me, including several spectators, was covered with burning gasoline. I pulled off my clothes and only got a few slight burns. Ben was standing on his bally platform waiting for us to finish. With great presence of mind he rushed into his top. Grabbing the big ten-gallon jar containing the two-headed baby, he rolled it back and forth across the platform until the flames were crushed out. It didn't do the baby any good but Ben explained later that the baby was made of terra cotta anyhow.

The spectators who got burned were pretty mad, but they weren't badly hurt. Bits of my preserve jar were driven into the wooden uprights on the platform so hard we never could get them out and they stayed in all season. We just broke off the protruding ends with pliers so they wouldn't cut our hands when we set-up the platform. After that, I always pressed out the cotton heads against the side of the bowl instead of flicking off the surplus gas.

I naturally felt indebted to Ben and we saw a good deal of each other until, a week or so later, Ben failed to show up at a new stop. His sex show wasn't much liked on the lot because some mark was always squawking to the police and that got the whole carny in trouble. I suppose Ben finally joined up with some rag show where his concession was more appreciated.

Krinko in the pit with a mark from the tip.

Krinko doing the nail-in-the-eye routine and catching the nail on a tin plate.

CHAPTER 9

When I first joined the carnival, my ambition had been to learn all the various side show acts. Now that my Fire and Sword routine was running smoothly, I decided to branch out a bit and pick up another act. My choice here was limited. I couldn't very well be a fat lady and May was very fussy about letting anyone handle her rattlesnakes. So I resolved to learn old man Krinko's torture act.

There's always a good future in show business for anyone who can do a first-class torture act. The public loves to see a performer sticking hatpins through his cheeks, driving nails into his eyes or dancing on broken glass. Krinko had even worked out a nice piece of audience participation by letting someone drive a nail through his tongue. The old fakir was billed as "The Oriental Pincushion" and he put on such a fine demonstration that in a couple of communities his performance was barred by the police.

Why people enjoy torture acts is something of a mystery. I suppose it's basically the same reason that kids like to watch a friend wiggle a loose tooth or crack his knuckles. Recently, the motion pictures have caught on to this important principle and it's a poor western that doesn't show the villain stamping on the hero's hand with hobnailed boots or working him over with an iron-toothed rake. Murder mysteries have very much the same appeal. As long as the public will fight for a newspaper that carries the headlines SIX KILLED BY HATCHET MURDERER they'll go to see torture acts. And the grislier the exhibitions are, the more the public will love 'em.

When I first joined the show, I took for granted that Krinko must fake his routine. After all, when you see someone pouring molten lead into his ears, walking on sharp swords, and sewing buttons on his eyelids, you naturally come to the conclusion that the guy is either a fake or not quite right in the head. Krinko was a smart old boy, so I supposed that the old man's routine was "grifted"—which is carny slang for faked.

I was wrong. The real explanation of Krinko's routine was considerably more astonishing than the effects themselves. He did use some trickery, but it wasn't the kind of trickery that most people would care to employ.

Krinko began his performance in a mild way by exhibiting a small nail and then putting the point of the nail in the corner of his left eye. Picking up a hammer, he would drive the nail into his eye with slow, even strokes. You could hold the nail to make sure it was going in—if you wanted to. Then, after showing his hands were empty, Krinko would explain that he was going to pass the nail through his nasal passage and into his right eye.

After a few facial contortions and groans, Krinko would hold out a tin dish and then press his right cheek. The nail would pop out of his right eye like a squeezed grape popping out of the skin. Krinko would catch the nail on the tin dish as it fell. The nail always hit the dish with a clang which added greatly to the effectiveness of the stunt.

For a long time I thought that Krinko must palm the nail in some way. This wasn't so. The real explanation depended on a little-known physiological law coupled with a complete disregard for danger. If you made a mistake in this trick, you were blinded for life.

Krinko used two identical nails. Before appearing in the pit, he would quietly slip one of the nails into the tear duct of his right eye. The tear duct is large enough to admit a small nail about the diameter of a hairpin and an inch long. When he put on his routine, Krinko would exhibit the other nail and place it against the duct in his left eye. The hammering was purely for effect as the nail slid in easily. After the nail had vanished, Krinko would make passes, supposedly to transfer the nail to the other eye. Then he pressed his right cheek and the second nail would leap out and clatter on the tin dish.

If there were any members of the audience who were still conscious after this demonstration, Krinko would take an ice pick, insert it up one of his nostrils, and then, using the hammer, drive the pick up his nose to the handle.

I was so sure the ice pick must fold back into the handle that I didn't even bother to examine it. Then one evening Krinko couldn't find the pick so he did the stunt with a long, ten-penny nail. There was no deception about the trick at all. Centuries ago, the fakirs must have discovered that it is possible to shove a thin metal rod up your nose and into the nasal passage for a surprising distance. It must be a horrible sensation but it can be done. I suppose ninety per cent of the people who saw this effect thought, as I had, that it was faked in some way. It is simply an amazing anatomical feat.

The Human Pincushion, as Krinko called the main part of his act, consisted of running long, jade-headed hatpins through his body. This grisly effect has become almost a hallmark of the Oriental fakir, so I was particularly interested in it. I had read many theories about this remarkable stunt. Most of the authorities believed that a fakir first has to put himself into a semi-hypnotic state. Others thought that a fakir, through yogism, had to achieve a state in which his mind was completely divorced from his body. Still others believed that the feat was faked in some way or the fakir doped himself up on drugs beforehand so he wouldn't feel the pain.

When I tried to learn the Human Pincushion routine, I discovered that all these theories are wrong. I never reached the degree of expertise that Krinko attained, but I was able to sew buttons on my wrists and then button my shirt sleeves to them. I could also run hatpins through my arms and the skin of my chest. But anything I did was kids' stuff compared to old man Krinko's routine.

Krinko started by running half a dozen of the long pins through the flesh of his forearms in a very casual, business-like way. Then with more ceremony he stuck one pin through both his cheeks, turning slowly so the writhing members of the audience could study the effect. Occasionally he would put his head against one of the centerpoles supporting the top of the tent and allow some member of the audience to run a pin through his cheeks and into the wood, thus nailing him to the centerpole.

When Krinko wanted to be really fancy, he would use two pins, one through each cheek, with the points coming out of his mouth. Then Krinko would hold the pins by their jade heads and wriggle them so that the ends protruding from his lips danced around. In some towns we played, so many women in the tip were taken sick by this exhibition that Krinko became worried. So he thoughtfully tied little tassels of brightly colored ribbon to the heads of the pins to make the act more appealing to the ladies.

Actually, I think women were less affected by the act than men. They just liked to put on more of a show. Even when I was on the bally platform outside the tent, I could always tell when Krinko was doing his torture act. Screaming women would come rushing out followed by men who had turned a light shade of green. The men usually refused to go back, but the ladies, after screaming, "Oh, it's so horrible I can't bear to look!" would return and watch with fascinated delight while Krinko stuck the pins in himself. Small boys especially loved the Human Pincushion routine. They'd stay for show after show until we had to run them out of the tent.

There was no self-hypnosis or yogism involved with Krinko's stunt. He had learned the routine in India as a kid. When Krinko was a child, his father had started him out as a Human Pincushion by pulling up a fold of the boy's skin and sticking pins through it. Of course, this was easier then actually forcing the pins through the flesh. After a few weeks, little Krinko got used to the pain and hardly felt it.

This isn't as surprising as it sounds. Probably a large part of the pain is really psychological. Having a long needle stuck into you is a very unpleasant idea. I've seen men faint when a doctor simply approaches them with a hypodermic needle. But the pain itself isn't great. Diabetics often shudder with agony the first time they have injections. Then after a few months, they think no more about getting a hypodermic stuck in them than they do of brushing their teeth.

Krinko explained that after a few weeks of putting the needles through his skin, he got so used to the sensation that his father could drive them through the boy's flesh. Then suddenly he suffered a violent revulsion about the whole affair. Just the sight of one of the long needles made him sick. This stage passed in a few days and he was able to continue with his awful act. Finally he could run the long skewers through the flesh on his hands, chest, arms, legs, belly, or even through his eyelids.

When I first tried the stunt, I found that I bled very badly. Krinko hardly bled at all as long as he continued to stick the skewers through those portions of his body that had become accustomed to the pain. But when he tried some new part of his body, he bled as badly as I did. Then after keeping it up for a few days he seemed to stop. I don't know if this was because he unconsciously learned where the blood vessels were and avoided them or whether his veins, like his nerves, in some way accustomed themselves to the process and shut off the flow of blood. Of course, a great deal depends on where you run the needles. There are certain parts of the body that don't bleed easily. But an eighth of an inch farther up or down may mean hitting an artery or puncturing a main blood vessel.

I got so that I could run six of the long skewers through the flesh of my forearms without much discomfort. Like Krinko, I found that after I'd done it a few times, I bled very little. The trick is to push the needles through with a quick, decided thrust. Then you don't bleed very much. Of course, the closer you keep them to the surface of your skin, the less chance you have of hitting a vein.

To me, the most remarkable part of this stunt was that the people who do it regularly for a living don't develop blood poisoning. Except for wiping the needles off with a dirty rag, Krinko never took any precautions. He told me that in India he had several times left the needles in his body for days until the protruding points got so rusted that he couldn't withdraw them, and they had to be cut off. He also said that during the First World War, he had had the shoulder patches of various British regiments sewn all over his back. His chest was covered with medals, pinned to the bare flesh, that soldiers had given him as a joke. He claimed he never suffered any ill effects from making a patchwork quilt out of himself.

However, if the needle wounds did get infected, Krinko would simply leave that portion of his arm alone for a few days until the injury healed. Whenever I tried the pincushion act, I always wiped my arm off with alcohol first and washed the skewers with some disinfectant. Krinko considered this sissy stuff. Once, after I'd finished giving him a lecture on tetanus, the old fakir picked up a rusty nail and ran it through the skin on the back of his hand to make a liar out of me.

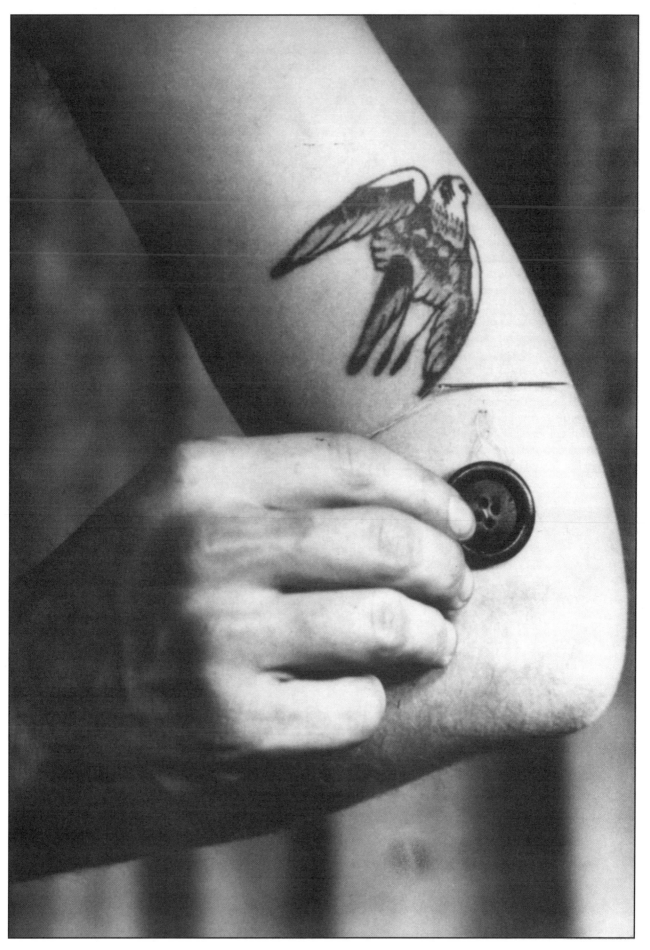

Sewing a button on arm (that's a tattoo of a hawk above it).

Nothing ever happened to him. I suppose the old guy was tough.

Krinko had been brought to the United States as a young man when an American impresario, touring India, saw the youthful yogi pulling a cart through the streets of Bombay by a hole in his tongue. When Krinko was a kid, his father had pierced his tongue with a heavy needle, leaving a short length of string threaded through the tongue to prevent the wound from growing together. The boy had been told to keep working the string back and forth as the wound healed to keep the string from adhering to the flesh. When the swelling and inflammation gradually began to go down, the child's father had worked sticks through the hole to make it bigger, until finally an iron hook could be thrust through the opening. By fastening a light chain to this hook and using the full strength of his neck muscles, Krinko could pull a cart with it. The hardest part of the stunt was to overcome the initial inertia of the cart and start it moving. After that, the cart's momentum kept it rolling and the fakir always made sure that the cart was placed on a slight incline.

Krinko had sometimes varied this routine by letting a member of the crowd drive a nail through his tongue and fasten him to a block of wood. Of course, he had to guide the nail to make sure it went through the hole already in his flesh. He still did the nail-through-tongue routine with the side show but he hadn't pulled a cart in years. There wasn't room enough for such a demonstration in a side show tent.

After working in carnivals for several months, I finally decided that there is almost no limit to the remarkable things that can be done with the human body. But before I realized this profound truth, I got the mistaken idea that because I knew a few carny routines, I was an authority on carny acts. When I was able to run half a dozen skewers through my arms and do the nail-in-the-eye act, I decided that there was nothing left for old man Krinko to teach me. Then one evening the old fakir resolved to show me up.

I was finishing my sword swallowing routine when Krinko called casually, "Hi, son, I want you to help me." I knew that after forty years in the show business, the old man needed my help like he needed a third leg, but I came over to his platform. Krinko was holding up a yard of red silk ribbon. After the tip had left my catwalk and collected around him, Krinko gravely rolled up the ribbon into a small ball and swallowed it.

Then Krinko pulled up his shirt, disclosing his great hairy belly. He picked up a razor blade and made a slight cut in his skin just above the navel. Reaching into the cut, he began to pull out the ribbon, inch by inch.

When he'd produced about a foot of it, I said, "Let me pull it out." I was certain that he must be palming

Krinko having tongue nailed to a barrel.

the ribbon. Krinko instantly put his hands on his sides so I've have a clear field. I took the ribbon and began to work it out. There wasn't the slightest doubt that the ribbon was coming from inside of him. I thought he might have made a small cut in his body, rolled up a duplicate into a ball, and stuck it into the wound. But this ribbon was paying out from somewhere inside the old man's body. I pulled out the whole yard of silk and was more astonished than anyone in the crowd.

Krinko knew he had me completely fooled and got a big kick out of it. For the next few days, he kept making cracks about Johnny-come-latelies who know all about torture acts and asking me if I'd mind giving him lessons in fakirism. The other members of the troupe took up the gag. Lu gave me a hot dog with a ribbon tied around it and asked me to produce the ribbon after I'd eaten the dog. I spent hours trying to figure out the stunt, but as far as I was concerned, it was still a miracle.

Krinko had never done the ribbon trick before in America, but after he saw the effect it produced on me, he started introducing it as a regular part of his act. As we were all working crowded together in the pit, he couldn't keep the effect a secret for long. So I soon discovered how the ribbon trick was done. As usual with side show tricks, the solution was more surprising than the effect.

Krinko used two duplicate ribbons. Before going on, he took one ribbon and threaded it on a long, flat needle such as women use to run elastic through their panties. Then the fakir took a big handful of skin on his side and pulled the skin away from his body as far as it would go. Taking the threaded needle, he ran it through the double fold of skin. When he let the skin snap back into place, the ribbon was threaded just beneath the skin, one end sticking out above his navel and the other reaching around almost to his back. Krinko took the dangling end of ribbon at his back and pulled it carefully until the ribbon in front was drawn flush with his flesh. The ribbon at his back was allowed to hang down his pants. After swallowing the duplicate ribbon, Krinko took care to make the cut in his belly over the spot where the needle had come out. Then he could pull the ribbon through as though he were pulling out the string in a pair of pajamas.

The most terrible feat Krinko performed was pouring "molten lead" into his eyes and ears. When the hissing lead hit his flesh and began to throw off steam, people in the tip fainted right and left as though you'd fired a charge of buckshot through the crowd. After the exhibition was over, Krinko would rise painfully from the table where he had been lying and grope around as though he were blind. Then slowly and dramatically he would open his eyes. I've seen people burst into tears from relief when they realized he wasn't blinded.

This act was so horrifying that the old man had to drop it out of his regular routine. Too many women were suing the show, claiming the sight had marked their unborn children. Yet this was the only one of Krinko's routines that was completely grifted and almost completely safe.

Krinko didn't use real lead for this effect. He used a compound of antimony which resembles lead so closely that it is almost impossible to tell them apart. Antimony has such a low melting point that you can hold a lighted match under a piece and it will melt like paraffin. The "molten" lead that Krinko poured over his eyes was no hotter than tallow drippings. Naturally, Krinko did everything possible to make the audience think he was using real lead. He melted the compound in a plumber's crucible, and used a blowtorch to generate heat, explaining that no ordinary flame was hot enough. You can adjust a blowtorch so it throws off almost no heat, but even so, the old fakir had to be careful that the crucible only got hot enough to dissolve the antimony without overheating. Actually, the warmth of your hand was almost enough to make the stuff pliable.

The most difficult feat Krinko performed was the Ladder of Swords. He walked barefoot up a step-ladder whose rungs were razor-edged swords. This feat wasn't grifted in any way, and was intensely dangerous. All you had to do was slip once and the swords would slice a hunk out of your leg as big as an old-fashioned sirloin steak. There was nothing you could grab for support as the other swords would have slit your hand to the bone. Yet this stunt never produced the effect on an audience that the lead-in-the-eyes did. People were positive that the ladder of swords was faked in some way while it never seemed to occur to them that the boiling lead might not be genuine. That's often the way with side show stunts. The really difficult feats are duds while the grifted stuff causes a sensation.

Krinko worked hard to convince the tip that his Ladder of Swords was genuine. He took the swords off the rack and sliced pieces of paper with them to prove they were sharp. Instead of being convinced, people thought that he only had part of the swords sharpened and the rest of the blade was blunt. Krinko tried passing the swords around and letting the audience examine them. One man was so sure the swords must have a dull area that he ran his hand along one of the blades. That was a mistake. The guy cut himself so badly that he had to be rushed to the hospital. The Ladder of Swords went over big that night, but you couldn't count on finding hecklers so obliging every evening.

The ladder stunt was based on a curious fact that few people know about. If you press a sharp cutting edge, like a razor, at right angles to your flesh, it won't cut you. But if you slide the blade in the slightest or try to force it in at an angle, you'll get hurt. To keep from being cut, you must maintain a steady even pressure, keeping the whole length of the blade in constant contact with some flat portion of your body.

When Krinko climbed the Ladder of Swords, he always climbed sideways, so that his feet were placed lengthwise along the blade, thus distributing his weight over as large an area as possible. He had to step slowly and carefully, making sure each time he took another step that his foot didn't tremble as he gradually put his full weight on it. Of course, he always checked to see that the swords were fixed tightly in the rack so there was no chance of having them wobble. The blades had to be perfectly horizontal. If they were set in the rack at a slant, the sharp edges would slice sideways through the sole of his foot.

I tried climbing the ladder a few times myself. Krinko stood alongside, holding my hand to steady me. Before I got down again, I was so scared that the sweat was running into my eyes and I could hardly see. After I'd made the ascent and descent a few times, old man Krinko told me to lay off it.

"Your knees shake too much," he said frankly. "Pretty soon you fall and cut off your leg. Big mess. You better forget that act." I took his advice.

My failure with the Ladder of Swords, coupled with a dislike of sticking skewers through myself that I didn't seem able to overcome, finally decided me against becoming a Human Pincushion. After all, my parents hadn't given me the right start in life. They hadn't pierced my tongue with a needle at an early age so I could use it to pull carts. They hadn't even inured me to pain by sticking needles through my belly when I was a baby. At my age, it was too late to start so I regretfully abandoned the project.

After seeing Krinko's act, I don't think I can be blamed for thinking I'd seen the ultimate in physiological miracles. But that was before the Human Ostrich joined our show.

While I was setting up my swords in the pit preparatory to the evening's show, Krinko came into the top with a stranger. The newcomer was nearly as tall as I was but so stoop-shouldered that he seemed almost hunchbacked. He had such protruding teeth that for an instant I thought he was a comedian wearing the celluloid buckteeth sold in novelty shows. He carried his head stuck forward like a tortoise and seemed to be constantly straining at something. I found later that this was because he was very shortsighted. He was wearing a long cape and an ancient opera hat with the nap much worn. He carried a silver-headed cane.

Krinko said proudly, "Slim, this famous Human Ostrich. He do very fine act. He join show now."

The Ostrich bowed and placing one hand on his shirt front said impressively, "If you put your ear against my chest, you can hear live frogs swimming around inside of me. There is no other man alive who can make this claim."

"Can you do it now?" I asked deeply interested.

The Ostrich made a deprecatory gesture with his hands and shoulders. "Not now, no. But in my act, yes."

"He do very high-class variety act, swallowing everything people in tip bring him," explained Krinko, regarding the Ostrich with open admiration. This was obviously the sort of act that the old fakir could understand and appreciate.

"I usually start out by eating some rings, streetcar tokens, a key ring—with keys—an old razor blade, and a couple of electric light bulbs," said the Ostrich with quiet pride. "After that, I go into my flourishes such as swallowing a chain and jumping up and down so the audience can hear it clink inside of me and end up with my smashing finale of eating live rats. I can give twelve shows a day, unless something sticks, as occasionally happens."

"What do you do then?" I asked.

"You should see my X-rays," said the Ostrich simply.

Captain Billy had joined us. "What do you do with the rats after you swallow them?" he wanted to know.

"Any object I swallow, I regurgitate afterward," explained the Ostrich. "The rats are never hurt. Neither are the frogs. Before swallowing a frog I always drink a quart of water to give the little fellow something to land in as frogs have feelings just like anyone else."

Captain Billy shook his head. "Krinko, the public'll never stand for it."

The Ostrich was very insulted by this remark. "I admit that in this country most people feel that a Human Ostrich isn't as high a type as a sword swallower or a tattooed man." This was said very sarcastically. "That may be true of the average Ostrich you see around carnival lots, who is nothing but a glass-and-razor blade eater. But I learned my art in the exacting Viennese Human Ostrich School. I had to leave the country during the German putsch, but I hope some day to return to my fatherland. When I do," he added severely, "I hope to leave behind me in this country an appreciation for regurgitation that was not here before."

The Ostrich spoke like an educated man, although with a strong foreign accent. I had never seen anyone like him in carnival before and looked forward with great respect to seeing his act that night.

The Ostrich began his act by borrowing some small objects from the tip and swallowing them. After getting some volunteers to examine his mouth to prove that he really did swallow the contributions, he very neatly regurgitated the collection without retching or unpleasant gagging. Then he swallowed two live white rats after first carefully brushing the little animals with a toothbrush to make sure they were clean. He brought up the rats one after the other and returned them to a small aquarium where he kept a number of the animals. The rats didn't seem any the worse for their experience and started cleaning their fur and whiskers very casually as though being swallowed was an everyday event for them, as indeed it probably was.

After the Ostrich had finished his act and waved the tip on to blow-off and Jolly Daisy, several people remained behind to talk to him. They all asked the same question—a question that was also of great interest to me. "Whatever made you start swallowing live rats for a living?" The Ostrich had what was obviously a stock answer to this question. He always replied, "One morning I simply thought, 'I want to swallow a

Krinko.

live rat.' So I did. Then it became a hobby with me. Other people go in for golf or bridge. I swallow rats."

After the last show that night, I asked the Ostrich how he was able to regurgitate objects so easily and simply. He smiled condescendingly, "I never intend to reveal my secret. I make my living from my art and naturally I don't want everyone to start swallowing rats. These things can become a fad. Look at the way all those college students started swallowing goldfish a few years ago."

Although the Ostrich was rather standoffish, we got to be fairly good friends in the next few weeks. He had a great liking for beer and often after the show we'd go to some little bar near the lot and drink beer for an hour or so before going to bed. During these nightly bouts, the Ostrich told me the story of his life.

The Ostrich was born in Germany. His family were Jews, and although Hitler had not yet appeared with his doctrine of racial supremacy, Jews were looked down upon by many Germans. Gangs of young toughs made life miserable for the Jewish children, and the gangling Ostrich, with his protruding teeth and humped back, was a particularly good target. He lived in terror of their abuse and his only happiness was to slip away to the traveling street carnivals and watch the beautifully dressed performers and listen to the music. The carnivals seemed particularly wonderful to him because they traveled all over Europe, from the minarets of Turkey to the fjords of Norway. He liked the side shows and the freaks above everything. Here were people who had started with everything against them, but they had had the courage to turn their misfortune into an asset, and instead of being ashamed of being different they flung their strangeness in the face of the world. As a result, they were happy and had escaped the cruel persecution that he was suffering.

While visiting carnivals, the Ostrich saw several performers who were able to swallow small objects and then regurgitate them. The Ostrich had learned their secret. To perform this feat, you must first swallow a small potato on the end of a string. Then you pull up the potato with the string, at the same time trying to eject it with your stomach muscles. This may make you feel unwell the first few times, but after six months of steady practice you will have such control over you stomach muscles that you can bring up any object you have swallowed without trouble. The Ostrich became fascinated by the subject of regurgitation and began to do research on it. He found that this controlling of the involuntary muscles is actually a crude form of yogism. Orientals practice it as a health measure. No one who can control his stomach muscles in this manner can become constipated as poor digestion is basically due to sluggishness of these very muscles. To a limited extent, young babies have this power naturally and so do certain animals like wolves. Trappers have found that it is extremely difficult to poison wolves because the animals can discharge the poisoned bait as soon as they feel the first warning pangs. After the Ostrich had learned the technique of regurgitation he used to pick up small sums of money by giving exhibitions of his powers before doctors in the Vienna schools.

The Ostrich had been troubled with indigestion as a young man, but after learning the technique of his act, he had never had another attack. "I always smile when people in the audience say, 'I'll bet you have awful belly aches with all that stuff you eat.'" The Ostrich explained, "I never have stomach troubles. Constant exercise of my stomach muscles has given me a much better digestive system than an ordinary man."

When Hitler marched into Austria, the Ostrich escaped to Switzerland, but he had no money and no particular qualifications for any trade. He was forced to make a living giving exhibitions of his peculiar powers in night clubs. One evening, a booking agent for American road shows saw him and offered the Ostrich a job in the United States. He had been working under canvas ever since.

"I enjoy the life, but my work is not without its dangers," the Ostrich admitted to me. "One of my best flourishes is to swallow a watch borrowed from the audience and then allow people to put their ears against my chest and listen to the ticking. Old and young enjoy this. While playing in Texas once, I experienced a good deal of difficulty as people refused to contribute watches, feeling they might not get them back. I offered to allow anyone to keep hold of the chain, but even this produced no results. At last, the manager of the side show I was with had an inspiration.

"'I'll post a reward of one hundred dollars to anyone who can produce a watch you can't swallow,' he told me. 'Everyone will be combing the family attics and the local pawn shops for giant watches. The publicity will be tremendous.'

"I felt a little nervous over this prospect as I was afraid someone might come in with an alarm clock tied to his wrist and I knew the manager would never forfeit that hundred dollars even if it killed me. For several days, everything went well. Then the blow came. An old cattleman stood up one evening holding a gigantic watch covered with an embossed scene of cattle punching. The sculptor had even included the cows' horns which stuck out from the surface of the case.

"'This would be difficult for some people to swallow,' said the manager, holding it up, 'But for the Ostrich it's just a joke,' and he handed the machine to me.

"I swallowed it bravely and immediately knew I was going to have trouble. Long experience has given me a sixth sense about these things. When I tried to bring it up, the cows' horns got stuck in my throat. I began to gasp for breath. I could feel myself turning blue in the face. I made one more effort and only succeeded in lodging the watch firmly in my throat, shutting off my windpipe. I began to suffocate. I tried to scream for help, but couldn't speak because of the peculiar circumstance I was in. Then I started to lose conscious-

THE GREAT WALDO
BIOGRAPHY

WHITE
MICE

?

WATCHES

?

RINGS

?

COINS

?

LEMONS

?

GOLDFISH

PRICE 10c

The Human Ostrich.

ness and fell to my knees. The cattleman jumped up shouting, 'You're trying to steal my watch, you dirty crook!' The manager was also mad at me and yelled, 'What's the matter, you sissy, are you trying to make me lose a hundred dollars?' I fainted from lack of air and fortunately this infuriated the manager and the cattleman so that they grabbed me by the feet and began to beat my head on the floor screaming, 'Cough up that watch!' The beating loosened the watch and it fell out. The manager returned it to its rightful owner who went back to his seat amid a burst of applause and the show continued as if nothing had happened."

The Ostrich told me that most of the men who do swallowing acts in carnivals don't know how to regurgitate and so must actually digest anything they eat. These men have to limit themselves to electric bulbs, old beer bottles, stones, hairpins, and razor blades. In the case of glass, the swallowers often cut their mouths while chewing it up, but once they have swallowed the stuff they are fairly safe. Apparently ground glass isn't the deadly substance people consider it and can usually be easily digested. However, many performers fake their act by putting chewing gum against their teeth and squeezing the bits of glass into it. Others secretly spit the fragments out while taking a drink of water, the splinters being invisible in a tumbler full of water. Still others simply keep the glass in their throats or cheeks. But many really swallow the objects and may go for years without trouble, as long as they take the precaution of chewing up the glass well beforehand and bending up the hairpins so they won't get caught crossways in their throats.

I was so impressed by the Ostrich's act that I begged Billie Callihan to come over some evening and see it. Billie dropped in between two of her shows and, decorously wrapped in her kimono, stood at the back of our tip watching the Ostrich with ill-concealed horror. Jolly Daisy had asked Billie and me for late supper that evening, so after the last show I joined them in the fat woman's living top. I asked Billie what she thought of the Ostrich.

"I think the people you're hiring in this Ten-in-One are getting queerer and queerer," said Billie frankly. "We've got some girls in the Model Show who maybe aren't all they oughta be, but at least they don't go around eating live rats. I can't figure out why the public wants to see a man swallowing rats and then bringing them up again. I think it's awful and I don't care what that Ostrich says—I'll bet it's cruel to the rats."

"I don't know what the rats think about it, but if I was a rat, I sure wouldn't like the idea," said Jolly Daisy. The fat lady had moved her chair close to her camp stove so she could do the cooking without having to get up. "Personally, I think an act like that lowers the whole tone of the show."

"The rats look healthy enough to me," I remarked. "What you girls don't understand is the imagination the Ostrich must have to think up such a routine."

"I got imagination too, but I don't do nothing like that," said Billie indignantly. "Compared to swallowing animals our Model Show is a high-class affair. We got a nice little orchestra and seeing us pose is very artistic."

"Billie's absolutely right," said Jolly Daisy, lifting the frying pan off the stove with a great spluttering of hot grease and serving us our fried steaks. "An act like the Ostrich's is undignified. I've been under canvas twenty years and I never done nothing yet that was undignified. I once worked with a show where the M.C. would drop a quarter in front of me and then tell me I could have it if I'd pick it up, but I wouldn't do it. It ain't dignified."

"I know just how you feel," agreed Billie warmly. "I've been in outfits where the manager wanted us girls to put on special acts for stag parties—you know, get up on a table and do an indecent routine. I'd never go for that. Those exhibitions pay well and some of the other girls would ask me why I wouldn't do it. I'd simply say to them, 'I guess I was brought up different from you. I was raised to be a lady. Maybe my folks made a mistake giving me high standards, but that's the way it is and I could never do anything like what you do.' Some of the girls would get mad at me, but I was only telling them the honest truth."

Billie spoke with deep sincerity. There is a regular series of gradation among posing girls. The girls that do nothing but pose look down on the girls who are willing to give indecent shows. These girls look down on others who are willing to put on public demonstrations of even more degrading practices. These, in turn, feel superior to common prostitutes. As far as I could learn, you never reached the bottom. No matter how low you went, there was always some poor creature still more degenerate than yourself.

Jolly Daisy changed the subject by saying, "I wish Slim would give up that Fire and Sword act of his. I can't see him from inside the blow-off, but every time he does that Fountain of Fire on the bally platform, the whole side of the top lights up and I sit there waiting to hear something explode. I don't see why a smart kid like him don't learn another act."

"Neither do I," agreed Billie warmly. "I suppose being a sword swallower and fire-eater ain't as bad as being a Human Ostrich, but it still's not a very high-class act."

"I make out all right," I said, secure in my knowledge that I was top salary with the show. "I've got the act worked out now so there isn't any danger."

"There's always danger," said the fat woman flatly. "Some day you'll get a backdraft while you'll be eating fire or one of them swords will chip and catch in your insides. Then it'll be 'please omit the flowers.' You better get another act."

"I've tried to learn old man Krinko's torture act, but it was a little too tough for me, " I explained.

The two women stared at me. "Well, you certainly pick the nice routines," said Billie in wonder.

"Sometimes I can't figure men out. There're plenty of nice, safe acts you could learn that would give you a chance at the big time. I'd try to pick up one of them, if I was you."

A few days later, an incident happened that made me think Billie might be right. I was in the pit with a good crowd around me and was just finishing my spiel before swallowing the neon tubes. I was standing with the red tube lighted and lying across the wiping cloth in my left hand. The yellow tube was also lighted and hanging over my sword rack. While I was talking, I saw the yellow tube suddenly go out.

Captain Billy was on the catwalk next to me. I saw he was looking at me strangely.

"That tube just went out. We must have blown a fuse," I called over to him.

"We didn't blow no fuse. Look at that tube in your hand," the captain called back.

I looked down at the tube. It had burst and for a foot along one side there was nothing but finely powdered glass. As the tubes were hitched in series, the other tube had gone out at the same time.

There had been no reason for the tube to break. There had been no noise and no warning. A moment later, I would have swallowed it. If the tube had broken inside of me, I would probably have been killed, for I could not have withdrawn the tube without cutting open the lining of my stomach on the jagged edges.

But at the time, I was only conscious that my act was being ruined. I cut off the current, connected the remaining tube directly to the transformer, and swallowed it. There happened to be a reporter in the tip that night. He wrote up the incident and for days later our show was packed by crowds hoping to see the other tube break inside of me.

I'd gone so long without an accident that I'd almost forgotten that my Fire and Sword routine was very dangerous. As Jolly Daisy said, sooner or later something would go wrong and I'd either be killed or seriously maimed. I didn't want to leave the carnival, but I began seriously to consider learning a less risky routine—at least something to enable me to rest now and then. I thought of several possibilities, but none of them seemed to fit the bill.

Late one rainy evening I was having a drink with the Impossible Possible in a little bar on the outskirts of Chicago. A man came into the bar looking very flustered and asked the bartender if he could use the telephone. "I just had a new lock put on my garage door and now I've lost the key," he complained.

The Impossible was obviously touched by the poor guy's distress. "What kind of a lock is it?" he asked.

The man told him, adding, "I'm afraid it'll have to be filed off because it's pickproof."

The Impossible smiled gently and remarked, "Let's take a look at it. Then we will see what we will see."

The man took us to his garage. The lock was a padlock with the keyhole in the bottom. The key for this type has notches in the tip instead of along the sides and when you shove it in, the lock jumps open. The Impossible took from his inside pocket a roll of soft cloth. He opened it, disclosing an assortment of tools as delicate as a set of dental instruments. But instead of using one of the tools, he selected a piece of thin, flat wood like the tongue depressors used by doctors. With a knife he took from the kit, the Impossible whittled the wood down to fit the keyhole. Then he stuck it in as though it were the key and jiggled the stick in and out. The notches inside the lock carved the soft wood into the shape of the key and then, of course, the stick became the key and the lock sprang open.

The Impossible offered to pick the ignition lock of the man's car for him, but the owner said that wasn't necessary. He had his car keys. He seemed in a hurry to get away from us and drove off without even thanking the Impossible.

Back in the bar, I asked the Impossible where he learned to pick locks.

"You learn all sorts of useful little things in carny life, m'boy," said the Impossible, allowing me to order him another shot of whiskey while he fitted a cigarette into his holder. "After Harry Houdini made lock-picking famous, escape artists broke out all over the country like a case of bad hives. Most of the performers spent very little time on their own routines. They were too busy trying to queer the acts of rival escapists. When Houdini introduced the Challenge Handcuff Escape, things became even worse. The Challenge act was an open invitation to louse up another performer's act."

I remembered reading about the Challenge Handcuff Escape. The performer issued a public challenge, agreeing to pay a certain sum of money to anyone who could handcuff him so he couldn't escape.

"I got a position as assistant to an escape artist named The Great Gambal," continued the Impossible, smiling reminiscently. "My main job was to go around and ruin the acts of other escape artists. Gambal couldn't do it himself because the escapists would have recognized him. He needed an innocent-looking young fellow for the work. I was innocent-looking in those days. My first job was to attend to an escape artist who was playing in a vaudeville house in the same town where we intended to open. Gambal decided to play a little prank on him.

"Well do I remember how we did it. We got an old pair of Bean Giant handcuffs and filed out the works so that once they were closed, nothing on earth, including the key, could ever open them again. With these cuffs in my pocket I went to take in the escape artist's act.

"When the escapist gave his challenge, I paraded up on the stage with some other people and waited my turn. Generally an escapist will insist that a pair of cuffs be locked and unlocked in front of him before he puts them on. But this man was doing a vaudeville turn and didn't have the time. I snapped one cuff around his wrist and the other to a bar running around the footlights. Then I ran."

"Did you collect the challenge money?" I asked.

The Impossible shook his head sadly. "We was robbed, m'boy. The theater was putting up the challenge money in this case and Gambal figured the management would have to pay off because the guy was chained there in plain view all through the rest of the show. They finally had to bring in a mechanic with a blowtorch to get him loose. The next evening Gambal went to the theater to collect the challenge money. When he came out he was so mad his face was white. The theater had guaranteed one hundred dollars to anyone who could lock the escapist up so he couldn't get loose, but the manager was dishonest and all Gambal could get out of him was a ten spot. That's the trouble with show business. There're too many crooks in it."

Suddenly I realized that here was the act for me. I would be an escape artist. It was nice, clean work without any danger attached and I might someday get to be a second Houdini. I broached the idea, and the Impossible was mildly enthusiastic.

"I haven't kept up with the new types of locks, but I can still show you the fundamentals," he told me. "Some years ago, one of the biggest lock companies used to send me their new models so I could pick them open and make suggestions. The companies were very cooperative in those days. But now they seem to take a sulky point of view toward the whole business. Too bad. However, if you're at all mechanically inclined, I see no reason why you shouldn't become the new King of Locks."

One of the rides.

I knew that old man Krinko would never let me give up my Fire and Sword act. But I thought I might do an escape act on the side. Then, when I became an expert at lock-picking, I could specialize in escapism and drop the more dangerous routines. I could hardly wait to tell Billie and the side show troupe about my new career. Once again, I was confident that I would make side show history.

CHAPTER 10

My first public demonstration of lock-picking came when a local committee locked me in a mailbag and dropped me into the Mississippi River. The stunt was supposed to draw a crowd and advertise the carnival. But the exhibition was only partially successful because when I didn't come up again, the crowd got tired of waiting and drifted away.

We had gathered by the river that afternoon surrounded by the type of crowd that usually turns out for a lynching. As I wasn't sure that I could pick the lock of the mailbag through the heavy cloth, I had secretly bribed a local boy to substitute a chain with a faked link for the real chain that came with the bag. I climbed inside the sack and the chain was securely locked around the mouth. As my assistant, with the help of two hefty farm hands dragged me to the end of the wharf, he put his mouth close to the bag and whispered, "I'm powerful sorry, but I never got no chance to switch the chains." Then they heaved me into the drink.

The chain and padlock acted as weights so I went down head foremost. I had to cut myself out of the bag with my pocket knife. It only took me about thirty seconds to get loose, but there was a strong current in the river and I was carried far downstream. When I came to the surface, I was a couple of hundred yards below the wharf. I was supposed to come up at the same spot where I'd gone—carrying the undamaged bag. I'd lost the bag, but I started to swim upstream underwater. Long before I got to the wharf, the crowd had gotten tired of waiting and had gone home. All in all, it was a pretty embarrassing experience.

The Impossible, who had been waiting for me on the wharf, told me he'd had a darn time of it too. The local hardware dealer who had loaned us the bag had raised hell when I didn't reappear carrying the bag as I'd promised. He told everybody that this was the last time he'd ever loan anything to carnival workers. "There were moments he became so aggressive that I was almost tempted to pay for the damn thing to shut him up," remarked the Impossible. The hardware dealer never did get his bag back and after that I limited myself to stage exhibitions.

At the Impossible's suggestion, I specialized in escaping from coffins. The Impossible wanted me to let the committees bury the coffin first, but I drew the line at that. When we opened in a new town, I'd go to the local undertaking parlor and offer them a lot of free publicity in exchange for escaping from one of their coffins. The parlor would exhibit the coffin in their window with a sign I provided, saying there was only enough air in a coffin to keep a man alive five minutes, so if I didn't escape in that time, I might as well stay where I was.

I always made the escape on a Saturday night. The afternoon before the show, I asked to have the coffin brought to the tent so we could build a stand for it on the inside platform. As soon as it was delivered, I'd take the bolts out of one side and put in some faked ones that opened in the middle. After that, the coffin never left the lot, but a few minutes before the escape, I had six canvasmen carry it into the tent to give the impression that it had only just arrived.

After I'd gotten in the coffin, a committee chosen from the tip would nail the lid on. Coffins have a crossbar running around the top and the lid was nailed into this so I could still get out the side once the grifted bolts had been loosened. A screen was put up between me and the tip so I could make my escape. Bronko, who acted as M.C., would stand on the platform in front of the screen and call off the seconds while the audience was waiting hopefully for me to suffocate.

I could get out of most coffins in less than a minute so to heighten the effect I'd sit on the box and read the *Billboard* until it was time to make a dramatic appearance. Bronko made me stop this because the tip could hear me turning the pages and the cowboy sometimes had to shout out the seconds to drown the noise I made.

I also did a handcuff escape, the cuffs being supplied by the local cops. This was easy. There are only about thirty-five types of cuffs in use, and the Impossible had master keys for all of them. But the average handcuff lock is so simple it's hardly worth while to use a key. Most of them spring open if you bang them against something hard. Policemen use cuffs only while transporting a criminal from one place to another, and the lawman is there all the time to make sure the prisoner doesn't have a chance to fool with the cuffs. Escaping from handcuffs is the simplest trick in an escapist's repertoire.

Opening pin-tumbler locks is much harder. Pin-tumblers are the toughest of all locks to pick. I did a challenge act, offering to pick open any locks brought to me by members of the tip. Whenever I saw a pin-tumbler coming up, I sweated until I had it open.

Pin-tumblers all work on the same basic principle. Inside the lock are a number of little cylinders, usually six or eight, that slide down into the keyhole. These cylinders or tumblers are each cut through at a different place and all these cuts must be perfectly lined up for the lock to open. When the key is put into the lock, it forces up all these tumblers which then drop down against the notched edges of the key. The key has been designed so that each bump on it pushes up its pin just the right distance for the pins to line up correctly. With all the pins in line, the key can turn and open the lock.

Because you cannot tell when all the tumblers have been lined up correctly, you must use a tension tool. This tool looks something like a tiny niblick. You put in the tension tool and turn it so that a pressure is constantly kept on the lock, then as soon as the tumblers are lined up, the lock will open.

With the tension tool in place, you begin to adjust the tumblers with a little pick that looks like the instrument a dentist uses to find holes in your teeth. I always covered myself with a black cloth when I was picking a lock so the tip couldn't see what I was doing. I used a little lipstick-sized flashlight such as women carry in their purses. I held it in my teeth and operated it by pressing the base with my tongue. A little cone of paper around the flash kept me from getting anything but a pinpoint of light right in the keyhole. All I needed to work was just an occasional flash of light.

Different types of locks require different picks. The Impossible made sets of picks for interested people as a sideline. He sold them for twenty-five dollars a set. But he was always careful to make sure first that his clients weren't crooks. He invariably asked them, "Do you intend to use these picks for any dishonest purpose?" His customers always said that they didn't.

Many people refuse to believe that locks can be picked even when they see it done. While we were playing in Illinois, I got an off-the-lot job one afternoon giving a show for some kids at a school. Naturally, I didn't show the children any lock-picking, so no one knew my talent along these lines. After the show, the principal remarked casually that it was a pity he had forgotten his keys as he wanted to make a phone call from his office. I decided I'd give the man a little surprise, so I went over and examined the door.

The lock was a lever, which means that instead of tumblers it had a series of little plates or levers that fitted into grooves in the bolt to keep it from sliding. Each of these levers had a notch in the end and the notches in the key corresponded to these lever notches. When the key was turned, it would lift all these levers together the right height, so the bolt could be pulled back. Levers are pretty good locks, so I was surprised when I opened it the first crack.

The principal stared from the open door to me for a moment and then said briskly, "Ah, someone must have left the door unlocked," and he went in to make his call.

While he was gone, I examined the lock. It had been made for master keying. The last lever was a master lever. When it was lifted, it lifted all the other levers with it. The regular key wouldn't go far enough to reach it, but there must have been an extra-long master key that was probably in the possession of the janitor. I decided the chances were that all the doors along the corridor had locks made the same way.

I decided I'd give the principal a thrill. By the time he'd finished phoning, I'd opened every door in the hall and had even picked open the cash drawer in the main

office. When the principal walked out, his face was really a study. Then he gave a little cough and said irritably, "Enough of this foolishness, boy. Help me lock up." I helped him close all the doors and, as we left, he rubbed his hands together proudly and said, "Ah, at last everything is safe!" He would have made a wonderful bank manager.

I don't mean to imply that lock-picking is easy. Even with the specially made picks, opening a good pin-tumbler lock is a job for an expert. Professional burglars seldom know anything about lock-picking. A burglar enters a house by jimmying open a window or cutting the lock out of the door with a drill. Even locksmiths rarely try picking a lock. They use a set of skeleton keys. If the locksmith's "skellies" don't work, he simply breaks the lock. Lock-picking is a stage effect and actually has very little practical use. I worked at it for several weeks, but finally I had to admit that I'd never become a good lock man. It requires a skill I didn't possess.

I decided to retire as an escapist after a little incident that occurred while the carnival was playing Indianapolis. I was featuring a Challenge Escape, offering to let any member of the tip tie me up with ropes and escape in three minutes. I supplied the ropes and made sure they were so heavy and so thoroughly waxed that no knots would hold. One evening some farm boys raised so much trouble about my ropes that I told them they could tie me up in any way they wished.

The boys came back in an hour with some fishline. They had dreamed up a rope tie that was a honey. They ran a slipknot around my neck so if I struggled at all, I'd strangle. Then they secured the line to other parts of my anatomy, arranging it in such a way that if I tried to wriggle myself clear, I'd be seriously injured—and I mean seriously.

I wasn't scared. I was petrified. Just before Bronko put the screen in front of me for my escape, old man Krinko waddled up to examine the ties. He clucked with admiration and congratulated the local boys on their ingenuity. When he left the platform, I had in my hand a razor blade and a skein of fishline left over from the tying. It was as simple as that. I cut myself free, stuck the cut line in my pocket and came out with the other length of line all carefully knotted and tangled. The best part of the trick was listening to the explanations the farm boys had for my escape.

I felt a sense of relief when I finally decided to give up lock-picking. There was too much mechanical business mixed up in the act to suit me. But I'd gone about as far as I could with fire-eating and sword swallowing and was still interested in acquiring a new routine.

I was tired of "stunt" acts and I wanted to learn something that would bring me into closer contact with the people in our tips.

I told Billie about my ambition a couple of weeks later. The Model Show girls were giving a dance in their top that afternoon and Billie had asked me. The girls had prepared a "home-cooked" meal for their escorts and even though most of it came out of cans, it was still pretty good. The girls had talked the show's orchestra into coming and we danced on the stage where the girls did their nightly strip. Billie and I were sitting out one dance in the back of the tent. I explained to her that I wanted to do a routine that depended on handling people rather than props. She didn't think much of the idea.

"You don't know enough about people to swing it, Slim," she told me. Billie had dressed carefully for the dance in a neat little skirt and blouse. She looked very young and ingenuous sitting on a pile of soft sawdust with her slender legs cocked up under her. "I could handle an act like that. I understand people. But you don't."

I didn't think Billie's experience with Steve and the Model Show talker showed much knowledge of how to handle people, but I didn't say anything.

"Now you take Aunt Matty," Billie went on. "She really knows how people think. That's why she can run a good mitt camp." Mitt camp is carny slang for a palmistry concession—a place where you can get your mitts read. "Of course, she's made a scientific study of palmistry too, so she knows what all those lines and things mean."

"That palmistry is all a fake, Billie," I told her. "Aunt Matty just tells the marks that they'll meet a tall, dark stranger, take a long trip, and get money from an unexpected source. There's nothing to it."

"You don't know anything about it," said Billie with surprising warmth. "Aunt Matty is real good. She told me I was going to have two disappointments in love and then meet my heart's desire. The two disappointments were Steve and our talker. How could Aunt Matty know I was going to meet them if it wasn't on my palm?"

"Aunt Matty is just a nice old lady with a good line," I said.

"She is not. Aunt Matty used to be a very important person. When she was a young girl she was being kept by one of the most important men in America."

Billie said this as though Aunt Matty had been one of the co-discoverers of radium, but I refused to be impressed.

"Who was the important man, Abraham Lincoln? Aunt Matty is darned near old enough to date back to him," I remarked with the intolerance of the young.

"He was a big New York club man. She was a chorus girl in a big musical hit back in the nineties sometime and he saw her and got her a lovely apartment and gave her money and jewels and things. I think men, in those days, must'a been a much higher type then than they are now. Anyhow, it was very romantic and she really loved him. She was all broke up when he finally had to get married and leave her."

"How do you know all this?" I demanded.

"Sometimes Aunt Matty comes to our top in the afternoon and plays our piano. She plays old, old songs from big musical hits that ran before we were born.

Her boy friend used to take her to all the musicals and when they got back to her apartment, she'd play the songs for him on a little piano she had. When he left her, the piano was the last thing she sold. Aunt Matty told me about it one afternoon. Sometimes when she plays the old songs, she puts her head down on the keyboard and cries and cries. I felt sorry for her so once I went into the top when she was crying and put my arms around her. That was the time she told me."

"Poor old lady," I said sadly. "I wonder how she ever ended up reading mitts in a Ten-in-One."

"Well, believe me, I'm never going to make the mistake that she did," said Billie with determination. "She stuck with that man for ten years until she was an old broken-down woman over thirty. It's all right to fool around with men while you're young, but any time a man wants me to spend that long with him he'll have to trot out a marriage certificate."

Aunt Matty and I had always been very good friends, but I'd never thought much about her palmistry routine. When I first joined the carnival, I'd been particularly attracted by the strange, esoteric quality that many side show acts possess. Until now I'd been so interested in learning the more spectacular routines that I'd almost forgotten about the pseudo-mystical acts like palmistry and mind reading that are as much a part of the standard side show exhibitions as fire-eating and sword swallowing. I decided to talk to Aunt Matty and see if there was anything to her palmistry act beside giving the marks a previously memorized spiel.

The next day I went to see Aunt Matty. The old lady lived in a trailer that wasn't much bigger than a doghouse but she kept it as neat as a bandbox. In spite of her ridiculous pompadour and old-fashioned clothes, Aunt Matty was a careful dresser. The white ruffles on her blouse were always starched and gleaming white. There was never a trace of lint on her black dress and her gray hair was invariably brushed and held neatly in place by a big tortoise-shell comb.

Aunt Matty was sitting outside her trailer when I came up. She had a small electric stove going, hooked to a connection in her trailer, and was having her eleven o'clock cup of tea. As always, she greeted me cordially and asked me to sit down. Aunt Matty was a palmistry enthusiast and she willingly explained to me about the Girdle of Venus, the Circle of Mars, the Mount of Saturn, and the various crisscrossing lines. Halfway through the first lesson, a terrible suspicion dawned on me.

"Say, you actually believe in this stuff!" I exclaimed. Aunt Matty regarded me gravely. "Certainly. I wouldn't tell people anything I didn't think was true."

This was such a radical departure from all carnival ethics that I couldn't believe my ears.

"But any doctor will tell you there's nothing to palmistry," I protested.

"That is simply because they haven't investigated the subject thoroughly," Aunt Matty gently explained.

Aunt Matty.

She was so obviously sincere that I began to wonder if maybe there wasn't something to palmistry. After taking a few more lessons and getting the general hang of the business, I plagued Aunt Matty to let me listen in on some of her palm-reading sessions. She gently refused.

"I regard my clients as a doctor does his patients. What they tell me and what I tell them is in strict confidence."

I argued that even doctors allow medical students to watch them operate and finally Aunt Matty reluctantly consented. Aunt Matty read palms in a tiny curtained booth near the entrance to the blow-off.

There obviously wasn't room for me as well as Aunt Matty and her client. Besides, Aunt Matty explained that my presence would make her customers nervous. So we decided it would be best for me to sit inside the blow-off and listen through the thin curtains.

In country districts, Aunt Matty usually opened her booth for business in the afternoon although the regular side show performance didn't begin until around six o'clock. She would stand outside the side show entrance in her gypsy costume beside an enormous cardboard human hand. Across the palm of the hand was a notice saying that the gypsy queen was available for private readings. A few people came on the midway in the afternoon because some of the rides were open then, but most of Aunt Matty's business came from word-of-mouth advertising. People who'd gotten a reading told their friends about her. Aunt Matty frequently did more business in the afternoons than in the evenings.

As I had nothing to do in the afternoons, I settled myself in the blow-off after lunch with a magazine and waited for Aunt Matty to bring in her first client. The first customer was a woman. I watched her come into the side show top with Aunt Matty through a division in the blow-off curtains. The mark was a plumpish, well-corseted lady, hovering between overripe youth and middle age. I saw them enter the booth and then settled myself to listen.

"Let me see your left hand," said Aunt Matty. There was a pause and then the palmist said, "I see something is troubling you. I feel it is either business, under which I include money matters; or affairs of the heart. Am I right?"

I chuckled to myself as virtually every problem can be classified under one of these headings. The woman gave an embarrassed laugh. "Well, sort of," she acknowledged. This wasn't much help, so Aunt Matty went on. "Now although you're the home-loving type, I can see great success for you in the business world."

"I guess you would, seeing as I'm the personal secretary to Mr. Boyman and he's the assistant vice-president of the Lynn Valley Meat Packing Corporation," said the woman proudly. "He said to me the other day, 'I don't know what I'll do when you get married and leave us, Miss Davis.' Well, I laughed the way you would, you know, and I said, 'I don't figure on getting married *yet*, Mr. Boyman. None of the men who've pro-

posed to me are what I want. I've got pretty high ideals about the man I intend to marry. Lot of men are giving me a big rush and spending of sorts of money on me. They're all right to run around with, but I just can't see marrying one of them.'"

"You remember I could tell immediately that you were in business," said Aunt Matty wisely. "Now here I see a man coming into your life."

"What's he like?" the woman's tone was faintly tinged with interest.

"He's an older man, distinguished-looking, dresses well and makes a great deal of money."

"That sounds like Mr. Boyman," said the woman with a forced laugh. "But he isn't coming into my life now."

"By coming into your life I mean he's beginning to take an interest in you," explained Aunt Matty. "Your lives have been running alongside each other and now they join. I'll have to cast his horoscope." Like many mentalists, Aunt Matty mixed several methods of clairvoyance together. "Do you happen to know when his birthday is?"

"It's September twenty-first," said the woman softly, and even *I* knew now that Aunt Matty was on the right track.

"The stars have been against you for some time," Aunt Matty continued. I could hear the confidence in her voice. "That is what has stood between you and him all these years."

"Well, maybe," said the woman doubtfully. "But I don't think it was altogether the stars. I've got a feeling it's his wife and three children that's been holding things up."

Aunt Matty said hurriedly, "Yes, I can see he's a married man. This must be another man I see."

"You . . . you don't see a divorce for Mr. Boyman?" said the woman timidly.

"No, I don't," said Aunt Matty very flatly.

"I didn't expect anything," said the woman in a regretful voice. "I gave up hoping years ago. When I get too old to work, he'll let me out and then what'll I do? You can't save anything on a woman's salary."

"The man I see can't be Mr. Boyman," said Aunt Matty commiseratingly. "It's someone else who wants to marry you that you haven't met yet."

"I'm sorry, but I don't want to hear about him," said the woman in a mournful voice. "I guess you got other customers out there and I'm taking more than my time. That was a real good fortune and I'm grateful for it."

Most of Aunt Matty's customers were women—about eighty per cent of them. But there were a number of men. I remember one especially—a thin, fidgety fellow who entered coughing apologetically. He wore glasses and Aunt Matty told me later that he had a nervous habit of continually taking them on and off.

"Just give me your hand," I heard Aunt Matty say. "No, the other hand. That's right." There was a pause while she examined the palm and then she repeated the business-health-love formula. The man coughed and laughed.

"Now that's right," he said and coughed again. "When you say I got money worries, you hit the nail right on the head, ma'am. I guess that's a pretty common complaint in these times, though. I hope you see some improvement for me."

"I see a change for the better, although not immediately," said Aunt Matty in her usual grave manner. "It will start in a few months and be so gradual that you may not notice it at first."

"I'm glad to hear that," said the man. "I got quite a family to support. My wife and four kids and then there's the old gentleman. He's my father. Been bedridden for years."

"That's a terrible thing, having a sick person in the house," suggested Aunt Matty.

"Oh, he's a fine old gentleman and he did a lot for me," said the man with honest feeling. "Once when I was a kid, he pawned some of his clothes to buy me food and medicine. He even bought me some toys at the same time. What I always think is, there's men who would have got the food and the medicine, but not many who'd a remembered to get a child toys so he wouldn't grieve."

"That was very thoughtful," agreed Aunt Matty. "He must be a lovely person."

"He is," was the sincere answer. "But he's been ill a long time now. You haven't any idea what a terrible expense doctors are until you actually have to pay their bills. My wife not only has to nurse the old gentleman, but do all the housework herself. As for our poor kids, the other children at school laugh at them because their clothes are so shabby. Often they come home crying. But we're all glad to help the old gentleman because the doctors say they think they can keep him alive another couple of years or even more. Now this is what I wanted to ask you. Father's been suffering a great deal these last three or four years. Do you think he's going to get any better?"

"When was he born?"

"August eighteenth, 1868. He's eighty-two."

There was a pause while Aunt Matty cast the horoscope. Then she reported. "I see a death in your family in the near future."

"Poor old gentleman," said her client with real regret. "I certainly hope you're wrong, ma'am. It's wonderful, though, how you folks can tell these things and how right you always are."

"Do you want your own reading next?" asked Aunt Matty.

"No thank you, ma'am. I just dropped in to see if there was any relief in sight for the old gentleman. Thank you very much," and he left.

Although Aunt Matty never gave exactly the same reading twice, she had certain standard formulas that I got to recognize. She once told me simply, "I divide all women into two main groups—those that are married and those who are just trying to be." In college I had been taught that modern woman doesn't regard marriage as the goal of her existence and is perfectly willing to compete with men on an equal footing. Aunt Matty had obviously never heard of this theory. She based all her readings on the principle that the woman who came to her were mainly interested in love problems. "I see that you're worried about some man," she generally began and her client would usually take it from there.

If her clients wouldn't talk, Aunt Matty tried one after another of her set formulas until she struck a responsive chord. "This is a very unusual palm . . . I've never seen one like it before in all my experience," she would say. "Haven't you often felt that you were a very unusual person—quite different from your friends and acquaintances?" This usually started a gush of words, but if it didn't Aunt Matty would try another lead. "Many men have been interested in you, but not the man you've always dreamed about. You're still waiting for Mr. Right to come along." If a client seemed suspicious or querulous, Aunt Matty would suggest, "I see someone is working against you. Don't you suspect that one of your female acquaintances is talking about you behind your back?" If the client showed some reaction, Aunt Matty would continue, "We'll see if your suspicions are correct. What is the first letter of your so-called friend's name?" The client would write the letter on a slip of paper and she and Aunt Matty would clasp hands over it. "Now spell out the name silently to yourself. So that I can keep in psychic rhythm with you, squeeze my hand at every letter." As Aunt Matty already knew the initial letter of the name, she could usually give a pretty good guess as to what it was when she knew the number of letters in it. The client would probably swear afterward that Aunt Matty had called out the name without being told a single thing. Aunt Matty always told the client to ignore the gossiper. "You are too far superior to such a person to descend to her level," Aunt Matty would explain.

Sometimes Aunt Matty would run into a client who refused to give her any help whatsoever. Aunt Matty never wasted any time on this type. She had a special spiel memorized for such occasions starting with, "You are a sensitive, intelligent person, but have had occasional bad breaks in the past that were not your fault. I see conditions improving for you, etc." She would reel this memorized speech off very fast and then say briefly, "Did I make any mistakes?" The client would have to admit the reading was basically correct and Aunt Matty would say, "One dollar, please." That would be that.

Occasionally Aunt Matty would look closely at a woman's hand and say suddenly, "When was the last time you contemplated suicide?" She never tried this dramatic question unless she knew the woman was married. According to her, virtually all married women contemplate suicide at some time or other. The client would often burst into tears and leave the booth groggy. This always greatly impressed any other marks who might be waiting to come in.

Usually Aunt Matty made a real effort to help her clients. If a woman said she was contemplating divorce, Aunt Matty would cast her horoscope and say, "The stars aren't propitious for divorce proceedings at the moment. The signs look better three months from now." By that time the woman would probably change her mind. If a young girl came into say she was planning to elope with a boy, Aunt Matty would ask her a few questions about her sweetheart and then cast the young couple's horoscopes. If she didn't like what the girl had told her, she would shake her head. "Your horoscopes show that you are not soul-mates," she would explain. If she were doubtful, Aunt Matty would ask the girl to bring in her boy friend so she could read his palm. If the boy made a good impression, Aunt Matty would suggest that the girl bring her parents to have their horoscopes cast. If Aunt Matty felt that the parents were being unreasonable, she would say, "I strongly suggest that you let the young couple get married—as soon as possible. I can see something in your daughter's palm that makes this very advisable." Although Aunt Matty never went into particulars, this usually resulted in cementing the match.

Aunt Matty did really believe in palmistry. She was a gentle, fundamentally honest person who would probably rather have starved to death than take money under false pretenses. The instructions in books of palmistry are so contradictory and confused that the final analysis is really up to the palmist herself. Aunt Matty knew people. It makes no difference to someone who has this gift, whether she uses palmistry, astrology, tea-leaf reading or handwriting. She can always give you a good reading—just as Sherlock Holmes was able to tell his clients' professions and temperaments at a glance. But the seer must employ some pseudo-scientific device to justify her readings—not only to her clients but also to herself. Otherwise she stands convicted in her own eyes as a hypocrite and very few people can go through life admitting that they are complete frauds.

Aunt Matty was a poor person's psychologist. She was, to the best of her ability, analyzing her clients' troubles and trying to guide them. I remember a prominent psychologist, who had worked for years among the Navajo Indians, saying to me, "The Indian medicine men are very poor doctors but they're excellent psychologists." Aunt Matty was a modern medicine man. When trained psychologists can give character readings at a dollar a throw, people like Aunt Matty will no longer be needed. But until then they fill a definite public need.

I developed a great admiration for Aunt Matty. As far as I was concerned, she was the best showman on the lot. She believed her own spiels. Not even Mountmorency at his best could compete with the gentle sincerity of the old soubrette. A few weeks later

when Aunt Matty left the Ten-in-One to open her own separate mitt camp concession with another carnival, we all greatly missed her.

I think Billie missed the old lady even more than we did. The girl had been spending more time at our top than she did at her own. Most of her visits were to Aunt Matty. I'd often see the two women sitting outside the palmist's little trailer, Aunt Matty knitting and Billie nervously puffing on a cigarette and talking a blue streak. What the two women talked about, I never knew, but after the palmist had gone, Billie seemed lonely. Often Billie and I would go on picnics or take in the afternoon shows at the local movie houses. From remarks Billie let drop, I guessed she was getting tired of the posing business and wanted to progress to something else—either the stage or marriage. I was in no position to help her with either ambition and Billie realized it. So although she was fond of me, Billie was rather restless on our dates, as though she knew that she was only killing time until something more important came along.

Krinko missed Aunt Matty also, but for purely practical reasons. Her loss left a gaping hole in the show. Then one evening the old fakir stumped triumphantly into the top to announce that he had cornered one of the top-notch mentalist teams in the country. "They called Mr. and Mrs. Moyer," he told us happily. "Read minds, make horoscopes, tell future, very talented. I no have to pay them . . . they pay me for chance to get at the public. All we need do is get tip for them. They do the rest."

The idea of an act paying the side show manager to be allowed to play was a new one to me. I couldn't understand how the Moyers expected to make money. But we all congratulated Krinko and awaited the arrival of the new act with great interest.

A couple of days later, I was coming back to the lot, after helping May take her snakes for a swim in a river. Sultan, May's big rock python, could glide through the dark-brown water like a streak of copper-colored light. He showed the most remarkable dexterity in coiling up his great body in little depressions you wouldn't have thought could hold a dog. The great snake would lie there, watching you with his unwinking black eyes, while you walked around and screamed yourself hoarse looking for him.

All in all, I was glad when May and I got them safely back to the lot. As I came up behind the side show top, I ran across a brand-new bright green living top hopping around as though it had sat down on an ant hill. First an arm would stick out of a flap. Then a head would poke out and suddenly go back again like a Punch and Judy show. It was a wonderful sight and I stopped to watch it.

Finally the whole top fell down and lay there panting. After a pause, the canvas began to twitch and a little wire-haired man followed by a woman four times his size came slowly crawling out. They sat down side by side, looking very tired, and stared at the big side show tent respectfully.

At last the woman said in a tone of voice most people reserve for speaking of the miracles of the Bible, "How do you suppose they ever put up one like that, Mr. Moyer?" She nodded a couple of her chins at the side show.

"It's just a knack," said the little man, panting but very confident. "You'n I could put up that big tent just like that," and he snapped his fingers, "if we knew how, now let's see." He scratched his cheeks with both hands. "Let's look at that big tent again and see how it's done."

Naturally there's no similarity between erecting a big circus tent like the side show top and putting up a little living tent. I came over and offered to help them. The fat woman smiled and got up to shake my hand. She seemed like a friendly person. But the little man was plainly on his dignity and simply nodded.

"This is the first time we ever worked under canvas, so we don't know nothing about tents," the woman explained to me.

"That Krinko who runs this concession oughta sent over half a dozen roustabouts to set up our tent," said the man, waving a hand at their tiny umbrella job. "Now that he's gotten us all signed up for the season, he's forgotten about us. Madam's absolutely right. We never worked in a carnival before and we wouldn't be now, except that I had a little trouble with them boardwalk pirates at Seaview where we generally spend the summer."

"What's your act?" I asked.

The little man gave me a terrible look while the woman cried out, "Oh, Mr. Moyer don't have an *act*. He does strictly scientific work only." She waved one hand at a stand with a poster on it which was about the only thing they'd managed to set up.

I walked over and examined it. There was a picture of a human head cut up into slices, each one marked with something like "Courage," "Truth," "Love," and a drawing below. "Love" was a couple sitting on a stone bench holding hands, and "Courage" was a man killing a lion with a sword.

I still didn't realize that these two were the world-famous mentalists Krinko had told us about. They seemed more like harmless lunatics. "What do you do, tell fortunes?" I asked.

That seemed to be the wrong thing to say too. The little man screamed, "Tell fortunes!" as if I'd insulted his mother. His wife moaned, "Tell fortunes! Oh no!"

She was going to say something more, but her husband interrupted her.

"Wait, let's be calm, Madam," he said, putting one hand on her shoulder. "Let's take this whole thing easy. Look!" he went on dramatically, coming over to me. "Look in my eyes!" he snapped his fingers and then stretched out his neck toward me. We stared at each other but nothing much seemed to happen. "It don't work so good because you're so much taller than me," he muttered, looking around for something to stand on. "Well, never mind about that." He snapped his fingers in front of my face again. "Now concentrate!"

"What on?" I asked. It seemed a natural question.

"Never mind about that now. Just concentrate. Project your thoughts like they was pictures so as to impress them on my highly sensitive brain. Now stand closer for the mental vibrations. Ah, I got it! Next kindly think of something not possibly known to me. Got it? Good!"

I tried to think of something quickly, but all I could think of was a fish dinner I'd eaten that noon.

"Now I read your mind like it was an open book; never having seen you, never having met you before." He intoned it like a chant. "You been thinking of something, right? Now I read your mind and tell you what you been thinking of. You been thinking I haven't got no real powers, that I can't read minds. Am I right, quick, tell me."

"No," I told him. "I didn't have much chance to think, but I was thinking about a certain fish dinner."

"You mean you never doubted my powers?"

"Possibly I did."

"That's the thought he picked up," explained Madam Moyer while her husband nodded wisely. "That was your main thought, so that's what he picked up."

I began to realize they had a system here and became more interested.

"You want to take in our performance tonight," urged Mr. Moyer. "It's wonderful how I can take a crowd of people and lay bare everything they're thinking. I don't use no hooks, wires, gimmicks, or other devices. I just work with my hands and this." He tapped his forehead.

The Moyers weren't exactly my idea of magicians, but I knew they were probably the closest thing to real magicians I was likely to meet. At last I was going to work with someone who claimed supernatural powers. With a light heart I started setting up their living top for them, looked forward to a very interesting acquaintanceship.

CHAPTER 11

Every performer I'd seen in carnival got his props together with the smooth efficiency of a well-oiled machine. The Moyers were an exception. Everyone with the show watched in fascinated astonishment while Mr. and Mrs. Moyer prepared to put on their act that evening. I wanted to help them, but the Moyers were so busy running back and forth between their car and the side show top carrying boxes of horoscopes and lucky charms that I didn't like to interfere. But finally Mr. Moyer dropped a crystal ball on his toe, and while he was howling and jumping around I asked Madam Moyer if there was anything I could do for them. She was carrying a pile of poles and red velvet drapes and I could see it would take them an hour to get the sawdust off the velvet as it was.

"Maybe you could set this booth up for us," said the Madam doubtfully. "We got it second-hand but the former owner didn't use it for anything but materializing ghosts and that oughtn't to have hurt it none. I know I got the directions for putting it up around here somewhere, because last week I tried to fit the crystal ball into its stand with them and got awful queer results."

Paul, the canvasman, and I got the booth up. Madam Moyer helped us. It was quite an undertaking, although later Paul was able to assemble it in five minutes when he didn't have to worry about getting Madam Moyer fastened up inside by mistake. When we finally finished, Mr. Moyer limped up and wanted to know where his dressing room was.

I suggested he dress in the blow-off. Jolly Daisy was still in her living top and that left the curtained-off section of the top empty except for Dot, the five-legged horse. But before retiring to the blow-off, the Moyers obviously wanted a chance to exhibit their really very handsome costumes before us. They unpacked a huge suitcase, putting on a sham discussion as to which of their several outfits they should wear. Mr. Moyer at last decided on a beautiful white satin turban, with a red jeweled spider in the center, and his tuxedo. He tried on the turban while his wife held a hand mirror and then turned to me proudly.

"I don't know if you've noticed it, but I'm a little shorter than you," he explained. Mr. Moyer was pushing five foot four. "This turban gives me a lot of height. Well, Madam, I guess we'd better dress for the show."

They went into the blow-off while I began to get my own apparatus ready. I was pouring gasoline into my burning and soaking bowls, when Madam Moyer dashed frantically out of the blow-off and loped across the sawdust toward me.

"Hurry!" she gasped. "The horse has swallowed Mr. Moyer's turban."

I raced for the entrance to the blow-off and pushed through the folded curtain. Inside there was only a single red bulb lighted but I could see Dot, the five-legged horse, standing in her little canvas-hung stall. The end of the turban was still hanging out of her mouth and Mr. Moyer was holding onto it for dear life.

"Kick her in the slats!" he panted. "She's got herself braced so I can't get no purchase. This is a hell of a thing to happen to a mentalist, I must say!"

When Dot saw me coming, she tried to do a quick swallowing job and nearly pulled Mr. Moyer into the stall. I rushed in and grabbed the sleeve. We whipsawed it back and forth until we got some slack and I could take a twist with the sleeve around my hand. After that it was just a matter of pulling. Madam Moyer wound the turban into shape again, moaning over it, and Mr. Moyer put it back on. It was a little damp.

He was very annoyed. "I'm liable to catch cold wearing it wet like this," he complained. "I think that darn brute's half-goat. You'd think they'd get a good act in here that wouldn't eat people's clothes."

I leaned over and scratched Dot's ear to show her the whole thing had been a misunderstanding. She pulled back with a snort, then bent over and began to nuzzle one of my buttons with her soft nose. I didn't need the button much anyway and while she was eating it, I stroked her neck. Dot was a nice horse, but as she had never been broken in, she was apt to be temperamental.

I'd have thought that the atmosphere of a carnival side show would have destroyed the air of solemn mystery necessary for a mind reading act. Actually, I don't suppose there's any better place to put on a mentalist demonstration than in a Ten-in-One. The whole mood of a side show top is mysterious. Once the tip has entered the tent and left behind the noise and lights of the midway, they find themselves in the quiet, not too brightly lighted top full of uncanny props and strange people. After the tip has watched a woman handle live rattlesnakes, a man eat fire, and a fakir walk barefoot up a ladder of sharp swords, it no longer seems illogical that a strange-looking little man wearing a huge turban can read their minds.

The Moyers worked from the inside platform. Mr. Moyer looked fine. His turban was almost dry and he had a blue cloak thrown over his evening clothes. Madam Moyer sat beside him on a folding chair in a blue evening dress that matched the cloak. Her bulk gave her a certain dignity. Mr. Moyer opened his patter in a quick, confident tone that didn't give people a chance to begin to doubt him.

"Friends, I am worried that you may confuse the performance we are going to present this evening with ordinary exhibitions of so-called fortunetellers and mind readers. I don't do fortunetelling as I am above it and also it's illegal in this state. I am a scientific thought-analyzer and tell your past, present, and future, describing your traits, temperments, likes and dislikes, never having seen you, never having met you before."

He took a packet of envelopes from the table beside him.

"First, I am going to give each and every one of you here tonight a free reading, such as you would have to pay from fifty cents to five dollars for elsewhere. But before I do, I want to introduce to you a wonderful little invention, brought from the sacred Lamas of Tibet, to be given away free!"

He held up a box full of beans.

"These beans are said to bring the owners good luck. Not only that, but they perfume the whole person, keep moths out of the clothing, prevent illness, attract members of the opposite sex, and bring success. At least, that is what is claimed for them by scientists and professors all over the world. All I claim is that they are genuine beans."

"Now," he went on, taking up a pile of colored papers, "I have a collection of forecasts for this year, personal forecasts for you personally. You notice each sheet is dated for a sign of the zodiac. Each and every one of you has been born under one of these signs because there's one for every month of the year and you had to be born in some month. I guess everybody here will grant me that."

He paused impressively and as no one spoke, he went on triumphantly.

"That being the case, it proves that astrology is a genuine science, endorsed by professors and doctors everywhere and you can't afford to be without one of these charts which tells you everything you might want to know; what sort of a girl you should marry, what illness you should beware of, or if you will travel, make money, have success or failure."

He stopped to adjust his cloak and to kick Madam Moyer who had fallen asleep. She awoke with a slight scream.

"Now folks, the value of these charts is one dollar and well worth it. You get three pages of reading matter and a handsome picture in three colors on the front. Tonight I am asking only fifty cents. In addition to that, you get absolutely free one of these genuinely lucky beans and a complete reading from Madam Moyer, who is a scientific palm reader, physiognomist, cartomancist, numerologist, and astrologer. Now I am going to pass among you with these beans and charts and who's the first?"

The whole side show troupe watched in wonder while the massacre was going on. I began to understand why the Moyers were able to pay old man Krinko to let them appear in the show. Their horoscopes were such an effective after-catch that all the couple needed was someone to collect a tip for them. They could do the rest. After Mr. Moyer had made sure that no one in the tip had any loose change left in his pocket, he proceeded to the next part of his act.

"Now, folks, everyone who has bought one of the horoscopes is entitled to ask Madam Moyer a question. As she can read your minds, all you need to do is think of your questions. But to help you concentrate, I'll distribute these cards and you can write your questions on them. All the ladies will want to know the real dope about their boy friends, husbands, or somebody else's husband. The men will find that Madam Moyer can advise them about financial matters, just as she has been doing for years for the leading bankers on Wall Street. Ask her about missing objects, like keys, jewelry, husbands or children. Simply write your question on one of these cards and then seal it in one of the individual envelopes which I'll hand you. I never see these questions in any way, shape, or form but please write plain."

He passed through the crowd, handing out the cards and the envelopes. I noticed that Paul had quietly joined the tip. Paul pretended to write on the card but I could tell by his actions that he was only going through the motions. Then the canvasman put the card in an envelope and sealed it up. Mr. Moyer collected it with the other envelopes on his way back to the platform. As the mentalist passed me, I saw him slip Paul's contribution to the bottom of the pile of envelopes in his hand.

Mr. Moyer climbed back on the platform and, picking off the top envelope, held it against his wife's forehead. After a few preliminary shudders, Madam Moyer pointed out over the tip's heads toward Paul.

"I get vibrations from over there," she announced. "I get the initial T. Has someone there the first name of Tom?"

Paul said that was he.

"You want to know about your brother, Tom. Is that right?" Paul called out that it was. "Your brother left home several years ago . . . four years, I think. Now concentrate on his name. I get it now. His name is John. I can see John very plainly. He's in a hotel in Chicago. He is partly bald and has a scar on his right wrist he got playing baseball with you. Am I correct in every detail?"

Paul acknowledged that it was wonderful.

"You want to know where you can reach him. Well, his address is North Capital Avenue 4567. You can write him there."

Paul said he'd do that. The tip was staring goggle-eyed. The Moyers had made a knockout impression, but Mr. Moyer didn't leave it at that.

"I've just picked up your last vibration!" he yelled. "You doubt Madam Moyer's powers! I'm going to read your question aloud so everyone can see the Madam got it correct." He tore open the envelope and pretended to read off the question. I knew Paul's envelope was at the bottom of the pile, so Mr. Moyer had now opened someone else's query. Mr. Moyer threw the card on the table in front of Madam Moyer very carelessly. "Now in front of all these people here, I'll tell you what you've got in you pockets." He called off a list of things and Paul, obviously very much abashed, admitted that he was right. "Now get out of here!" thundered Mr. Moyer. "And if there are any more skeptics in the audience, I'll treat them the same way."

Paul slunk away with everyone in the tip laughing at him. Obviously no one would try to interrupt the act now for fear of being made a fool of like Paul. Mr. Moyer picked up another envelope and held it against his wife's head. She read off the message lying on the table in front of her as though it were the one her husband was holding. Mr. Moyer became worried about her interpretation, so he opened the envelope in his hand to check it. Thus keeping one message ahead, they went through the whole pile of envelopes.

I was disappointed that a mentalist's routine was so simple. I had expected a really ingenious exhibition of sleight-of-hand. But the Moyers were certainly taking in the cash. After finishing the message-reading, Mr. Moyer announced that anyone wishing a more complete reading could see Madam Moyer in her booth, and have his personal problems solved for him at one dollar a problem. This started a stampede to the red velvet booth. By the end of the evening, I computed that the couple must have taken in over a hundred bucks. Even if they had a sixty-forty split with old man Krinko, this wasn't bad. I decided to investigate mentalism more thoroughly.

After listening to the couple for several evenings, I decided that the Moyers' basic technique lay in their manner of answering the questions submitted to them. How they managed to find out what was in the

Mr. Moyer doing his mind-reading routine.

envelopes was unimportant. There are literally hundreds of methods known to magicians for finding out what is in a sealed envelope. But the method itself is nothing; the manner in which it is presented is vital. I noticed that the Moyers never simply read out a message. They went through a very complicated process that immeasurably heightened the effect.

The Moyers' presentation was so effective that even I occasionally wondered if they didn't have flashes of genuine mental telepathy. One evening while the couple was doing their act, Madam Moyer announced, "I get a mental vibration from someone in the audience about a financial deal." She paused, groaned, and rubbed her forehead as if in pain. "I think it's about the sale of a car. Is anyone here thinking about selling a car?"

A woman who had written one of the questions held up her hand. Madam Moyer continued. "You are wondering if your husband will succeed in selling his car, aren't you?" The woman admitted that she was anxious about the sale. "Well, I see that he will sell the car, but not for as much as you were hoping to get." Then Madam Moyer sighed and leaned back in her chair as though the reading were over.

Suddenly Mr. Moyer said to the woman. "I think Madam can even tell you the name of the town where your husband has gone to sell the car. But you'll have to concentrate on the name." Madam Moyer made a great mental effort, but couldn't get the name. Mr. Moyer turned to the tip. "All of you will have to help Madam. This is very difficult. Will you all concentrate . . . concentrate." He raised his clenched fists. There was a pause while Madam Moyer groaned and struggled as if in childbirth. Finally she cried out triumphantly, "The town is Monksford!"

This produced a sensation. Mr. Moyer held up his hand for silence. "Now concentrate on your name, remembering that neither Madam or I have ever seen or met you before. Try to project your name as though you were a radio station sending out waves." Madam Moyer groaned, pressing her temples with her fingertips. The tip was absolutely quiet. Finally Madam said, "I see the letter B. Yes, it's a B. Your name . . . your name is . . . is Betty?"

The crowd burst into applause. The Moyers seemed to be struggling against some tremendous cosmic force. Everyone was straining to help the couple in their fight. If some skeptic had gotten up and tried to expose the mentalists, I think the crowd might have lynched him.

When the applause had died down, Mr. Moyer said, "Now concentrate on your husband's name. He isn't even in this tent but miles away in Monksford trying to sell his car. That makes getting his name through vibrations much harder. Everyone here will have to help us on this."

I saw women in the tip twisting their handkerchiefs in anxiety as Madam Moyer fought to get the name. When she finally cried out, "The name is William!" people cheered with relieved tension.

Everyone except the most cynical skeptics wants to believe in the supernatural. To the tip, the Moyers weren't side show performers doing an act. They were magicians in the tradition of Chaldea and Egypt. They were gratifying a human desire nearly as deep and basic as the sexual urge. The Moyers had the same direct contact with the tip that a medicine man has with a primitive tribe.

After each show, Mr. Moyer tore up the messages and tossed them behind the inside platform. When the last performance was over that evening, I went behind the platform and collected the torn slips. I screwed one of the loosened electric bulbs into the socket so I would have some light and began to put the pieces of paper together. I finally located the woman's slip about the car. She had written, "Bill is going to Monksford to sell our car. Will he sell it?" The message was signed "Betty."

If Madam Moyer had simply read out the message as it had been written, most of the effectiveness of her performance would have been lost. By pretending to get bits of information from the woman by mental telepathy, the Moyers built up a simple stunt into an awe-provoking miracle.

While I was assembling the other slips, I heard a noise behind me. The Moyers had seen the light and returned to the side show top to investigate. Mr. Moyer came toward me bristling like an angry mouse.

"Trying to steal my act, are you?" he yelled, his shrill voice going up into an infuriated squeak. "You better stick to your swords and leave things requiring an eddecation to the eddecated."

"I didn't think you'd mind if I just looked over the old billets," I explained. "I'm very much interested in mentalism."

Madam Moyer, who had indignantly clumped up behind her husband, gave a contemptuous snort. Mr. Moyer continued to glower at me suspiciously.

"I used to be a pretty fair magician," I urged. "Maybe I could help you work some good sleight-of-hand moves into your racket."

At the word "racket," both the Moyers stiffened. Mr. Moyer drew himself up until he was nearly on tiptoes.

"You have insulted the esoteric macrocosm!" he told me. "You have violated the talismanic occult. You have profaned the secrets of the Kabala! The time has come to give you the works!"

"Oh, no, not that, Mr. Moyer!" cried his fat wife, her line of chins shaking with apprehension. "Maybe he'll say he's sorry and lay off spying on us."

But the little man had already begun to tuck up his cuffs. I wondered if he were going to fight me. "It's too late for half-measures now, Madam," he told her sternly. Then he turned to me. "Clasp your hands!" he ordered. I did. "Tighter! Tighter!" He began to run his hands over my wrists. "Tighter yet! Now your hands have grown together. You are unable to unclasp them. Try it!"

This is an old test that stage hypnotists use to see if a subject is susceptible to hypnosis. I unclasped my hands easily. Instead of being disconcerted, Mr. Moyer turned to his wife triumphantly.

"See, no powers of concentration," he remarked.

She shook her head sadly.

"No will power, no determination."

"Poor boy!" Madam Moyer admitted.

"Low-grade moron!" agreed Mr. Moyer. He turned to me. "Look, punk, what do you know of the hidden mysteries of ancient Egypt? What about the weird powers of the Orient? Do you know that the yogis of India possess powers that enable them to rule the world?"

"Then why don't they rule the world?" I asked.

"What? Well, for the same reason you don't rule the world. Because they can't, that's why," said Mr. Moyer irritably. While I was trying to figure this one out, he added, "I hope you see now this is too big for you to handle. You better forget the whole thing and go on swallowing swords before the occult forces jump you."

The Moyers were rather cool to me after this interview, but I was very much interested in them. For some time now, I'd been wondering about my future in carnival. I didn't want to be a sword swallower the rest of my life. I'd hoped vaguely that carny might lead into a regular career and mentalism seemed to fit the bill. Men like Dunninger, the radio mind reader, have made a very good thing out of mentalism. Mind reading is good, clean work with plenty of opportunities for breaking into the big time. After watching the Moyers for a while, I felt there wasn't anything they did that I couldn't do, so I decided to study their "science." But before I had a chance to work anything out, a disaster hit the carnival that very nearly closed the whole organization down for the rest of the season.

CHAPTER 12

The carnival was playing a small resort town high up in the Ozarks. A great river had cut its way through the hills, gouging out a tremendous chasm almost a mile deep. A little town was glued to one side of this gorge; all the streets canted at a forty-degree slant. An enormous hotel, set high above the village, dominated everything but a great suspension bridge flung across the abyss. From our lot, the bridge looked like a child's construction toy and the great steel girders seemed to be made of the finest filigree work. In the early morning, mists from the river hung around the bridge like curls of smoke and white sea gulls flew over and under the great highway.

To support the gigantic cement foot of the bridge, a platform of earth had been raised beneath the beginning of the span. On this artificial lot, the carny was set-up. It was the only flat piece of ground in town. Of course, it was much too small and the tops had been framed so closely together that their guy ropes overlapped and the stakes of one show were almost against the sidewalls of its neighbors. There was room for only a few of the little living tops and most of the cars and trailers had to be parked elsewhere.

Everyone with the carnival was feeling very contented. We had had an exceptionally good season and in a couple of more weeks, the carnival would begin to play its close-of-season "still dates"—showing in conjunction with local fairs. "Still dates" are usually the most profitable part of the season because the fairs draw enormous crowds and the shows have no trouble getting their tips. For the last month, the weather was made to order for outdoor shows—cool but not chilly, with brilliant blue skies and enough tang in the air to make people want to get in their cars and start driving.

One afternoon while we were playing the bridge lot, Captain Billy, the Bronkos, the Impossible, and Billie and I decided to have a picnic. Carrying our food in paper bags, we crossed the sawdust-covered pavement beside the carny and struck out through the little town. A trail led from the village up the side of the gorge and we followed it until we came to a good picnic spot under some pine trees. From the brown mat of pine needles, we had a fine view of the whole canyon. We could see the bridge below us apparently floating in space. The air was so clear that every detail of the car-

nival was as sharp as though we were standing on the lot looking at the familiar set-up through the wrong end of a telescope. The brown canvas shone in the afternoon sunlight and the ebony shadows of the tops stood out hard and clean-cut against the yellow sawdust of the midway. The brilliant banners flapped in the easy breeze. They were the brightest spots of color on the midway except for the painted horses on the merry-go-round. Around the perfect circle of the tents stood a few trucks, axle-deep in the high grass. Behind the tops, some women were washing clothes. Men were sleeping in the sun. Some kids from the town were playing tag among the guy ropes. Somewhere a man was singing to a guitar. The carny had never looked more peaceful or more secure.

After we'd finished eating, everyone lay back on the soft pine needles, luxuriating in the wonderful weather and the glorious view. The Impossible had taken the precaution of bringing along a couple of bottles of beer and stacking them under a tree where they'd keep cool. He opened one of the bottles now and sat with it in his hand, looking benignly out over the river and the great hanging bridge.

"My heart has always been in the Middle West," said the old fellow contentedly. "According to rumor I was born somewhere near these parts. I believe that Mother was playing the tank towns when the blessed event came off. Ah, what a fine woman she was! The dear old lady never licked me but once. That was the time I forgot to put the hammer under the counter that she used to hit the marks over the head."

"Did all your folks run flat joints?" asked Lu curiously. A "flat joint" is the carny name for a gambling wheel that can be operated on a flat counter or hung against a flat backdrop.

"It was something of a family tradition," admitted the Impossible, taking another drink of beer from the bottle and wiping his whiskers. "But we have always been very versatile. I was once impresario of a repertoire group. In my youth, I owned a flea circus. I was working in a dime museum at the time. My performance went on at the same time as the Oriental Dancing Girls, as the two shows attracted a different type of clientele. My show was a definitely higher class of entertainment, however, because my fleas wore clothes which is more than you can say for the girls."

I was afraid Billie might take offense at this crack, but she only giggled. Billie was lying on her back beside me with her arm over her eyes to keep out the sun. She looked far more desirable stretched out on the soft pine needles than she had naked in the Model Show.

Captain Billy, who was sprawled out beside us, remarked, "When I was in merchant service, I used to collect fleas for flea circuses. Got ten cents apiece for them. It's only certain kinds of fleas you can train, though. In some places the fleas you get play dead and you can blow them around like dust. They're no good for show business."

"Human fleas are the only sort you can use," agreed the Impossible. "My circus opened with a parade of the fleas around the ring, led by Napoleon, the French flea, carrying a banner. I had several big production numbers, such as the Ben Hur chariot race, 'La Castina,' the Spanish flea who danced with castanets, and Daredevil David who did a Leap for Life off the top of a fountain pen. It was the only outfit I've ever been with that the performers didn't complain about the food. They had no cause to—they ate me. I was probably the most flea-bitten man in America."

I never knew how seriously to take the Impossible's reminiscences. All I could say was that I'd have enjoyed seeing the circus.

"Yes, it was quite a spectacle, m'boy. Unfortunately, my fleas perished in a conflagration. My car caught on fire one night. The police dragged me away while I was trying to rescue my cast. I screamed at them, 'There are forty fleas dying in that car,' but they wouldn't pay attention to me."

Suddenly a moaning sound came from the tall pines around us. Everyone sat up. Far down the river, the cliffs came together in a great V and through this cut showed a blue-black mass of clouds. In front of this terrible backdrop, golden streaks of lightning flickered spasmodically. A strong, damp wind began to blow in our faces and wave the little rock plants on the boulders. There was a terrible suggestiveness about the breeze. The trees seemed to sense it and tremble as it tickled their branches.

"We'd better get back to the show," said Captain Billy, rising abruptly. We hurriedly packed up what was left of the picnic and began to trot downhill toward the carny.

By the time we reached the village the wind had risen to a gale. Dust and rubbish were whirling about the streets and people were hastily slamming their windows shut against the coming storm. The clouds had covered half the sky now, and abruptly the sun was blotted out.

"We'd better get going, boys," said Captain Billy to Bronko and me. "This looks like a blow-down. They'll need us to drive stakes."

We ran ahead and left the women. Heavy drops of rain began to fall, pitting the dry dust in the gutters. The wind was tearing at shutters and ripping dead branches from the shade trees. The whole town seemed to sway with the fury of the storm. Houses gave the impression of holding onto their roofs. The storm was sweeping up the gorge and the village was almost as high as the thunderclouds. As a result, the lightning flashes seemed to be in the streets and the thunderclaps made the windows rattle beside me. The inky heart of the clouds was almost overhead but still only a few raindrops had fallen. Then as we reached the lot, some heavenly force really pulled out the plug. A quick flurry of drops followed by an avalanche of water broke over the town. In a moment the buildings were hidden by a sheet of rain. Before we could get to

the side show, the hard, dry surface of the lot was transformed into a mud pie.

As I ran under the marquee, I passed little bunches of canvasmen racing to double-stake the big shows before the full force of the gale reached us. I saw the carny's boss canvasman, his face slashed with rain, standing in the midway shouting, "Tear-down for a blow!" Dropping the big tops would take a couple of hours and there wasn't time for that, but everything that could be torn-down was being dropped as fast as possible. The storm had come up so suddenly that almost none of the shows were prepared to meet it. The canvas top of the bingo concession rolled past me, torn from its wooden supports by the wind. I saw Mountmorency and Paul, our canvasman, desperately trying to drop our banner line. The wind had bellowed out the banners like sails and they were almost unmanageable. I ran to help the two men.

The wind had become so terrible we could hardly stand against it. "Let the banners go and throw the blow lines over the top!" yelled Bronko. "That's worth more than the front." The blow lines are long lines, weighted at one end so they can be thrown over a tent. They are used to give the top additional support in bad storms.

As the cowboy spoke, Krinko came waddling toward us with the long blow lines coiled in his hand. He tried to speak to us but the scream of the wind was too shrill. Paul seemed to understand him. He waved his hand and loped around the tail of the tent to the back.

Bronko snatched one of the ropes from the old fakir and flung the weighted end over the top. Paul must have grabbed it from the other side, for the line began to twitch and tighten as if by itself. While the two men were fastening the blow lines to stakes, Krinko and I went around the top, double-staking the important guys. This was done by driving in an extra stake behind the one already holding the guy and then throwing a double tie around the two together. Bronko and Captain Billy dropped the banner line and then came to help us.

When we had the top fairly secure, we stopped for breath. Most of the midway seemed to be underwater. The ride boys on the Ridee-O were still working hard to cover the seats with the oilcloth slip covers, for once the leather cushions got wet it took them days to dry out. The wind had begun to slacken a bit although the rain, if anything, had increased. It seemed almost like a falling wall of water.

But there was still enough of a gale to do considerable damage. I saw the green umbrella living top of the Moyers turned almost inside out. It was held to the centerpole only by an extra tie-down rope I had put in for them when I set the top up. While we watched, the canvas was carried away, revealing the little man and his huge wife clinging to the centerpole in terror. The storm swept in around them and in a minute both were soaked to the skin. The wind hurled their possessions across the lot, doing particularly well with a cardboard

Blow-down.

After the blow-down.

box full of 'scopes which it distributed like a varicolored snowstorm over the midway.

Mr. Moyer made a bolt for one of the open concessions that still retained its top. His wife lumbered after him, holding a folded newspaper over her head as protection against the rain. As the little man rushed across the midway, a remarkable thing happened. He suddenly rolled over like a shot rabbit and lay kicking in the deep water.

I ran toward the mentalist to help him up. Moyer didn't move. I thought he must have had a stroke. As I splashed through the soggy sawdust toward him, I felt the ground begin to tingle strangely under my feet. Suddenly I got a shock that threw me backward.

Captain Billy dragged me to my feet. I was numb all over.

"The juice men ran a cut-in line under the midway here and I guess they didn't bury it deep enough," said Captain Billy. "When the ground's wet like this, you can feel it."

"Damned if you can't," I said, rubbing myself.

We found a board and threw it across the wet ground. I tight-rope-walked out to the end of it and pulled Moyer in by his coat, but not without a few unpleasant shocks. The little man was still conscious but he was half-stunned. We rubbed him until he could stand and then left him in the hands of his anxious wife.

The storm was particularly hard on the freaks and animals. I found Jolly Daisy sitting in her living top wrapped up like a giant cocoon in blankets and coats. The top was still standing, but the wind had ripped open the front flap and the rain was whipping through the little tent. But when I burst in, the fat lady waved me away.

"You help the men save the big top, Slim," she said calmly. "Come back and get me later. I'll be all right. I ain't going to melt."

Dot, the five-legged horse, had escaped and we found her hours later standing forlornly in a field with her back turned to the wind. May, the snake charmer, had the worst time of all. In an effort to save her precious snakes she tried to drag a huge, glass-fronted box full of rattlers off a table. The box was too heavy for her and she fell backward with the box crashing down on top of her. The glass shattered into pieces and there were rattlesnakes all over the top. Our lights had gone out and we had to help May collect the snakes with pocket flashlights. May could handle the snakes with reasonable impunity, when the reptiles were calm and simply being lifted in and out of their boxes. Rattlesnakes that have been kept in captivity for some time become so listless they show little desire to bite and often even refuse to eat. Also, like any other animal, they become used to being handled and don't resent it. But these snakes were loose and frightened. While I was searching among the catwalks for them, a snake's rattle would suddenly go off like a hive of bees right beside my foot. The noise was enormously magnified by the confines of the tent and you couldn't tell where it was coming from. I'm ordinarily not afraid of snakes, but I really was sweating by the time May got her pets back. May refused to pin their heads down with a stake before picking them up as I would have done. While I held a flashlight on the reptile, May would go down on her knees and slowly hold out her hands under the snake's body and lift him up.

"You can tell if a rattlesnake is really angry by the way he uses his tongue," May assured me later. "Snake's hear with their tongue, you know, so if a snake keeps his tongue extended and rigid, he's frightened and dangerous. When he begins to flicker it in and out, he's relaxing."

I had occasionally handled May's rattlers on bright, sunny days while she was changing the paper in their boxes or washing them. But I wouldn't have picked up one of those raging creatures with my bare hands in the middle of a storm if they'd given me the carnival—and I didn't care how the snakes were holding their tongues.

The next day was gin clear. A burning sun in the absolutely cloudless sky dried the soggy canvas by noon, but the carny had been badly damaged. The fronts had sunk at weird angles into the soft ground and most of the tops were leaning over on their sides, their sidewalls flapping helplessly. The gambling joints were nothing but sticks with shreds of canvas hanging to them. The rides listed in every direction. The hot sun seemed to have dried the sawdust on the midway but when I kicked the stuff with my foot, it was a caked, damp mass underneath.

In spite of everything, the show opened that evening. The sawdust truck went around the midway and spread a new layer of sawdust. The men followed behind with rakes and spread the soft material over the old midway. The fresh, yellow ring improved the appearance of the lot somewhat but we had no lights and most of the shows had to open with kerosene flares and Coleman lanterns.

Mr. Moyer was still laid up from the effects of the underground juice line, so we had to open without the mentalist act. To make matters worse, the Human Ostrich found that all his rats had been drowned during the storm. The Ostrich kept the rats in a large aquarium covered with half-inch mesh wire and the aquarium had been under a leak in the tent's roof.

Krinko was more worried over the loss of the rats than he was about the mentalist act, although the Moyers had been our biggest draw. The Ostrich's routine was just the kind of entertainment the old fakir could appreciate. The Ostrich reminded Krinko that he could still swallow his goldfish and frogs, but the fakir said they didn't have the personalities that the rats did. Krinko wandered away disconsolately. The Ostrich shook his head sadly as the old fakir stumped out of the top.

"Of course, the old man is right—there's something about swallowing live rats that appeals to the popular imagination," he admitted. "But I know I can't get any white rats in this town and naturally I don't want to swallow any wild animals."

In spite of everything, we had a pretty good tip that evening. I did my Fire and Swords, and then the Ostrich started on his routine. He was halfway through when Krinko came waddling eagerly into the top, triumphantly holding a large wire rat trap containing two of the largest, toughest-looking rats I have ever seen. They were covered with long hair and were biting the bars with their yellow teeth. Krinko forced his way through the tip, put the cage on the Ostrich's table, and announced proudly, "Now folks, you next see the great Human Ostrich swallow live rats. No one else do this effect." He nodded to the Ostrich and clumped off happily to his own catwalk.

The Ostrich looked at the rats in horror and I didn't blame him. But he was too much of a showman to refuse the challenge. Fortunately, the Ostrich had a specially-made cigarette, heavily saturated with nicotine. Sometimes even his pet white rats resented being swallowed and then the Ostrich would light this reinforced stogie and puff smoke in their faces until they got groggy enough to be gulped down.

With shaking fingers the Ostrich lit his special cigarette. Then, opening the trap, he grabbed one of the rats by the tail and hauled it out. Holding the struggling animal in front of him, he puffed smoke into the rat's eyes. The rat hiccuped, kicked and relaxed. The Ostrich swallowed him.

Suddenly a look of horror appeared on the Ostrich's thin features. He stood statue-still for an instant and then clapped one hand to his chest. "That rat has recovered!" he gasped. "I didn't give him enough smoke. This is a horrible position to be in!"

I could dimly hear muffled squeals come from the inside the Ostrich. It seemed as though I could even see his belly expanding and contracting as the rat rolled around inside of him. The tip was fascinated. "Does he always do this?" I heard one woman ask a friend wonderingly, "I'd think it would be an awfully unpleasant way to earn a living."

The Ostrich was clutching his sides with both hands. He was gradually turning a curious greenish-yellow color. "Hurry up and regurgitate him, " I urged.

"I can't," moaned the Ostrich. "Every time I try, he grabs hold of the lining of my stomach."

I had an inspiration. The Ostrich also did a Human Fountain Act. For this routine, he swallowed twenty glasses of water in half a minute and then regurgitated the water slowly while Bronko played "Indian Love Call" on his guitar. There was a full pitcher of water beside him on his table. I grabbed it up and shoved it into the Ostrich's hands. He drank a couple of quarts and then looked up relieved.

"He's swimming for his life," he announced.

"Quick, regurgitate him and the water," I begged.

The Ostrich made a great effort. Rat and water came up. It was quite a sight. Women in the tip screamed and fought their way blindly toward the open air. Several men reeled over and fell weakly against the inside platform. But a number of people were totally unaffected and continued to watch with deep interest. One of this group, an old farmer, warmly congratulated the Ostrich who had collapsed on his catwalk.

"I been to see every tent show in these parts for the last forty year," he assured the exhausted Ostrich. "But I never seen an act better'n that one. You got something real unusual there and don't let anybody tell you different."

The Ostrich was moody for the next couple of days and refused to go on with his act. He claimed he'd strained something inside of him and his whole career might be imperiled. Then early one morning, he packed his props in the back of his old car and disappeared. We never saw him again, but I later heard through the carnival grapevine that he had joined a carnival playing South America and that his remarkable performance had gone over well with the Latins.

With the Ostrich gone and the Moyers unable to perform, we were very shorthanded. Krinko tried desperately to pick up some new acts before the carny played its fair dates, but it was pretty late in the season. Most acts already had their commitments, for the fair season is the biggest time for the out-of-door show business. Fortunately for us, the carnival manager decided to keep the organization on the bridge lot for another week so the shows could make repairs.

The next day, we tore down the side show top and spread out the great mass of canvas on the side of the hill. From a little distance, it looked as though half an acre of ground had suddenly turned brown. We all gave Paul a hand sewing up the rents that had been made by the storm and the repeated folding of the great canvas sections. Then Captain Billy and Krinko paraffined the canvas to make it waterproof. Our top was so old that patches of it were worn almost paper-thin and these sections wouldn't take the paraffin. Captain Billy, who was supervising the job, got discouraged.

"It'd be easier to paraffin ourselves and let the top go," he suggested. "We wouldn't have to worry about the tip getting wet. When it rains, we don't have a tip anyhow."

While we were waiting for the paraffin to dry, I went back to the cook shack to get something to eat. As I was crossing the midway I heard Madam Moyer calling to me. She was standing in front of her restored living top waving a colored scarf to attract my attention. I strolled over to her.

"Mr. Moyer's still weak from his turrible experience," she told me solemnly. The couple had scarcely appeared on the lot since the day of the blow-down. "But he says he wants to see you. He's laying down inside."

I ducked into the little top, Madam Moyer wheezing after me. Mr. Moyer was lying on an army cot with a damp cloth on his forehead and a bottle of beer in his hand.

"How do you feel?" I asked.

He groaned. "I'll tell you, Slim, I was about ready to kick the bucket—I mean superimpose myself on the

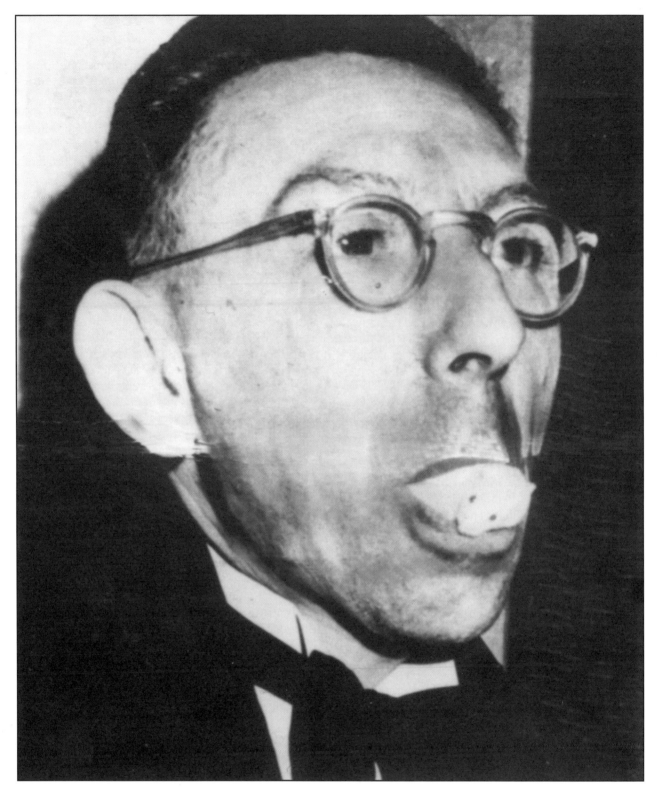

Human Ostrich swallowing a rat.

infinite," he said gravely. "Another shot of that juice and you'd have been planting me."

"I'm glad I pulled you out in time."

Mr. Moyer and his wife exchanged glances.

"Well, yes, you did," said Mr. Moyer in the tone of one giving the devil his due. "You did and I'm not one to forget it. From now on, I'm going to overlook the fact that you've been trying to sneak my act."

The little man said this as solemnly as though he were forgiving his worst enemy.

"Oh, ain't that grand!" exclaimed his wife, speaking to her husband, but addressing me. "I think that's real big of you, Mr. Moyer."

"I feel like it's the least I can do, seein' as how you saved my life," said the little man, gravely taking another drink of beer. "I guess you'd like to be a mentalist yourself. Well, to put on a good mentalist act, you gotta be partly psychic. You want to study yourself first, like the yogis in India do. Ask yourself, 'What am I? Whence came I? Whither am I going? What in hell is it all about?' We all live in this vale of tears, or as you probably call it, the world. But why?"

"Gosh, I don't know, Mr. Moyer," said his wife, obviously deeply impressed. "Why?"

"Well, that's the secret," explained her husband. "Only a few adepts like me know and we ain't telling." He took another drink of beer.

I asked Mr. Moyer if he'd ever had any flashes of real clairvoyance while presenting his routine. The little man was very indignant.

"Just because I use a few little innocent deceptions don't mean I ain't a genuine psychic. Lots of times I'll look at a woman and say 'Didn't your husband run away from you some years ago?' Plenty of times she'll admit I'm right. After you've been in this business as long as I have, you can spot a woman whose husband has left her. She usually has a couple of kids tagging her and she looks worn out and defiant at the same time. Then I sometimes notice a girl staring up at me twisting her hands, scared to speak. Right away I know she's in trouble over some man."

"Do you call that being a mind reader?" I asked.

"Sure, I read their minds, don't I?" demanded Mr. Moyer, annoyed. "But for a regular act I can't count on things like that, so I gotta use my one-ahead system for the billet reading. Just the same, I believe a mentalist should always be honest—honest in a reasonable way, of course. I always keep faith with the public by never doing anything grifted that they can catch me at."

Madam Moyer broke in angrily, "Those debunkers who claim all mind readers are lazy crooks ought to see the time we've spent steaming open envelopes, listening in for hours on party lines, and digging in garbage heaps for old letters. In all the years Mr. Moyer's been in business, he's never charged more than fifty cents a reading. For that, the marks got a horoscope with five pages and three colors, and a complete life reading telling them who to marry, when they should have children and what business they ought to go into. Those 'scopes cost us a dollar fifty a gross and in country districts we throw in High John Conquer Root that cures cancer, makes childbirth easy, and restores virility to men."

"That's right," agreed Mr. Moyer solemnly. "I don't guess that root does the marks any real harm and the advice I give them on things like sex is just what a psychologist would charge them ten dollars for and maybe not have had my experience."

Mr. Moyer admitted the real reason he was taking such a generous attitude about my stealing his act was because he and Madam Moyer had decided to leave the carnival. After his experience with the cut-in juice line, Mr. Moyer had come to the conclusion that carny life was too tough for him. The couple had telegraphed their agent and his answer had just arrived that morning. He had gotten them a job playing night clubs in the East during the winter months. The Moyers were going to leave as soon as Mr. Moyer felt well enough to travel.

During the next few days, I spent as much time as possible with the couple learning all I could about their technique. Mr. Moyer sold me an old crystal ball he had and a small black draped table that I could use for my act. When the couple finally departed, I felt I was able to walk into a radio broadcasting studio and challenge Dunninger.

With both the Ostrich and the Moyers gone, our show had shrunk to a Five-in-One, not counting Jolly Daisy and Dot in the blow-off. Losing the mentalist act was the worst blow because the Moyers had not only been a big attraction, but they had paid Krinko for the privilege of working in the top. Everyone in the side show felt very depressed except me. I was confident that I could put on a better mentalist routine with one hand tied behind me than the Moyers had ever dreamed about. Before joining the carnival, I'd worked for years as a magician and had a good knowledge of sleight-of-hand. I'd studied the Moyers' act carefully and I thought I could say, without boasting, that I had as good a stage presence as Mr. Moyer. All I needed was an assistant and I decided to sound out Billie Callihan.

My feelings were very hurt when Billie was obviously doubtful of my ability to carry a mentalist act. "I don't think you're the type, Slim," she told me frankly, when I broached the subject the day before we left the bridge lot for our first fair date. "You don't look like a mind reader. You look like a young kid. It's all right as long as you're swallowing a sword or breathing out fire. But a mind reader has got to inspire confidence."

"What do you mean, I don't inspire confidence?" I said indignantly. "If the marks had confidence in Mr. Moyer, I ought to be able to run for president."

"You're different from the Moyers," said Billie seriously. "I saw the Moyers' act one Saturday afternoon when our Model Show wasn't open yet. As soon as Mr. Moyer went into his spiel, I had gooseflesh all over me. But with you doing it, I'd just feel 'Look at that nice young guy pretending he's a mind reader.'"

"You feel that way because you know me so well," I told her. "The marks will never think of that."

"You wait and see. The marks are dumb but not that dumb," said Billie gravely.

I thought Billie was crazy. I decided to give my first show with Paul, our canvasman, as my assistant. I'd worked out a method of billet reading far superior to the Moyers' routine. In my system, the billets never left the tips' hands. I intended to use a clipboard with a sheet of paper fastened to it. The paper was divided by a series of horizontal perforations into a dozen small slips. A mark could write his message on the bottom slip, tear it off, and then pass the board on to the next customer. When all the slips had been written on I'd read off the messages from the platform without ever leaving my seat or even touching the board.

The clipboard was grifted by having a sheet of carbon paper inserted under its brightly colored tissue paper covering. I was going to have Paul, our canvasman, pass the board around. When all the slips of paper were torn off, he'd retire off stage with the empty board. Then he'd take off the clip at the top of the board and pull out the carbon paper. The carbon had a sheet of plain paper fastened to it and on this paper would be a copy of all the questions the marks had written. Paul would copy these questions onto a small square of cardboard and when he came on stage to hand me my crystal-gazing globe, he'd drop the cardboard into a little shelf behind my table that magicians call a "servante." It was a sure-fire system and very dramatic.

I talked to Krinko into letting me present the routine on the next lot. Krinko was doubtful but told me to go ahead. I drilled Paul in the very simple part he had to play and we were all ready to go.

The first night on the new lot, I started off my new routine with the opening tip. Everything went very well until the time came for Paul to copy out the messages on the slip of cardboard. Apparently our canvasman wasn't used to writing and he took an unconsciously long time to write out the messages. Paul couldn't simply drop the paper that had been in the clipboard into the servante because it was too big. I stalled as long as I could, telling the tip about the wonders of mentalism and asking them to concentrate on their messages. Finally I called, "Now my assistant will bring out my crystal-gazing ball."

Paul was working away on the messages, hidden from the tip by a pile of props. Instead of bringing me the ball and the cardboard, he held up five fingers, to indicate he still had five messages to go. I went into another spiel. By this time the tip was getting restless. I finally shouted again to Paul to bring in the ball. He held up three fingers. I lost my temper. "God damn it, bring in the ball!" I roared.

"I can't!" Paul shouted back, equally mad. "I can't read their writing."

The tip howled. Bronko instantly went into his whip-cracking routine and I slunk off the stage. I might have been a failure as a mentalist, but I certainly was a success as a comedian. When I came out to do my Fire and Sword routine, the tip burst into bellows of laughter at the sight of me. They laughed steadily all through my act and left the top hee-hawing and slapping each other on the back.

At the request of everyone with the side show, I resigned as a mentalist. I was still feeling bitter about my failure when I ran into the Impossible one afternoon in the cook shack.

Now that we were going to play the fair dates where supervision would be stricter, the carnival manager had passed the word among the joint men that the grift was out. They'd have to run their shows on the level. The Impossible had smiled knowingly when he heard this new ruling. "The manager'll change his mind the first week after the rides don't hit," he prophesied confidently. But as long as we were playing fair dates, not only the rides but all the concessions could count on a good return. I knew the Impossible was worried, because without the grift, his wheel couldn't make much money.

When I sat down beside him, the Impossible was hunched over a bowl of chili looking like a bewhiskered spider. He greeted me with his usual cheerfulness.

"I'm sorry to hear your new act was a failure, m'boy," he said, guiding a spoonful of chili through the jungle. "Ah, you should never have tried to learn a mentalist routine from a couple like the Moyers. A good mentalist can get more money out of the public than the U.S. Treasury. But I've seen the Moyers let people walk out of your top with money still in their pockets. No real student of the occult can be successful if he's going to be as inefficient as that."

"I supposed you used to be a mentalist yourself at some time or other," I remarked somewhat bitterly.

"One of the best, m'boy. I had a very nice little code routine worked out for me and my assistant. I'd sit on the platform while he walked through the tip and the marks handed him objects. I could call out anything they gave him even though I was blindfolded. We didn't have to speak a word. But one day we were picked up by the lawmen for finding a lost gold mine for a mark through psychic vibrations. It turned out that the mine was a piece of property that I happened to own under another name. Unfortunately, the judge was wearing his spectacles and recognized my assistant. That broke up our team. I've never really regretted it, however. I suspected the boy was holding out some of the money he collected from the tip and I can't bear dishonesty."

"It's a pity you got out of the racket," I said and told him what the Moyers had been making a week. The Impossible drank his chili sauce thoughtfully.

"That's only chicken feed to what a good man could take in, but it makes you think," he remarked reflectively. "The nice thing about a mentalist act is that it doesn't require any apparatus. In case you have to leave town in a hurry, that's a great advantage. The only apparatus I ever used was a ten-spot to slip the cops and sometimes they'd extend me credit. But before I could do a mind reading turn, I'd need an assistant."

"I'm the assistant," I told him. "Let's talk to old man Krinko."

A week later the Impossible Possible and I opened in the side show as a mentalist team. ✒

CHAPTER 13

In our regular routine, the Impossible would sit blindfolded on the inside platform and I'd walk through the tip touching watches, rings, purses or anything else handed to me. The Impossible would name them. I never spoke directly to him and never said anything when an object was handed to me. I'd simply concentrate for a moment and then pass on, asking for something else. It was while I was asking for the next object that I'd signal the preceding one. Different positions of my hands and body represented different letters so I could spell out the name of anything given to me. As the Impossible could see through the blindfold, he was able to watch my motions. Actually, the Impossible preferred to work in a blindfold. He said it shaded his eyes and enabled him to see better.

I was a little surprised to find out that the audience accepted us as real mind readers. A mind reader today has the same advantage a magician had in the Middle Ages—people actually believe in him. A magician is a juggler and if he makes a mistake the audience reasons he's no good. But the more mistakes a mentalist makes, the more people are impressed by what a difficult job he must be doing. After the Impossible and I got really expert with the code, we had a lot of trouble remembering to make enough mistakes to keep the act convincing. It's very hard to make realistic mistakes and our biggest sensation came one evening when we got our signals mixed.

A woman had handed me a wad of chewing gum. I signaled "gum" but the Impossible called out that she'd given me a piece of wood. I signaled again. The Impossible went into a trance and announced it was an eraser.

Unfortunately, he was too far away to see the gum even with the shade of his blindfold. I couldn't very well make the woman go up on the platform so I signaled again, making enough gestures to flag down a plane on a carrier. Finally the Impossible said triumphantly, "I see it clearly now . . . a jar of glue!"

There were some tough kids in the tip and they started giving me the raspberry. I walked out in front of the tip, waited until the Impossible got his blindfold adjusted and then, in plain sight of everyone, openly and deliberately went through the code of motions. I knew we were cooked with that tip anyhow and I was sore at the Impossible for not getting my signal. The

Impossible hedged around a little and then said despairingly, "Sorry, I can't make a damn thing out of it but 'gum.' "

I hope I may drop dead if we didn't get a solid minute of applause. I heard a woman say delightedly to her husband, "There! I told you it was real! They wouldn't have to keep trying like that if it wasn't." We picked up a number of private bookings from that slip and achieved quite a local reputation. The Impossible told me later that he got the original signal of "gum" but could only think of resin from a tree. Then he guessed art gum, used by artists, as we were playing near an artists' colony. Finally in desperation he turned to spruce gum, a glue used in laboratories.

Just as the Moyers never called out exactly what was written on a message, so the Impossible would always give whatever information I sent him an elaborate build-up. If I signaled "watch," the Impossible would say, "I see a round object. There are figures on it. I think it is a watch. Is that correct?" While he was going through this routine, I'd be selecting my next object from the crowd and meanwhile send him the type of watch, the time on it, and any initials that might be on the back. While he was calling off this information, I'd be deep in the crowd getting still another object. Even someone who knew our system would have had trouble telling exactly when I sent my signals.

As we got more expert, I had only to signal the first letter or two of common objects for the Impossible to get them. Finally, I only had to begin to make the gesture and he could usually spot it. If he was wrong, he'd just say the mental vibrations weren't strong enough and I'd go ahead and spell the word out. Then the Impossible started calling articles before I made any signals.

This was considerably surprising. The Impossible told me he's always had psychic powers, but couldn't count on them for regular work. I was willing to believe him. Then one day he said jokingly, "M'boy, I can always tell if you're going to send the letter 'V' or 'Z.' You have trouble with them and stiffen up a little first."

I got to thinking this over and finally decided he had gotten to know me so well he could actually spot the microscopic movements I made preparatory to sending certain letters. He probably did it almost unconsciously. The sender and receiver of a mind reading team get into a sort of rhythm after a while and good guesswork can do the rest. Since then, I've met many mind readers who honestly believed that occasionally they have flashes of real psychic power. I think they had simply carried their methods to such a degree of skill, they finally ended up fooling themselves.

My training as a magician often hurt me as a mentalist. I hated to see a trick go wrong, but the Impossible would gamble on a long shot as calmly as a card player drawing to fill an inside straight. While we were playing one of the fair dates, the Impossible and I dropped into a little novelty shop to buy a few gross of horoscopes. The shop also sold novelty postcards. The

Kids looking at our banner line.

cards had a suggestive picture on them accompanied by an appropriate phrase. The proprietor noticed me thumbing over the stack.

"We're having a lot of trouble with the printers this year," he told me sadly. "They aren't making anything but that type called 'Daddy's Slipping.'"

A couple of weeks after this chat, we were playing near a small town in Kentucky. The Impossible was calling out objects and I asked the local doctor for something. Instead of handing me an article, he called out:

"This is the first year I've only gotten one dirty postcard. If you fellows are mind readers, tell me what it is."

I'd forgotten all about the novelty dealer and was about to brush off the doctor with one of our standard routines. Suddenly the Impossible called out, "Daddy's Slipping." I glanced at the doctor to see if he'd been hit. The man's face was really a study. He hung around the show for days after that begging the Impossible to tell him how it was done. He used to invite the whole Ten-in-One troupe out to a bar, hoping to get us so liquored up we wouldn't realize what we were saying. He certainly didn't know much about carnival people.

The Impossible kept watching for long shots all the time and they turned up surprisingly often. We were once asked to give a free show at a hospital for the patients. The doctor who spoke to us had a curious name like Gusselhoffer. I went to a stationary store to get some special carbon paper we needed for the act. The girl behind the counter said to come back in a few hours. "Ask for me—my name's Gusselhoffer," she added.

"Isn't there a doctor up at the hospital by that name?" I asked.

She nodded. "He's my brother," and she told me a couple of stories about their childhood.

The afternoon when the Impossible and I gave the show at the hospital, we made medical history. We heard afterward that Dr. Gusselhoffer read a paper at a medical dinner explaining the scientific principles that made mind reading possible. "The telepathist does not necessarily receive the thoughts the subject is thinking at the moment," he explained. "He may, instead, pick up memories on the stream of consciousness that the subject has not thought of for years and has all but forgotten." The doctor sent us a copy of his paper and the Impossible and I read it with interest. Unfortunately, the doctor also sent his sister a copy. They were good sports, though, and didn't give us away. Of course, they couldn't very well without making the doctor look like a fool.

I'd always supposed that a mentalist needed a lot of paid sticks in the tip. It's too expensive to hire sticks and people will volunteer for the job if you give them a little encouragement. I used to stand near the entrance of the top selling paper-bound books of astrology, palmistry and dreams. When I saw a likely-looking man, I'd stop him and say, "Would you like a completely free reading by the Great Impossible Possible?" If he said he would, I'd add, "Please give me your name and date of birth. The Impossible Possible will give you your reading from the platform."

After we'd finished our routine with the code, the Impossible would announce, "I'm getting a strong vibration from someone with the initials J.S. Now I get the name . . . John Smith. Will you think of the date of your birth, Mr. Smith? I get October 27, 1911. Is that right and have we ever met before? Now I see you have an artistic nature . . ." and so on. Of course, Mr. Smith understood how the Impossible knew his birth date and name, but to the rest of the tip it seemed as though the Impossible had picked the information out of the air. Then I'd go around collecting dollar bills from persons who wanted a private reading after the show.

Sometimes we varied the routine. I'd stop a few people entering the top, ask them to write questions on slips of paper, and then keep the slips. To make it easy, I'd provide the slips and one of our paper-bound books for them to write on. The Impossible told me he could often sense what was on the slips by psychic vibrations, but just in case he couldn't I always took the precaution of putting some carbon paper under the cover of the book. During the show, the Impossible would pass out slips to everyone in the tip, asking them to retain the slips. "There'll be no collecting of messages in this show!" the Impossible would say emphatically. "That leads to abuses!" Then he'd read the messages I'd gotten for him in the lobby while the rest of the tip stood around clutching their slips waiting for him to get around to them, which he never did.

The Impossible always put mechanical gadgets in the same class as magicians and detectives—enemies of the human race. Once I managed to talk him into using a mechanical ringing bell. The bell was worked by a thread, but the principle was so clever that even the Impossible was impressed. We used it for private shows.

In one spot where we played, a wealthy lady called us in so often for private shows that the Impossible began calling her his annuity. We were working in her living room before a group of well-to-do marks that the Impossible felt sure were good for half a dozen more dates. I was just about to demonstrate the ringing bell when our hostess stopped me.

"Please, one moment!" she called lightly. Hurrying over, she located the thread to the bell and carefully broke it. "I happened to notice that thread lying on the floor and I was afraid you might trip over it," she explained. "Now do please go on with your fascinating demonstration!" She sat down again, all starry-eyed and eager. That was the last time I ever persuaded the Impossible to use anything mechanical.

I never saw the Impossible caught but once, and that was by dishonest methods. We'd been engaged for a private show by a wealthy gentleman who later became the country's leading financier. The Impossible's eyes were causing him trouble and I used to cover him with a black cloth, handing him the carbon copies of the messages at the same time. He'd get out a flashlight, put on his glasses, and sit there in comfort reading out the messages.

That afternoon the Impossible was reading away and I was off preparing for the next effect. Suddenly I heard a ripping noise. I looked up and was surprised to see the financier's little son calmly ripping up the Impossible's covering cloth with a jackknife. I grabbed the little brat by the seat of his pants, but it was too late. The cloth fell open, disclosing the Impossible with his slips and flashlight.

We were just giving a show, not claiming supernatural powers, but even so the Impossible was annoyed. Afterward, he went over to the kid's father and suggested payment for the cloth. The multimillionaire smiled.

"The little fellow has an inquiring mind," he said indulgently. "A little needle and thread will fix everything—just a little needle and thread."

The Impossible and I also did a good deal of free publicity, especially in small towns, that not only benefited our show but the whole carnival. In some spots, the Impossible ran a daily column in the local newspaper answering all personal problems himself. For this purpose, he carried around a bunch of letters to mail to himself. But if we were playing a spot for more than a few days, he didn't need the fake letters as he got plenty of real ones. In some places, he drove a car through the streets blindfolded, using, naturally, his transparent blindfold. He would also hypnotize a girl and leave her in the window of the leading dry goods store, find lost chickens for neighboring farmers by casting their horoscopes, and eat at the main restaurant in town daily while wearing his turban. Naturally, he got his meals free in return for the publicity. Every store where he pulled these stunts benefited by the advertising so we were very popular with the various chambers of commerce. And no one had to pay for it . . . except, of course, the public.

Simply finding out what the people had written in the messages wasn't enough. The Impossible also had to answer the damn things. Sometimes this was difficult to do. Questions such as "Is my boyfriend true to me or has he gone back to his wife?" require tactful handling in a mixed tip.

Sometimes an unscrupulous person in the tip would ask us a trick question. As we always had more messages than the Impossible could answer, I'd simply destroy these billets. But occasionally I'd make a mistake. Once I let a message through to the Impossible that read, "If you know so damn much, tell me how and when my son died. Signed Joe Brown." Instead of being rattled, the Impossible announced, "Excuse me, ladies and gentlemen, if I take a moment to bring consolation to an unhappy man among you. Mr. Brown, while reading these vibrations, I happened to tune in on your mental wave length. You lost a son some time ago, am I right? You are thinking about your son now. Mr. Brown, I can't answer your mental question about your boy's death . . . because he isn't dead! To a true psychic, there is no such thing as death . . . We simply pass into another existence. I trust this solves your puzzled state of mind. I suggest we all observe five seconds of silence as a tribute to Mr. Brown." This gave the whole show a nice atmosphere and also held Mr. Brown.

The Impossible had a very effective way of selling one of our extra money items, the *Gypsy's Dream Book*. While I was going through the tip with my copies, the Impossible would announce, "Friends, I want to be fair with you. Please do not write, as many people have, asking for more copies of this remarkable book. Because of the delicate nature of the book, it cannot be sent through the mails." That statement always caused a spurt in our sales.

In one town where we played, the editor of the local newspaper must have been an amateur magician. He ran an editorial, full of ponderous humor, denouncing our act and supposedly exposing our methods. The exposé was crazy. To accomplish the effects he ascribed to us, we would have had to carry around enough mechanical apparatus to outfit a panzer division. It was a pity that we couldn't expose the editor by telling how we really did the stuff, but that would hardly have been practical. I read the exposé strictly for laughs, but the Impossible denounced it with honest indignation.

"What do you care?" I asked him. "It won't make any difference in our take. And after all, our routine is grifted."

"M'boy, we may be running a grifted act," said the Impossible seriously. "But it's the way we make a living. This fellow is trying to hurt us. I've never deliberately set out to hurt anybody in my life. I've never given a mark a destructive reading. I've always tried to help them."

Looking at the Impossible, I could tell he was sincere. But I would have liked to have gotten a relief map of the old man's conscience sometime.

Girl Show on midway.

Sideshow ticket seller with girls from the Girl Show.

CHAPTER 14

We'd finished with our still dates and the carnival swung south over what Mountmorency called "the grits and fatback south." In a few more weeks it would be winter and the carnival would have to go into winter quarters, but as long as the talkers could still turn a tip, the carnival kept running. I didn't want the season ever to end. I was perfectly contented. Everyone in the side show troupe was my friend. The Impossible was always available either for a drinking bout or a flow of amazing reminiscences. And I spent nearly every afternoon with Billie Callihan—picnicking, dancing, or taking long walks together in the country.

Then one day Billie told me she'd decided to get married.

The announcement shot so many different kinds of emotions through me that I felt like an engine that has been thrown into five gears at the same time. I hadn't even known Billie had been seeing anyone else. I couldn't imagine the carny without Billie. I was glad for Billie, sorry for myself, and above all puzzled over the identity of her fiancé. I thought he might be another Steve or a smoothie like the former Model Show talker. But this time Billie had apparently selected very well.

"He's a young guy in town here, a couple of years older than me," Billie explained softly. We were sitting in my car on the edge of a high bluff that commanded a magnificent view of a little valley, checkerboarded with tiny farms and stained soft pastel colors by the first autumn frost. "He thinks I'm just some potatoes, Slim. He had me out to his house for lunch yesterday so his folks could meet me. You know, a lot of these small town families wouldn't want their son to marry a carny, but these people really looked up to me like I was a famous actress or something. He had all his brothers and aunts and cousins in and they asked me about the places I'd been and admired my clothes and, gee, I never felt so important in all my life."

"How did you meet this guy?" I asked. I knew in many of the rural communities the natives regarded carnies with as much admiration as people in larger communities regard motion picture stars. But I was still surprised to hear of the family's reaction to Billie.

"There was a local dance and I went with some of the girls. I met him there. His name's Bud—at least, that's what his folks call him. He fell in love with me right off.

I told him I was an actress with the carny, and invited him to see our act. It was all right to do that because we don't do a strip here; just our dance number."

The community where we were playing was very strict and Frisco hadn't been able to fix the local lawmen. So the girls performed in their bras and trunks and were quite as decently covered as though wearing two-piece bathing suits. For the blow-off, they simply rolled their bras and trunks tighter to show an inch or so more flesh. I suppose Billie's boy friend took for granted that was all the girls ever did.

"Well, Billie, it looks like you were fixed for life," I said, a little regretfully.

"That's the way I look at it," said Billie matter-of-factly. "Of course, if you'd told me a year ago I'd marry a small town boy and settle down in a little hick town, I'd have laughed at you. But that's the way it is. His father owns a factory where they make arch supports for people's shoes. At least they call it a factory . . . they only got three or four people working there. Anyhow, he's pretty well off. And it's nice to find a man in love with me instead of me being in love with him."

I had about fifty dollars saved up and the next day I gave it to Billie for her trousseau. She thanked me politely but without too much enthusiasm. Later, Billie introduced me to her fiancé. He was a pleasant-faced young man who gave the impression of being years younger than Billie. He was obviously very nervous, but tried hard to seem at ease. He told me that Billie was going to stay with his family until they could get married. I liked him and thought that Billie was lucky.

The next lot was a long jump of two hundred miles. One afternoon after we'd been on the lot a couple of days, I was walking across the midway on my way to the cook shack when I saw Billie coming toward me. I stared at her as though she were a ghost. I'd said good-bye to Billie at the last lot, and she and her Bud had gone off to price furniture.

"Billie!" I yelled. "What are you doing here?"

Billie looked up and I saw her face was drawn and tired as though she'd had a bad night.

"Hello, Slim," she said, making an effort to keep her voice natural. "How's tips at the Ten-in-One?"

"Aren't you married?"

"No, I couldn't go through with it."

"What the hell happened? I thought Bud was a wonderful guy."

"It wasn't Bud's fault. He's all right. But the minute I walked into Bud's home with my suitcases I started to get cold feet. Last evening I was sitting talking to his ma and his sisters and all of a sudden I thought, 'My God, I'm going to spend the rest of my life doing this. I'm going to have to stay in this little town until I die, talking to these women and living with Bud.' I couldn't do it, Slim. I went upstairs and packed my bags and sneaked out the back door. Then I caught a bus for the lot."

"What's Bud going to think when he finds you're gone?"

"I don't know. I'm really sorry for Bud, but I wouldn't have made him a good wife. Do you think I'm terrible, Slim?"

"Well, if you didn't love the guy, I guess you did the smart thing," I said slowly. "Did you have any trouble with Frisco about getting your job back?"

"No, the other girls even had my dressing table set up for me before they knew I was coming back and Frisco hadn't bothered to change the routine around to cover my spot. It was like they expected me to be there." Billie spoke wonderingly.

I left Billie and walked on slowly down the midway. As I approached the cook shack, I saw Frisco standing in the shade of one of the little gambling booths watching me. He was leaning on a cane and smoking a gigantic cigar.

"Hello, Slim," he said as I came up to him. "You look worried. Figuring you damn near lost your girl on that last lot?"

"You damn near lost her too," I remarked.

The big man mouthed the cigar. "I didn't come near losing no girl, Slim," he said gently. "Neither did you. Billie'll always be around. She thinks she wants to get married and settle down, but she won't never leave the carny. Twenty years from now she'll be an old broad working the popcorn concession."

The confidence in his voice irritated me. "How can you be so sure?" I demanded.

The big cigar traveled back and forth. "Because I know women, son, I deal in 'em. I'm putting the girls in a burlesque when the carny closes next week and we'll go on the road again next summer. Billie'll be there if you want to see her again. But if you're smart, you won't see her. Because you'll be through with carny by then."

"How come?"

"Because you can do better for yourself than working in a Ten-in-One. It's all right for some people, but it's a rough life. If I was you when the carny goes into winter quarters, I'd kiss the whole business good-bye and strike out for yourself somewheres else."

That talk with Frisco left me uneasy. If Billie didn't want to marry somebody like Bud, what did she want? For that matter, what did I want? Life in the carny had been so interesting I'd simply drifted along without thinking about the future. But with the carnival getting ready to close for the winter, I realized I'd have to do some worrying. Eventually I'd have to decide whether I wanted to spend the rest of my life under canvas or whether I'd look for another way to make a living.

Although the talk with Frisco had started me thinking, it was a little incident that happened to Jolly Daisy which really made me worry about carnival life.

While we were playing our still dates, a young southern boy had attached himself to our show as a sort of supernumerary canvasman. While driving between lots, Captain Billy had seen the fellow hitch-hiking and given him a lift in the truck. His name was Cal and he seemed to have no home and no place to go. Krinko gave him a job helping Paul set up the top and do the endless odd jobs necessary around a carnival. I don't think Cal would have lasted more than a couple of weeks with the show if Jolly Daisy hadn't adopted him as her protégé.

Cal had a gentle, horselike face covered with scraggly down that turned into wiry bristles on his chin. His only clothing was an old coat with a strip of soiled white lining hanging down behind like a tail and a pair of ancient pants held sketchily together by safety pins. Cal was certainly willing. If for some reason you asked him to stand up, Cal immediately obliged and then remained standing until someone suggested that he sit down again. If you asked him to hand you a certain prop during your act, he was happy to do it, but it never seemed to occur to him that the next evening you would need that same prop at the same moment in your routine.

One of Cal's tasks was to hold a pleated page from *The Billboard* while Bronko cut off strips of the folded paper with his whip. Lu usually did this routine task but sometimes she was out on the bally platform and then Cal was pressed into service. There was only one thing you had to remember for this job—to hold the paper out stiffly so it would offer enough resistance to the whip lash to be cut. Cal never mastered this art. He would hold the paper all right while Bronko cut off a couple of pieces from the end. Then his mind would start to wander and he would let the paper droop. Bronko would crack the whip but the snapper on the end of the lash would simply knock the paper back and forth without cutting it.

Jolly Daisy first became interested in Cal when Bronko started cutting off the boy's nose. As a climax to his whip-snapping routine, the cowboy would cut a cigarette out of his assistant's mouth. The assistant had to keep his head thrown back and the cigarette sticking out straight, otherwise his nose got in the way of the whip lash. Cal was continually letting the cigarette hang down and as a result Bronko kept slicing off the end of the boy's nose. Apparently Cal, in addition to not having a very active mind, had absolutely no feelings for he didn't seem to mind losing part of his nose every time Bronko did the stunt. In fact, Cal was rather proud of it. He kept showing his mutilated nose to people on the lot and asking them if they noticed how it was getting smaller every day.

Cal found a strong supporter in Jolly Daisy. She could watch the pit acts through a slit in the blow-off curtains and as soon as Bronko produced his whips, the fat lady would scream, "Don't you slice off no more of that poor boy's face. I'm telling you, don't you dare!" This naturally made Bronko nervous and his whip work became very wild. The cowboy finally complained to Krinko that Cal and Jolly Daisy, between them, were ruining his act. Krinko would have let the boy go if Jolly Daisy hadn't interfered and

Cal holding papers for Bronko's whip-cracking act.

agreed to pay his wages if he'd set up and tear down her living top, drive her between lots, and do a few other simple chores.

I thought this was very motherly of Jolly Daisy. Then one evening while I was helping the fat lady get from her living top to the blow-off, I discovered that Daisy's interest in Cal was more complicated.

"Cal is terrible fond of children," the fat lady told me. We had reached the rear entrance of the side show and she was holding on to the canvas flap while resting. "I seen him playing ball with some of the towny kids that come on the lot in the afternoon. He'd make a great father for a kid on account of he's not too old and can fool around with children hisself."

"He seems to me sort of young to get married," I said with a sinking feeling for I knew what was in Jolly Daisy's mind.

"Oh, he's been married once already," the fat lady assured me. "He and his wife got divorced or something. Cal's a lot more grown up than you realize. He's a real thinker. Says plenty of interesting things sometimes. All he needs is an older woman to look after him some."

Cal.

I had my own ideas about what kind of a father Cal would make to a convent-raised, twelve-year-old girl who had just discovered her mother was a side show freak, but I didn't say anything.

A few evenings after my talk with the fat lady, the troupe was in the top getting ready for the evening show. I was up on the inside platform helping the Impossible get our few props ready. Old man Krinko came in followed by a brisk, bespectacled man who was leading a gawky young girl by the hand. The girl was about as homely a looking specimen as I've seen. She was thin as a sidepole and wearing a dress so short it ended several inches above her knees. Her scrawny legs were bare. Her long face was a curious mixture of childish innocence and vacant stupidity. She seemed about fourteen years old.

Krinko stumped over to the pit chain and pointed to Cal who was helping Bronko coil up his spinning ropes. "There he is," said the old fakir bluntly.

Cal looked up carelessly and then stared at the girl in surprise, but without any trace of dismay.

"Hi, Bet," he said. "How'd you get here?"

"This man brung me," said the girl indifferently. She didn't pay any attention to Cal. She was staring in frank amazement at Jolly Daisy. The fat woman was sitting on a chair by the pit, chatting with the rest of us

until it was time for her to go into the blow-off. The girl pointed at her. "Is she real?" the child demanded.

"Sure she is," said Cal proudly. "She's a genuine freak. She's the fattest woman in the world."

The man with the spectacles interrupted to say with professional heartiness, "Well, Betsy, aren't you glad to see your husband again?"

Betsy didn't answer him. She had just seen Captain Billy who was sitting on his bed of nails stripped to the waist. "What's that stuff all over him?" she demanded, pointing to the tattooed man with the same decisive gesture.

"That's tattooing. It won't come off," Cal explained. Eagerly, he began to point out the other acts. "That there is May who can handle rattlesnakes without getting bit and that's Bronko who does a whip act. Look what he done to my nose." Cal gingerly but proudly felt the end of his nose.

The girl stared at her husband's injury with the same interest she'd shown for everything else. The bespectacled man broke in again.

"So you're Cal," he said cordially. "I'm certainly glad to meet you. You've got a wonderful little baby girl at home, son. Wouldn't you like to see her?"

"I've seen her," said Cal without interest. Then he went on enthusiastically, "Look, Bet, there's a five-legged horse in that place—we call it the blow-off—and that man with the whiskers can read your mind . . ."

"Come, come," said the man with the glasses a little testily. "This is very interesting, son, but you want to go back to your wife and child, don't you?"

"Do I have to?" asked Cal slowly.

Krinko said, "Sure you got to. This man from Welfare Agency. Lawmen been looking for you. You go home now."

Cal began to blubber, wiping his nose on his frayed sleeve. "I don't want to go home. I want to stay here with the show."

Jolly Daisy broke in. The fat woman had been listening in a sort of numbed horror to this conversation. Now she spoke.

"Sure you gotta go home, Cal," she said sadly but a little angrily. "You got a kid to support. What's the matter with you, ain't you got no feelings for your own kid?"

Cal suddenly had an idea. "Say, couldn't you send Bet my wages and let me work here for nothing? I don't need no money. I can sleep in one of the trucks and the guy at the cook shack'll always give me stuff to eat that he was going to throw away. It won't do me no good to go home. I ain't got no money to give Bet."

Jolly Daisy sighed. Then she felt in her vast bosom until she came up with a little bag that was fastened around her neck. With difficulty, she pulled open the drawstrings of the bag and reluctantly produced a small role of bills. She counted out half of them.

"Here, you take this," she said, holding them out to the boy. "You take this and buy something nice for the baby. Don't you go running away from home no more. It ain't right. This money'll keep you going for awhile."

"Why, I think that's wonderful!" said the Welfare man with his artificial enthusiasm. "If you're careful of it, that money will carry you along nicely for some time. Aren't you going to thank the lady?"

"Thanks," said Cal taking the money reluctantly. "But I sure wish I could stay with the show."

"You better go now," said Krinko. Cal departed with his wife and Welfare man, the girl still looking back over her shoulder at the wonders of the pit.

Daisy rose without comment and waddled into the blow-off without help. Later in the evening, I took time off to slip into the blow-off between shows and tell her I was sorry.

"Well, I'm glad I found out when I did," said the fat lady soberly. "I wouldn't want to have nothing to do with somebody who didn't have no more natural feelings than to run off and leave his own baby. I'm certainly surprised at that boy. I didn't think he was like that at all."

"As you say, it's lucky you found out in time," I agreed.

Jolly Daisy sighed. "I could of taken him away from her. You saw that yourself. He didn't want to go back to her. He wanted to stay here with me. But I'll never take a man away from his woman. A woman done that to me once. She stole a man of mine. It's an awful mean trick and I swore then that I'd never steal another woman's man."

I didn't say anything. Jolly Daisy's version of the facts obviously made her feel better and that was all I cared about.

The fat woman sat staring at the ridiculous little pink bows on her huge shoes. Then she sighed.

"It's all my own fault for trying to get married and pretend I'm a normal woman. I ain't normal and there's no use in pretending I am. I'm a freak . . . jest like you and everyone else in a carny."

"Everyone with a carny isn't a freak, Daisy," I ventured.

"Oh yes they are. Maybe it don't show on the outside like it does with me, but everybody 'with it' is some kind of freak. They ain't none of them normal. Look at May, crazy in love with her snakes, and Captain Billy having himself covered with tattooing trying to be an out-and-out freak like me, and even you—a college graduate swallowing swords and eating fire when you knew all along it was liable to kill you. I'm a freak because I gotta be, but somebody like you is making a freak out of himself because deep down inside you've got a craving for it. And the longer you're 'with it,' the more of a freak you'll get until pretty soon you can't be happy anywhere except in the carny where there're other freaks for you to be with."

Although the fat woman was speaking in a dull, monotonous voice I felt my flesh crawl as though she were delivering a curse.

Jolly Daisy in the pit with Bronko.

For the first time Daisy raised her eyes and looked at me. Usually the fat woman's face was young and full of life, but now the folds of fat seemed to hang from it and she looked very old.

"What country do you think you've been living in for the last six months?"

"The United States, I suppose."

"No, you ain't. The United States stops at the marquee out there." Daisy pointed at the canvas walls in the direction of the main gate of the carnival. "You been living in a world that ain't on any map. When you was a kid, did you ever think about running away to fairyland? I sure did. Well, this is fairyland. It ain't a real world. There was good things and bad things about fairyland. There's adventures and no responsibilities and fun and you'll never have to grow up. But if you never grow up, that means you can never have a home or a family."

We could hear Krinko's voice as he prepared to turn the tip in the blow-off. Jolly Daisy automatically picked up a little hand mirror from the table beside her and began to adjust her hair.

"I didn't have no real choice, Slim. But you got one. Scram out of here before you turn into a freak like everybody else. You may think it's fun never to grow up, but maybe someday you'll want to, and by that time it'll be too late. O.K., here comes the tip. You better get back to the pit."

I ducked out under the blow-off curtain as the tip came pouring in.

I'd recently had a chance to leave the carnival and start a career for myself. Ever since high school, I'd wanted to be a writer. While I was in college, I had sold that one article to the *Saturday Evening Post*, but I hadn't had any more luck for a long time afterward. But while we were playing out fair dates, I'd borrowed a typewriter from the carnival manager and written an article entitled "How to Swallow a Sword." I had signed the manuscript with my carnival name—"The Great Zadma"—and sent it to *Collier's* magazine. *Collier's* had bought the article and asked for more. *The Reader's Digest* had republished it, paying me almost as much as I'd gotten for the original sale. There was a chance I could make a living as a free-lance writer.

But I didn't want to leave carny life. I liked it. I liked the people. I liked traveling. I thought Daisy was bitter and probably exaggerated the hold that life under canvas exerts on people. But the sincerity in the fat woman's voice bothered me. I was still thinking about it as I climbed up on the inside platform to help the Impossible cut up the paper billets we used for the mind reading.

"Our mentalist routine is beginning to attract national attention, m'boy," remarked the Impossible to me as we stacked the billets. "My various skills have always made me much sought after—in fact in Texas they were once using bloodhounds. But we've recently had an offer that is on the up and up. I received word this afternoon that a big booking agent from Chicago is coming over tomorrow to catch our act. When the carny closes next week, we'll go to Chicago for the winter. You'll like Chicago, m'boy. It's full of temptations for a young man and I'll personally introduce you to some of the best of them."

Listening to the Impossible, I felt that here at least was somebody who couldn't be said to be living in fairyland. The Impossible might have his faults but he was no crackpot. He was a living refutation of Jolly Daisy's remarks about carnies. If we got the Chicago bookings, we were set. It might well be the beginning of a great career for us both. I didn't see any reason why we couldn't become as famous as Houdini or Dunninger.

The booking agent turned up the next afternoon. He was a squat, bald little man, very jovial and gave the impression of being as hard as the head of a sledge. He took in our act that evening. Afterward, he came over shaking his head.

"Well, it's lucky I came down here to catch your act myself," he admitted. "I'd never have believed that same old corn could go over so big. It's the same stuff mentalists have been doing for years but the rubes eat it up. I guess it's like you fellows say, there's one born every minute, eh?"

The Impossible eyed the little fat man unpleasantly. "This was the ordinary part of the act you saw this evening. I can assure you both my assistant and I have flashes of real psychic power. As you doubtless know, the researches of Professor J.B. Rhine of Duke University have definitely proven the existence of telepathy and clairvoyance and we have frequently demonstrated both phenomena in our performances."

"I'm glad to hear that," said the agent genially. "Because what I saw tonight was sure straight off the cob."

"Do we get the Chicago bookings?" I asked.

"Oh, sure, sure. You put the stuff across. That's all I'm interested in. I'll be around after the last show to discuss terms."

The agent came around while we were packing up our props for the night. The Impossible asked the man to hand him our crystal ball. As the agent lifted it, a low, moaning hum seemed to come from the crystal. The man was so startled he nearly dropped it.

"The glass must pick up some kind of vibration from the street noises," he said puzzled. Again the hum came, this time apparently from our table. We all jumped.

"Say, are you doing this?" the agent asked the Impossible suspiciously.

"My friend, there would be no point in my trying to fool you," said the Impossible seriously. "This curious phenomena has happened a few times before. I can't control it and I can't explain it. I can only believe it may be a spirit guide sent from some higher power to show us that occultism is real. If so, it will be worth a fortune."

The agent was fascinated. We found the sound could answer questions—one buzz for yes and two for no. The agent tried every way he could think of to explain the phenomenon. Sometimes the sound came from the platform, sometimes, from the pit, sometimes from the sidewalls. Finally the man broke down.

"I think there's something big here . . . maybe bigger than any of us realize," he said at last. "You know, I've always believed there was something to this occult business—some power around us we don't know about. There're lots of things in this world we can't understand. Look at radio—fifty years ago people would have called it witchcraft. Now I don't say this is supernatural, but it looks like you've stumbled on something pretty remarkable. Maybe we've made history tonight right in this side show tent."

After the agent had left, I said to the Impossible, "What's the grift?"

"I give you my word, m'boy, this whole thing is a mystery to me," the Impossible gravely assured me.

I was not unnaturally a little suspicious of the Impossible, but I thought by this time I knew all his tricks and there didn't seem to be any way he could be causing the noise. I knew the history of spiritualism is studded with similar inexplicable occurrences and I decided to keep an open mind on this one.

Everyone with the side show had lined up a job for the winter. May had gotten a job with a roadside zoo in Florida exhibiting her snakes. Jolly Daisy was spending the winter in a New York dime museum. Captain Billy was joining a traveling circus playing the Gulf states and the Bronkos had been signed up by a small radio station to sing cowboy songs. Old Man Krinko was taking Dot, the five-legged horse, south with him and putting her out to pasture while he spent the winter months getting a new top and making arrangements for the next season. Mountmorency had gotten a job at an amusement park. The Impossible and I were packing up, ready to leave for Chicago.

The booking agent turned up next day still very much excited by our spirit guide. He had even bought a notebook to keep a record of the mysterious noise's answers to his questions. The Impossible and I had rooms in a small hotel. That evening, the Impossible ran into an old friend of his in the lobby who was en route for the Mexican border. While the two men were talking over old times in the bar, the agent and I went up to our rooms to get ready for the séance. The Impossible came up a little later with a hand bell he'd borrowed from the desk clerk. He thought our spirit friend might consent to ring it.

We sat in semi-darkness concentrating, but the spirit guide refused to come. The Impossible got very angry. "That drunken bum!" he kept muttering. Finally he stamped out of the room, saying he'd be right back.

While he was gone, the maid came in and turned down the dark counterpane on the bed. Across the white sheet lay a tiny black line, leading from the bell to the open window. After six months in the mentalist racket, I knew a black silk thread when I saw one.

Unfortunately, so did the booking agent. We went downstairs and found the Impossible in an alley back of the hotel. He was trying to explain to his stewed friend how to pull the thread and make the bell ring.

"There's a very reliable little clockwork motor made for that," I told him. "Only you don't like mechanical devices."

The Impossible turned around. "Ah, so there you are!" he remarked pleasantly. Then addressing the furious booking agent he explained, "You said last night that you couldn't understand how the marks could be fooled by an old codger like me using methods that went out with the shell-and-pea game. I thought you'd be interested to see how it was done."

The agent stood there breathing deeply. "How did you make that hum?" he managed to ask.

The Impossible looked up thoughtfully at the stars. "Ever hear of a Punch and Judy show? Old-fashioned things, I'm afraid. Used to run one. Have to be something of a ventriloquist. What you heard was the ventriloquist drone—the first sound a Punch man learns to make."

The booking agent didn't have a very strong sense of humor and we never did get those Chicago bookings. Later that night I sat on a chair in our hotel room watching the Impossible lie on the bed and drink straight rye while he chuckled over the expression on the agent's face.

"But what good did it do?" I finally asked. "You must have known the guy would be sore. Now we've lost our bookings."

"Don't worry about a thing, m'boy," said the Impossible contentedly. "I know of a carnival playing the South this winter and the gaffer that runs the Ten-in-One is a friend of mine. He's got a mentalist act, but you can do your Fire and Sword routine and I'll set-up my flat joint. I never meant to play Chicago for more than a couple of months anyhow. I'm a carny man."

"Didn't you ever want to hit the big time?"

"I did try it a few times, but I get asthma away from the smell of sawdust."

"Then you deliberately queered our chance of going to Chicago because you wanted to stay in carnival?"

"Not exactly, m'boy. I didn't like that booking agent, and to me the sweetest music in the world is the squealing of a sucker who thinks he's a wisenheimer and finds he's just another mark. Speaking of music, did I ever tell you about the time I was playing in the circuit with a couple of parrots who sang the 'Miserere' from *Il Trovatore*—one singing bass and the other soprano?"

While I was listening to the story about the parrots, I made my decision. That night I packed my suitcase, left a note for the Impossible and started east in my car. In my inside pocket was the letter from *Collier's* asking for a series of articles based on carnival life. And on the seat beside me was a second-hand typewriter I'd purchased from the carnival manager. ✐

V/Search Mail Order Catalog

ZINES! Vol. 1: Incendiary Inverviews with Self Publishers

In the past two decades a quiet revolution has gained force: over 50,000 "zines" (independent, not-for-profit self-publication) have emerged and spread—mostly through the mail, with little publicity. Flaunting off-beat interests, extreme personal revelations and social activism, zines directly counter the *pseudo-communication* and glossy lies of the mainstream media monopoly. These interviews with a dozen zine creators capture all the excitement associated with uncensored freedom of expression, while offering insight, inspiration and delight. Included are: *Beer Frame, Crap Hound, Fat Girl, Thrift SCORE, Bunny Hop, OUTPUNK, Housewife Turned Assassin, Meat Hook, X-Ray* and more! "Will inspire the most confirmed couch potato to make a zine."—*Last Gasp Newsletter*

8½x11", 184 pp, illustrations, quotations, zine directory, index. PB, $18.99.

RE/Search 12: MODERN PRIMITIVES

BEST-SELLER. The *New York Times* called this "the Bible of the underground tattooing and body piercing movement." *Modern Primitives* launched an entire 90's subculture. Crammed with illustrations & information, it's now considered a classic. Thoroughly investigates ancient human decoration practices such as tattooing, piercing, scarification and more. 279 eye-opening photos and graphics; 22 in-depth interviews with some of the most colorful people on the planet..

"Dispassionate ethnography that lets people put their behavior in its own context."—*VOICE LITERARY SUPPLEMENT* *"The photographs and illustrations are both explicit and astounding . . . provides fascinating food for thought."—IRON HORSE*

8½x11", 212 pp, 279 photos and illus. PB, $17.99.

RE/Search 14 & 15: INCREDIBLY STRANGE MUSIC Vols. 1 & 2

Surveys the territory of neglected "garage sale" records (mostly from the '50s-'70s). **Genres examined** include: "easy listening," "exotica," "celebrity." Also recordings by (singing) cops, (polka-playing) priests, undertakers, religious ventriloquists, astronauts, opera-singing parrots, beatnik & hippie records, and gospel by blind teenagers with bouffant hairdos. **"This book will change your life."—*MIRABELLA*** *"Alfred Hitchcock's Music to Be Murdered By is just the tip of the iceberg . . . a catalog of the wackiest discs ever made, goes where few audiophiles have ever gone."—ENT. WEEKLY* **"A must read."—*HIGH PERFORMANCE***

8½x11", 208 pp, over 200 photos. PB, $17.99 (each).

RE/Search 10: INCREDIBLY STRANGE FILMS

Spotlighting unhailed directors–Herscell Gordon Lewis, Russ Meyer, Larry Cohen, Ray Dennis Steckler, Ted V. Mikels, Doris Wishman & others–who have been critically consigned to the ghettos of gore and sexploitation films.. 13 interviews, numerous essays, A-Z of film personalities, "Favorite Films" list, quotations, bibliography, filmography, film synopses, & index. **"Flicks like these are subversive alternatives to the mind control propagated by the mainstream media."—*IRON HORSE*** **"Whether discussing the ethics of sex and violence on the screen, film censorship, or their personal motivations . . . the interviews are intelligent, enthusiastic and articulate."—*SMALL PRESS*** *"This book directly sparked the reissue of thousands of amazing films on video, opening minds as well as eyes."—VIDEO COLLECTOR*

8½x11", 224 pp, 157 photos & illustrations. PB, $17.99

RE/Search 11: PRANKS!

A prank is a "trick, a mischievous act, a ludicrous act." Although not regarded as poetic or artistic acts, pranks constitute an art form and genre in themselves. Here pranksters such as Timothy Leary, Abbie Hoffman, Monte Cazazza, Jello Biafra, Earth First!, Joe Coleman, Karen Finley, John Waters and Henry Rollins (and more) challenge the sovereign authority of words, images & behavioral convention. This iconoclastic compendium will dazzle and delight all lovers of humor, satire and irony.

"The definitive treatment of the subject, offering extensive interviews with 36 contemporary tricksters."—*WASHINGTON POST* *"This book has inspired a new genre of prank phone call recordings, performances and videos based on pranking, and other dubious achievements."—COMIC REVUE*

8 ½x11", 240 pp, 164 illus. PB, $19.99.

RE/Search 13: ANGRY WOMEN

16 cutting-edge performance artists discuss critical questions such as: How can revolutionary feminism encompass wild sex, humor, beauty, spirituality plus radical politics? How can a powerful movement for social change be inclusionary? A wide range of topics is discussed *passionately.* Armed with contempt for dogma, stereotype & cliche, these creative visionaries probe deeply into our social foundation of taboos, beliefs and totalitarian linguistic contradictions from whence spring (as well as thwart) our theories, imaginings, behavior and dreams. Includes interviews with Karen Finley, Annie Sprinkle, Diamanda Galás, bell hooks, Kathy Acker, Avital Ronnell, Lydia Lunch, Sapphire, Susie Bright, Valie Export, and more . . .

"The view here is largely pro-sex, pro-porn, and pro-choice."—*THE VILLAGE VOICE* **"Every interview contains brilliant moments of wisdom."—*AMERICAN BOOK REVIEW.***

8½x11", 240 pp, 135 illustrations. PB, $18.99.

V/Search Mail Order Catalog

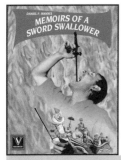

MEMOIRS OF A SWORD SWALLOWER by Daniel P. Mannix

"I probably never would have become America's leading fire-eater if Flamo the Great hadn't happened to explode that night . . ." So begins this true story of life with a traveling carnival, peopled by amazing characters (the Human Ostrich, the Human Salamander, Jolly Daisy, etc) who commit outrageous feats of wizardry. Under the tutelage of a veteran "carny," The Impossible Possible, Mannix was eating fire on stage the next night. This is one of the only *authentic* narratives revealing the "tricks" (or more often, the lack thereof) and skills involved in a sideshow, and is invaluable to those aspiring to this profession. NEW! OVER 50 RARE PHOTOS taken by Mannix in the 1930's and never before seen! Sideshow aficionados will delight in finally being able to see some of their favorite "stars" captured in candid moments. This edition definitely supersedes all previous editions. 8½x11", 128pp, 50+ photos, index, descriptive table of contents. **PB, $15.99.**

FREAKS: We Who Are Not As Others by Daniel P. Mannix

A fascinating classic book, based on Mannix's personal acquaintance with sideshow stars such as the Alligator Man and the Monkey Woman. Read all about the notorious love affairs of midgets; the amazing story of the Elephant Boy; the unusual amours of Jolly Daisy, the fat woman; the famous pinhead who inspired Verdi's *Rigoletto;* the tragedy of Betty Lou Williams and her parasitic twin; the black midget, only 34 inches tall, who was happily married to a 264-pound wife; the human torso who could sew, crochet and type, etc. Plus bizarre accounts of normal humans turned into freaks—either voluntarily or by evil design! Includes additional material from the author's personal collection. **88 astounding photos. 8½x11", 124 pp, illustrated. PB, $13.99.**

BOB FLANAGAN, SUPER-MASOCHIST

Bob Flanagan, 1952-1996, lived longer than any other person with Cystic Fibrosis, thanks to his extreme masochistic practices. Eye-opening photos; intense interviews. **128pp, illus. PB, $14.99.**

THE RE/SEARCH GUIDE TO BODILY FLUIDS by Paul Spinrad

Mucus, saliva, sweat, vomit, urine, farts, feces, earwax and more are humorously (and seriously) described in this anthropological/historical investigation. **8½x11", 148pp. PB, $15.99.**

THE CONFESSIONS OF WANDA VON SACHER-MASOCH

The wife of the man responsible for the term "masochism" describes her life, an adventure in deciphering the meaning of love in all its extremes. **8½x11", 136pp, photos. PB, $13.99.**

THE TORTURE GARDEN by Octave Mirbeau

A gothic classic about the art of torture as practiced in a fantastic 19th century Chinese garden. Will sicken, deprave and delight modern readers. **8½x11", 120pp, photos. PB, $13.99.**

ATROCITY EXHIBITION by J.G. Ballard

The author of *CRASH* (made into a film by David Cronenberg) reveals his futuristic imagination in all its perverse splendor in this extraordinary work. **8½x11", 136pp, photos and illustrations. PB, $13.99. HB, signed limited edition, $50.00.**

WILD WIVES by Charles Willeford

A sleazy tale of deception and doom by the master of hard-boiled dialogue. "Willeford never puts a foot wrong . . . an entertainment to relish."—*New Yorker.* **5x7", 108pp. PB, $10.99.**

HIGH PRIEST OF CALIFORNIA by Charles Willeford

This tale of a ruthless used car salesman obsessed with seducing a married woman strips bare the American 50's landscape of lust and denial. *Noir* & *Nasty!* **5x7", 148pp. PB, $10.99.**

RE/Search 8/9: J.G. BALLARD

The definitive introduction to the most incredibly prophetic writer of the 20th century. Ballard's imagination has no equal. Inspiring and essential. **8½x11", 176pp, illus. PB, $17.99.**

RE/Search 6/7: INDUSTRIAL CULTURE HANDBOOK

This book launched a movement of musicians including Nine Inch Nails. Performance art and noise music pushed beyond the cutting edge. Amazing! **8½x11", 140pp, 179 illus. PB, $15.99.**

RE/Search 4/5: W.S. BURROUGHS, BRION GYSIN, THROBBING GRISTLE

William Burroughs, Brion Gysin & Throbbing Gristle talk about advanced ideas involving the social control process, creativity and the future. **8½x11", 100pp, 58 photos. PB, $15.99.**

RE/Search 1,2,3: THE TABLOID ISSUES

Deep into the heart of the Control Process. Preoccupation: Creativity & Survival, past, present & future. These are the early tabloid issues, 11x17", full of photos and innovative graphics. ♦ **#1:** J.G. Ballard ♦ Cabaret Voltaire ♦ Julio Cortazar ♦ Octavio Paz ♦ Sun Ra ♦ The Slits ♦ Robert K. Brown (editor *Soldier of Fortune*) ♦ Conspiracy Theory Guide ♦ Punk Prostitutes ♦ and more. ♦ **#2:** DNA ♦ James Blood Ulmer ♦ Z'ev ♦ Aboriginal Music ♦ West African Music Guide ♦ Surveillance Technology ♦ Monte Cazazza on poisons ♦ Diane Di Prima ♦ Seda ♦ German Electronic Music Chart ♦ Isabelle Eberhardt ♦ and more. ♦ **#3:** Fela ♦ New Brain Research ♦ The Rattlesnake Man ♦ Sordide Sentimental ♦ New Guinea ♦ Kathy Acker ♦ Sado-Masochism ♦ Joe Dante ♦ Johanna Went ♦ SPK ♦ Flipper ♦ Physical Modification of Women (anticipated *Modern Primitives*) ♦ and more. **$8 each, full set for $20 WHILE THEY LAST!!**

V/Search Mail Order Catalog

Incredibly Strange Music CD, Vol. One

This is an amazing anthology of outstanding, hard-to-find musical/spoken word gems from LPs that are as scarce as hen's teeth. *Vol. One* contains "Up, Up & Away" played on an unbelievably out-of-tune sitar, "The Will to Fail" (hilarious) and "A Cosmic Telephone Call," etc. These tracks must be heard to be believed! CD **$16**; cassette only **$8** (two for **$10!!!**)

Incredibly Strange Music CD, Vol. Two

Lucia Pamela's barnyard frenzy "Walking on the Moon"; "How to Speak Hip" by Del Close & John Brent; "Join the Gospel Express" by singing ventriloquist doll Little Marcy; "Bumble Bee Bolero," "Terror" by Bas Sheva; "Billy Mure's "Chopsticks Guitar"; "The Letter" by the Nirvana Sitar & String Group, and many more musical gems. Full liner notes. CD **$16**

Ken Nordine COLORS A kaleidoscope of riotous sound and imagery. The pioneer of "Word Jazz" delivers "good lines" which are as smooth as water, inviting the listener to embark upon a musical fantasy evoking ethereal images of every poetic hue. An essential addition to the musical library of the hip connoisseur. Contains extra tracks not on original vinyl record. CD **$16**

Eden Ahbez EDEN'S ISLAND Released in 1960 on Del-Fi records, it "is a bizarre cross between exotica, '50's pop, and Beat-Era lyricism, whose genius was probably unintentional." In *Incredibly Strange Music, Vol. I*, Mickey McGowan calls *Eden's Island* "one of the truly strange masterpieces on record." Contains additional tracks not on the original, rare LP. Hard-to-find CD **$16**

THE ESSENTIAL PERREY & KINGSLEY Two fantastic, classic LPs (*The In Sound from Way Out* and *Kaleidoscopic Vibrations*) combined on one hard-to-find, currently out-of-print CD available exclusively from RE/Search mail orders. This CD contains *all* the tracks recorded by the Perrey-Kingsley duo. Recordings were painstakingly spliced together by hand in a labor of love. CD **$16**

SEARCH & DESTROY Incomplete Set, #1-2, 4-11

"Living the punk life, 1976-1979." Incendiary interviews, passionate photographs, art brutal. Corrosive minimalist documentation of the only youth rebellion of the seventies. The philosophy and culture, before the mass media takeover and inevitable cloning. Crammed with information and inspiration. *The real thing.*
#1) Nuns, Crime #2) Devo, Clash, Ramones, Iggy, Weirdos, Patti Smith, Avengers, Dils #4) Iggy, Dead Boys, Bobby Death, Jordan & the Ants, Mumps, Helen Wheels, Patti Smith #5) Sex Pistols, Nico, Screamers, Crisis, Crime, Talking Heads #6) Throbbing Gristle, Clash, Nico, Pere Ubu, UXA, Negative Trend, Sleepers, Buzzcocks #7) John Waters, Devo, DNA, Cabaret Voltaire, Roky Erickson #8) Mutants, Cramps, Siouxsie, Chrome #9) Dead Kennedys, X, David Lynch, Pere Ubu, DOA #10) WSB, JGB, Plugz, X, #11: All-photo supplement. Tabloid format, 11x17." Only small quantity left! $5 each; **$39** for incomplete set.

TATTOOTIME #2: Tattoo Magic. This issue examines all facets of Magic & the Occult. Tattooed charms, sacred calligraphy, dragons and Christian/Coptic tattoos. Great intv with Richard O. Tyler on "Uranian Tattoo Magic." Plus before and after photos of "Inventive cover work," and an essay on the tattoo as used for magical purposes in ancient cultures across the globe. **$10**

TATTOOTIME #3: Music & Sea Tattoos. Mermaids, pirates, fish, punk rock tattoos, Sailors & Tattoos, Pinky Yun interview, Dan Thome, etc. A great essay by deceased tattoo artist Greg Irons on the mysterious and compelling tattoo image known as the "Sailor's Grave," and a long essay on the popular image, "Rock of Ages." Japan's tattoo revolution is described by Bob Basile. **$15**

TATTOOTIME #5: Art From the Heart. Hundreds of color photographs, in-depth articles on tattooers, contemporary tattooing in Samoa, weirdo monster tattoos, and much more. A fascinating and lengthy autobiographical interview with Michael Malone provides a by-the-numbers introduction to the nuts and bolts of launching a professional career in tattooing. **$20**

ORDERING INFORMATION

**MAIL: V/SEARCH Publications
20 ROMOLO #B
SAN FRANCISCO, CA 94133**

OR

**PHONE: Call Monday through Friday, 10 AM to 6 PM PST
TEL (415) 362-1465 FAX (415)362-0742**

Cash, Check or Money Order Payable to V/Search Publications OR Charge to Credit Card: VISA or MASTERCARD Only

SHIPPING & HANDLING CHARGES

DOMESTIC CUSTOMERS: first item $4; add $1 per additional item; for priority mail add $1 per order.
INTERNATIONAL CUSTOMERS: SEAMAIL: first item $6; add $2 per each additional item;
AIRMAIL: first item $15; add $12 per additional item.

PAYMENT IN U.S. DOLLARS ONLY

ATTENTION CANADIAN CUSTOMERS: We *do not* accept personal checks even from a U.S. dollar account!
Send Cash or International Money Orders Only! (available from the post office)

To order: send your name, address and check or credit card information *including expiration date and telephone number*. For full catalog send SASE or 2 IRCs. CA residents please add 8½% sales tax. *HAVE YOU ORDERED FROM US BEFORE? Let us know!*

Index

Snake charmer.